Men of Peace

World War II Conscientious Objectors

Mary R. Hopkins, Editor

Foreword by Duane L. Cady

Published by *Producciones de la Hamaca*, Caye Caulker, Belize
<producciones-hamaca.com>

ISBN: 978-976-8142-23-8

Photos: Most of the men who were interviewed submitted two photos of themselves, one taken during the 1940s and one taken recently.

TABLE OF CONTENTS

Acknowledgements

This collection from World War II conscientious objectors (COs)[17] began in the Fall of 2005 when I consulted four Quakers: Stephen Angell, a lifelong peace activist; Allan Brick, a professor of literature and a Korean War CO; Teresa Engeman, an editor and wordsmith; and Patricia Hunt, widow of a pacifist and a retired employee of the American Friends Service Committee.[4] They became a Clearness Committee[52] and encouraged me to go forward.

Then Edith Ballard volunteered in 2006 to help find World War II COs to be interviewed. She kept a card file and emailed me daily reports as she shook these elderly gentlemen out of their quiet retirement lives. They didn't have a chance. Then she died on May 2, 2007, a month after our deadline had passed when we had over fifty interviews in my computer. A great deal of credit for the rich fullness of this book goes to her.

The volunteer interviewers and transcribers are indicated in a footnote at the beginning of each interview. They include Barbara Anspach, F. Evert Bartholomew, Connie Bimber, Allan Brick, Duane L. Cady, Kathleen Davidson, Beth Edelstein, Terry Engeman, Philip Greenspan, Melba C. Gulick, Neil Hartman, Lorina Hall, Mary R. Hopkins, Doug Johnston, Peggy and Bill Kidwell, Susan Knox, Reverend Deb Oskin, Kathryn Parke, Kirk B. Roose, Ruth C. Schwaegerle, Linda and Mike Sears, Virginia Major Thomas, Wendy Underhill, Mary Way. Although different interviewers were involved, each CO was asked the same questions. The announcement and guidelines, including the questions, are found in the Appendix (*p. 379*). Each one of the interviewers and transcribers deserves credit for making this a readable book.

---

[17] *See #17 in Endnotes, beginning on p. 359*

Too many stories had to be put aside as unsatisfactory in one respect or another, but all material submitted was sent to the archives in the Swarthmore College Peace Collection. When I had about thirty usable interviews sorted into chapters, I needed readers. Allan Brick, Charles Foster, The Rt. Rev. William Jones, Elsie Landstrom, Jane Mullins, Gail Newbold, and Ingeborg Snipes kindly reviewed them and were not shy about making valuable suggestions.

When a preview version of the book was available, we enlisted Don Bender, Duane Cady, Mary Ann Downey, Johan Maurer, Patricia McBee, J. E. McNeil, Mary Ellen McNish, and Murray Polner to provide further guidance as we put on the finishing touches.

All royalties will go to American Friends Service Committee,[4] Center on Conscience and War,[11] Fellowship of Reconcilliation,[25] and other non-profit organizations which will support future COs.

My daughter, Virginia Hopkins, has many books to her credit. From beginning to end she has been a ready resource as I phoned for guidance on what the next step should be. Every mother should have such a child.

Judy Lumb eagerly edited, designed and published this book under the non-profit publisher, *Produciones de la Hamaca*. Her life lived among many cultures, including Quaker, brought valuable insights to this project.

I am grateful to each and every one of you, as well as those who have sustained interest in the project as the years have slipped by.

Mary R. Hopkins

Foreword

We live in a "warist" world, that is, a world of deep prejudice that takes war for granted. War is simply what nations do, and most nations—especially the United States—take great pride in doing war very well. Like racism and sexism, "warism" is poisonous. It distorts our judgments and leads many to rationalize behavior we may not have chosen had we been free of the bias favoring our endorsement of war. War has been sold as our sacred obligation, especially World War II.

As WW II veterans have aged they have come to be called "the greatest generation." In this book we hear from men of that same generation who marched to a different drummer, who stood against participation in war and did so as a matter of moral conscience, who swam against the prevailing current, no small undertaking in the United States, the dominant military nation on earth.

Since the 1960s, that is, since the height of political resistance to the U.S. war in Vietnam, moral rejection of war—pacifism—while not commonplace has become somewhat accepted and expected. But in the 1930s and 1940s, during the build-up to and through the duration of World War II—the good war—pacifists were an endangered species. Young men were under particular pressure to serve their country in the effort to stop Hitler and the Nazis. Still, thousands refused to register for the draft and thousands more registered as conscientious objectors (COs), most often on religious grounds.

During World War I, COs often ended up in prison for refusing military service. By the beginning of World War II the traditional peace churches had secured provision for CO registration with Selective Service. If the

CO status was approved by the candidate's local draft board, he was subject to the draft, but assigned to "alternative service doing work of national importance." The Quakers, Mennonites, and Brethren sponsored and directed Civilian Public Service (CPS) camps wherein COs served the country working in hospitals and schools, doing forestry, teaching in poverty areas, helping in mental institutions, and even serving as medical test subjects for studies on hepatitis, starvation, sleep deprivation, lice treatment, and more.

Some COs resented the "slavery" of the CPS camps where wages were unheard of, and tiny allowances of a few dollars a month "pocket money" were typical. A few resisters simply walked out of the camps, going AWOL at first, and later, to prison. Some COs organized to resist the peace church cooperation with Selective Service in providing and administering the alternative service camps, arguing that a more radical resistance to conscription was needed to witness against war. The musings of the CPS "veterans" on the politics of alternative service is a window into a missing piece of American history.

Men of Peace gives over thirty WW II COs an opportunity to tell their own stories of conscientious objection, and to do so in their own words. These are stories rarely told beyond immediate families and close friends, stories lost and neglected, stories left out of most textbook accounts of World War II. This collection of first-hand accounts gives readers a glimpse into the lives of pacifists who somehow found the courage to question and even reject war on ethical grounds. Often their ethics followed their religious upbringing, whether they had grown up in a traditional peace church (i.e., Quakers, Mennonites, or Brethren) or as Methodists, Congregationalists, Presbyterians, Lutherans, Catholics, or Jews. Sometimes the moral position came out of less structured spirituality and even from secular moral reflection without reference to organized religion. Always individuals followed their conscience. For some it was easy, but others struggled through torturous decision-making processes. Some felt supported by family and friends, but many were quite alone without pacifist parents, friends, or mentors. Some suffered no ill effects of choosing conscientious objection while others lost jobs, relationships, and even careers due to prejudice against pacifism. Each individual's experience is unique. Together these personal stories are pieces of a much larger mosaic, the mostly invisible history of American moral resistance to World War II.

Readers will find fascinating the variety of lives led by these COs following the World War II conscientious objector experience. Many were and are activists in subsequent anti-war efforts, but others have not been activists. Several have made significant contributions to dismantling America's racial segregation practices and many participated in the U.S. Civil Rights movement. Some have worked in international development to end colonialism or to reduce hunger and achieve self-sufficiency among ordinary people in "developing" nations.

Many have worked—and continue to work—on behalf of various organizations, such as, the Fellowship of Reconciliation, the Congress on Racial Equality, the Alternatives to Violence Project, and many, many others. Happily, Editor Mary Hopkins provides very useful endnotes wherein a host of acronyms are spelled-out, organizations explained, and dropped names are identified with short biographies. The index at the end of the book proves helpful as well. The book is so rich with information that many will begin researching through the index and find themselves drawn into the personal stories.

Historians, peace advocates, pacifists, students, as well as general readers will find this well worth their time. Since each man of peace tells his own story in his own words, selections vary widely in style and content. All follow one broad format, but each respondent goes his own way. The result is a bit uneven but all the more rewarding for the genuineness that radiates from every page. Perhaps most remarkable is that the authors range in age from their late eighties to their mid nineties. The cumulative effect of reading every selection is powerful. We can only hope that we might accomplish half as much in our lifetimes and be as articulate, generous, and open in passing our stories to future generations.

This is an important book. Readers will be grateful for the men of peace who first lived, and now share, these experiences, and to Mary Hopkins for her persistence in seeing this project through to publication while these men of peace were still available for their testimonies. A reading of *Men of Peace* will provoke more than a few smiles, more than a few tears, and, one can hope, many, many young people to think hard about who they are and where they stand on war. For this last result, future generations will be forever grateful.

Duane L. Cady

Duane L. Cady is Professor of Philosophy at Hamline University in St. Paul, Minnesota. He is author of *From Warism to Pacifism: A Moral Continuum* (1989; expanded edition, 2010) and *Moral Vision: How Everyday Life Shapes Ethical Thinking* (2005), co-author of *Humanitarian Intervention: Just War vs. Pacifism* (1996), co-editor of three anthologies, and author of more than fifty articles on political philosophy, especially on morality, violence, and non-violence. He is a past President of Concerned Philosophers for Peace and served six years on the National Council of the Fellowship of Reconciliation.

Preface

In 1940 the Selective Training and Service Act required male citizens of the United States to register for induction into the armed services. Provision was made for conscientious objectors. Almost 12,000 men claimed the conscientious objector[17] (CO) exemption and were assigned to "alternative service doing work of national importance," while another 6,000 went to prison for refusing to register at all.

Since World War II the pacifist stance has become more socially acceptable in Western society. World War II was the "good war." How could a young man refuse to defend his country, thereby committing himself to a path held in contempt by the society in which he lived? Common sense should have told him that he might never be able to find a wife, a decent job, or benefit from all the perks with which a government rewards its warriors.

Why is a pacific human male so rare? What is his character? Was he born a pacifist? How do we parent him? Is the culture in which he grows up paramount? Are religion and education important? Could a book that introduces these rare souls help others find their core values when faced with social pressures to act violently?

These men do not fall into convenient categories. By and large they are intelligent humanitarians. They come from all walks of life, parts of the United States and vocations. As each man, in his own words, tells his story, I gain a deeper understanding of what living with a clear conscience means to some and how much it means to me. How could these driven young men have lived otherwise?

What I lacked as a young person in the 1940s, and what we don't have today, are role models, or an archetype for a Man of Peace. Gandhi and Martin Luther King, Jr. cannot carry the entire load. All of those who helped to put this book together hope that young people can find inspirational role models here. If this book helps to lift such an ideal figure into our collective consciousness, my life work, and the work of the many men and women who have lived their lives by the principles of peace, will be validated.

Mary R. Hopkins, Editor

Chapter One
Led By Conscience

Chapter One
Led By Conscience

Calhoun D. Geiger

F. Warren Wilson

Henry Ormsby

Warren D. Sawyer

First we meet four men who grew up in a white, Protestant, Bible-based culture. The decades were economically difficult and still bruised by World War I. Our first was loosely home schooled while the others finished high school before they chose a vocation. One thirsted for international experiences in order to make sense of his world. We must ask, "Why did each one turn away from the priorities of their community and nation when they were called to arms? What more imperative call did they hear?"

Without the benefits of a college education, they made their decisions on firm grounds provided by their families, churches or the personal and idiosyncratic philosophy of life that they worked out for themselves. They firmly trusted their inner wisdom. Calhoun Geiger names it as having been led by the spirit. These are men who have few if any regrets, and, by all accounts, their consciences are clear.

Calhoun D. Geiger *(1917-2009)*

"All of these questions hark back to this feeling I have of having been led by the Spirit through almost all these ups and downs."

My father was a very active and forceful farmer who started us off as soon as possible taking part in whatever was going on. I remember once he was plowing a field and I was following along behind. He stopped suddenly and said "Come on here Calhoun. You can do this as well as I can." I was small enough so I had to reach up to the plow handles. I realized later that old John Deere plow was being guided by my father's time-to-time touch with his skilled hands, but I thought I was guiding it entirely. That was the way we were encouraged by Father and Mother, and one or two uncles and one aunt that were part of the family.

I was home schooled through the eighth grade. I remember reading some rather interesting things. After eighth grade I enrolled in two correspondence courses from the University of Florida at Gainesville, which was a relatively short distance from our home, an English course and a geometry course. Because my father was active in the timber industry, I figured the geometry would help me when it came to figuring out timber values.

Interviewed by Kathleen Davidson and Doug Johnston, January 31, 2007. Parts of this interview are from Leadings Along The Way: Stories from the Life of Calhoun D. Geiger. *1998*[30]

I was about 24 when Pearl Harbor hit. I was doing general farming that included raising a good deal of sugar cane, making cane syrup nearly every year, and planting corn, sweet potatoes, and such. We ate great quantities of sweet potatoes because they were relatively easy to grow.

Becoming a conscientious objector (CO)[17] didn't come on very suddenly. When the World War II draft began to make a noise, I asked myself a bunch of questions. I came from a family that had been very much a Bible-studying family, as long as I can remember. During all my early childhood and growing-up years in rural Florida, reading the Bible was a daily occupation with the family. It was during that time that I came to a quotation in the Sermon on the Mount, "Love your enemies. Do good to those who hate you and spitefully use you."

About that time the Methodist Church nationally had made some quite strong and outspoken anti-war statements. These gave much food for thought and discussion as we tried to think through where we were and should be in the midst of the gathering war clouds in Europe.

I soon found myself asking, quite unwillingly at first, some serious questions: "If it comes to it, what should I do?" My brother Van and I rather surprised each other when we discovered we were thinking much the same thoughts, asking ourselves almost the same questions. We spent many hours thinking and talking together, along with two double-first cousins who felt like siblings to us.

Out of all this a question came to me quite suddenly, "What is the point of studying the life of a man who lived 2,000 years ago and taught and lived a life of absolute love, if it does not apply to me right now?" In my thinking, I carefully weighed, again and again, "What does 'blessed are the peacemakers' mean for my life? Or 'Love your enemies, do good to those who hate you and spitefully use you'?" Then came the question "Refuse to register and go to prison, or register as a conscientious objector?" After many more hours of talking and walking in the woods, all four of us—my brother, the two cousins, and I—all registered as COs.

The draft board was composed of several people that my father knew well and who had been in school with him. When I was drafted I received a questionnaire to fill out that went to the draft board after I had answered the questions. The Secretary of the draft board was a life-long acquaintance of my family. She told us what was going on in the draft board. When they got my CO application, she lost no time in reporting to us. She said one member of the Board who had been a childhood schoolmate of my father's, said, "That's one of Ed Geiger's boys. I know his daddy from way back yonder, and he always knew where he stood and what he stood for and why he stood there, so I'm not about to tangle with any of his youngsters. She knew what the answer was going to be and, sure enough, they didn't even ask me to appear before the board. They simply okayed my application to be accepted as a CO.

There was some challenge from the outside. I remember particularly an old WWI veteran, Percy Smith, was always very friendly to me, but he could hardly stand the CO position, which was so much a part of my life at that time.

My first assignment in Civilian Public Service (CPS) was to Buck Creek Camp near Marion, North Carolina, working on the Blue Ridge Parkway, which was a brand new highway at that time. We were dynamiting rocks that were sticking out too far to leave the highway as smooth as possible. Another important reason we were sent there was to fight forest fires. We also worked on Crabtree Meadow, a rather carefully developed picnic and camping area. But in the middle of the day, the Park Service Supervisor might suddenly say "Stop your work and rest for a few minutes. We've got a fire burning up the road apiece that we've got to go and put out." We were then taken to some place where there was a fire. It was at the time of the chestnut blight and all the chestnut trees all over that part of the country at least had died, so we were set to sawing down those chestnut trees and hauling them to sawmills to make picnic tables for use along the parkway.

After we had been there about five months, a superintendent and one or two employees of the Eastern State Hospital at Williamsburg, Virginia, came to recruit some of us. The hospital had been started by order of King George III, so it was older than the United States of America because that was before the Revolutionary War. It was commonly said around there that it had changed very little since old George gave the order to start the hospital, which was to some extent true. The buildings were old and not in the best shape, and the treatment of the patients was considerably primitive. Of course, back then they didn't have anything like the medications we have today for treating schizophrenia or the other ailments the patients came with. My brother and I both volunteered to go there because it seemed to us a situation of rather serious human need and more important than working on the parkway or fighting forest fires, as important as those things were. And we were both there for something like five years.

I was single. Virgie and I had written letters back and forth all during those years. When I was on night duty on the famous ward, said to be the violent ward, I would write letters all night long to Virgie. When I got my discharge at the end of the war and went home, she had been writing to me, and I to her quite steadily, and we understood our situation pretty well. We were married not too long after I got home.

I didn't spend much time choosing my work. The first thing I did was to settle back into where I had left off.

Father was still active in the farming and forestry work, so I simply joined him. The paper industry was just coming in, so the market for wood to make paper was beginning to boom. Virgie and I built a house for ourselves. I had inherited my grandfather's farm, which was only a short distance from my home. My grandfather's old house was pretty much eaten up by termites by that time, so we dismantled the old house where my father and his eight brothers and sisters had all mostly grown up. We saved the heartwood, and it made a pretty solid house.

The judge, who was the granddaddy and supervisor of the Jacksonville Boys Clubs, had been a longtime friend of the family. One day he said to me, "Now Calhoun I think it is time for you to quit just growing taters and sugarcane and corn, and come help me work with troubled boys." That is what started me in the Boys Clubs business. So I joined his staff of the Boys Clubs operation and pretty much moved out of farming, though I continued it to some extent.

During the war I had become acquainted with Quaker COs and found my thinking much in line with theirs. So after Virgie and I were married, it was rather a simple step for us to be involved in the founding of the Jacksonville, Florida, Friends Meeting.

Soon a couple of interesting people, Mr. and Mrs. Derbyshire, came to our Friends Meeting. As we became acquainted, we found that both of them were much concerned over the strict segregation within the Girl Scout organization. Mrs. Derbyshire was one of the leaders of the North Florida Council of the Girl Scouts. The only established camp in the region was for use of white Girl Scouts only. Black Scouts were not permitted there, even when it was not being used by white groups. A timber company had donated a reasonably attractive tract of land for the development of a camp for black Girl Scouts, but little money was available for the development of that site and building facilities. Our Meeting contributed many hours and most of the materials for the construction of an initial modest lodge building. The construction was done under the direction of a skillful black carpenter with some of us as well as parents of some of the girls working together as his helpers. Thus Camp Chanyata gradually took shape.

I was appointed Chairman of the Facilities Committee for the Girl Scout Council. Then came time for the annual meeting of the North Florida Council, which was customarily a very important and well attended occasion. Exhibits were to be set up on a large stage in the auditorium of the YWCA, depicting activities of the Girl Scouts. By this time I had become quite well acquainted with the activities of many of the troops, both black and white. As plans for the great occasion developed, I became increasingly disturbed by the fact that the troops for black girls were almost entirely left out. When I raised the questions about it in a planning session, the answer was a sort of embarrassed "Oh, but we have never worked together with them."

When I remonstrated, "Is it not right that we should all be working together?," The answer was a clear though rather weak, "Well, yes, it is right." I followed up with something like, "If we are clear that it is right, it seems we should move in the faith that we can and should all work together."

So exhibits were rearranged and on the night of the great meeting celebrating a year's work, we had black and white girls in uniform on the stage at the same time working together on their various projects. In Girl Scouts, I was told, this was the first time that had ever occurred. After that, I was called on by various churches and civic organizations from time to time to talk about desegregation efforts. And people never tired of introducing me as a Girl Scout!

Not long after the famous Girl Scout annual meeting, word was sent to me that it was urgent that I be at a council meeting at the YWCA. No reason was given for the urgency of my attending. At the meeting various business matters were first taken care of, then the announcement was made that Calhoun Geiger had been named by the Girl Scouts of America, as Man of the Year. I received a certificate signed by various officials of the organization, so stating. Not long after this, both established camps, as well as many individual Girl Scout troops, were integrated.

We fairly often had school classes coming to visit our home place to walk in the woods, pick wildflowers, and such. On these occasions we always tried to spend as much time with the children as possible, guiding them to particularly beautiful or interesting spots. We had a picnic lunch on the lawn in front of our house. On several occasions we had classes from a private school for black girls that was run by the Methodist Church. It had an integrated staff of dedicated teachers, and we always had a fine time with them when they visited our place. The picnic lunch on the lawn became a regular part of the day.

On one such occasion, wrong eyes must have taken in what was going on, for that evening as Virgie and I were eating supper in the back part of our house, we heard something crash against the front. I ran out the front door and heard someone running fast through the Palmetto scrub toward the highway some 200 feet from our house. A moment later a car door slammed and the car tore off down the road. But what I also saw was a burning cross by the side of the road, a short distance from the house. I told Virgie to keep a lookout and I would go and see about putting the fire out. There was no one in sight, but the cross was burning brightly. I kicked it over and with my heavy work shoes stamped out the fire to be sure it did not set fire to our woodland.

While I was still pretty actively connected to the Boys Clubs the call came from the American Friends Service Committee (AFSC).[4] As a CO I had worked in programs run by AFSC, so they had been very much acquainted with some of my doings. I was the Director of the Conscientious Objector Unit at the hospital. By the time we had been there three years our number had grown to eighty-one COs.

So we moved to High Point, North Carolina, where I was working in the Peace Program at the Southeastern Regional office of the American Friends Service Committee, which was a general all-inclusive educational program. That was a big move for us in 1956. We had two children, and Edward was born the next year, in 1957. I was traveling a great deal. They would give me pointers as to where they wanted me to go with the Friends Service Committee ideals. My work as a peace activist was challenging for our family because I had to travel a lot. I remember going to Texas for rather extended periods and then getting back home again as quickly as I could before I had to go in some other direction.

From time to time I ran into people who were unfriendly to the AFSC. I remember being asked to give a talk in a church in Texas on a Sunday evening. I gave my talk which was essentially centered on the CO idea. The church building was fairly new, with sweeping glass walls going up in two directions from the pulpit. When I got through, quite a number of people wanted to join me for a little more talk so we went out in the parking lot and continued talking. It was all fairly friendly, though there may have been a few who were somewhat antagonistic, too. All at once there was an explosion and we got showered with chips of broken glass. Fortunately nobody got hurt, but that elegant glass front of the building was destroyed. I always wondered if they made a mistake and waited too long, if they were planning to have that glass come down while I was in there. It might have finished me. Through all this, as with other situations of some danger and discouragement, the leading of the spirit was crystal clear, that I must not stop or hesitate as long as there was a road ahead, no matter how dark it was.

Then Seth Hinshaw and Binford Farlow came from the North Carolina Yearly Meeting to tell us that the long-time director of Quaker Lake Camp and a good friend of mine, Orval Dillon, had decided it was time to retire. Would we be interested in that job? The family conferences were brief as we felt clear that it was the right next step.

I had fairly strong feelings and ideas about how a Quaker-established camp for children should be planned and carried out. Clearly, it seemed right that we should have time set aside for sharing together about our faith, the values of simplicity, helping others, alternatives to violence, quiet time or meditation, listening to the call of the inner light or the Holy Spirit, and the importance of integrating all of these as vital parts of our daily lives as we live and work and play together each day. Such tasks as helping with food preparation, clean-up, and simple maintenance jobs are valuable experiences, and can be made both interesting and exciting when combined with the right dose of ingenuity.

Our staff were mostly either high-school or young college-aged folk, who had volunteered for all or part of a summer of caring for children. Their energy spoke eloquently of the sincerity and dedication of most of these young folk. And in all the planning and living out of the summer camp sessions, we wanted to remember that camp is camp. Of equal importance was to remember that our charges had come to Quaker Lake for fun and recreation, and a camp program must have this as a major part. So swimming, hay rides, games of many sorts, masquerades, treasure hunts and the like all had their place.

We were at Quaker Lake and the groups from Carolina Friends School (CFS) had been coming there for retreats, so we had got fairly well acquainted with CFS and they had got to know us reasonably well. They sent Don Wells over to buttonhole me, would I be willing to come to the school? He and I sat down on the little porch outside the kitchen at Quaker Lake and he said pretty bluntly, "We think we have a place for you at CFS. What do you think of that idea?" I said, "Well, this is kind of sudden but it certainly has possibilities for me. What do you want me to do if I come there?" And so we discussed the various possibilities and he said, "We are in the midst of various problems that we'd like you to help us with. One is to clean up the language at the school and another is starting this school service program involving the students in everything that goes on, whether it's building new buildings or simply cleaning up the campus or whatever." And I said, "In other words you hope I can be helpful in just doing whatever needs to be done?" And he agreed.

The language was really troubling to me at CFS because anything the students said was colored with cuss words. Anytime I heard one of these unseemly expressions, like when a student wanted to go in a building and the door was locked and she hollered out something unseemly, I just quietly said to her, "Now if you had said 'would you please open that door?' without putting that language in, wouldn't it have been more effective?" And she reckoned so. That was the way I went about it all the time. As the years went by and I needed to slow down, it seemed the right time for me to give up the full-time work there. I now serve on the school's board of directors, and occasionally in a sort of consultant capacity, as former staff clerk.

I can't come up with a good answer to what am I proudest of and I haven't come up with any pointed regrets. The fact is, all of these questions sort of hark back to this feeling of having been led by the Spirit through almost all the ups and downs. I realize that I didn't have faith enough that an end to war was going to happen, but I certainly dream that maybe someday this endless war spirit that is so much everywhere will disappear and people will learn that there is a better way than that of war. I would advise young people to think seriously about being COs and simply refusing to take part in what is obviously the wrong way. The CO experience provided me a core from which a lot has grown.

From the first I can remember, I never had any clear picture of what I should do with my life. On the surface it might seem that my life has been one of drifting rather aimlessly from one thing to the next. I never achieved even a high school diploma. Each job I had was clearly the best possible preparation and training for the one that came next. It has not always been easy to follow the leading, when it did not fit with our ideas of what we thought we would like to do, but the leading was always there, and became unmistakably clear as we listened.

F. Warren Wilson (1926)

"I do not wear my faith on my sleeve or a chip on my shoulder but in a pocket where it can be quickly brought out and referenced."

My childhood was spent in a devoutly religious structured family. However, that same family was socially dysfunctional. Much of that dysfunction sprang from religion and politics. In this family, I was taught both love and hate. My Father was an Independent Evangelist, Paulinist,[49] Republican and a quasi-Pacifist. Mother was a very independent housewife, anti-Paulinist, Democrat and hated the communists, but also had deep-rooted suspicions of government in general and, specifically, the military. She taught love but would have pressed the atomic bomb button and destroyed Russia, believing she was doing the will of God.

At age nine, I came under the influence of a truly loving Sunday school teacher who led me to accept Jesus Christ as my Savior. This occurred in San Antonio, Texas in a Freewill Methodist Church.

By 1939, I had stepped up to a very clear line in the sand, "Love your enemies." By the time I was fifteen, I knew Japan was negotiating with USA to leave their islands. The USA's presence was depriving the resource-starved island nation of Japan of numerous natural resources that were essential to their existence. On December 7, 1941, the Japanese Ambassador was in Washington, DC warning them that a refusal to negotiate would mean war.

I argued at the time that the bombing of Pearl Harbor was not the "sneak attack" claimed by the U.S. propaganda machine. I was in the ninth grade in Louisville, Kentucky when this event occurred. At that early age, I had fully arrived at the CO position which included a refusal to salute or pledge to the American flag. In fact, I disliked all flags. At this time I was a devout believer but not a member of any church.

I had a great interest in fine art. The highest point of interest came in Louisville, Kentucky, while I attended the ninth grade art class. I entered a painting in the statewide art contest. This piece won first place and was on display in the Governor's Mansion all summer. My Art teacher was a strong, encouraging mentor. She understood my pacifist stand and at a time when war was approaching, she did not discourage my stand.

My secondary interest came in my tenth grade when I took woodworking at Ahrens Trade School in Louisville, Kentucky. That year I designed and constructed a secretary desk from a picture in a catalog. This, too, was entered in a statewide competition winning first place. Like my painting, the desk was displayed all summer in the Governor's Mansion. My instructor, Mr. Schell, saw my hidden skill and helped mentor me when I thought I could not do it. A second generation German, he also

listened when I shared my conscientious objector stand and never discouraged me.

My interest in competitive sports began in the seventh grade in Rialto, California. I was on the tennis team, was handball champion and won a blue ribbon in high-jump at two track meets. I also placed in other jumps and relays. I have maintained profound interest in competitive sports; especially tennis. No one in my family or friends had any interest in the arts or sports so I was largely self-motivated. Neither did I have any mentors when it came to being a conscientious objector.

My father was proud of his sixth grade education. My mother attended one year of Girl's Finishing School after High School. To my parents, higher education was of no real value in the grand scheme of things and they looked on higher education with a deep sense of suspicion. However, it would be grossly unfair to my parents if I failed to acknowledge the relatively high level of education they both achieved on their own initiative.

Despite working from six to ten hours every night after school, I carried a B+ average through the middle of the eleventh grade. Eighteen-year-olds were being drafted out of high school, so I justified leaving school in the middle of the eleventh grade. Later in life when I applied for management positions, I tested out at graduate school levels. Like my parents, I learned how to learn by life experiences.

I was sixteen and arrived at my position solely because of my knowledge of and love for Jesus Christ. I had almost no major supporters and the world around me served as major detractors. This condition did not change until I registered at age eighteen with the Elizabethtown, Kentucky, draft board.

I taught the adult men's Sunday school class in the Cecilia, Kentucky Methodist Church. One of the five draft board members sat under my teaching in that class. He knew the integrity of my faith position and other draft board members became ardent supporters of me. General Hershey[34] had every intention of incarcerating me and would have if it had not been for the support of these men. I was drafted and sent to Bedford, Virginia, then Belden, California, and finally back to New Windsor, Maryland. I spent eighteen months in CPS.[14]

I spent most of my adult working life in the printing industry. I did not deliberately choose this vocation but it seemed to almost be a part of some grand plan. In my first printing experience, while in the tenth grade, I operated a sixteen station collator. We collated, bound, and trimmed magazines. When I was sent to New Windsor as a CO, they saw my resume and I was given the job of managing their print shop. Here I learned to cold set type and run the old snapper printing machine. New Windsor purchased a small offset press so I became an offset pressman.

When I married and came to Dayton, Ohio, I learned the trade of making offset printing plates. This job paid poorly. There was an opening in the printing division at Wright Patterson Air Force Base that offered double the pay I was making, but I turned down the offer because of my peace position.

I do not wear my faith on my sleeve or a chip on my shoulder but in a pocket where it can be quickly brought out and referenced. There are many places where I cannot work but I do not consider this a personal loss.

Then I took a big step up when I pursued a job opening as a supervisor of the "in house" printing department of the Standard Register Company. To apply for this position, I was put through a battery of psychological testing. In reviewing my test results, the employment manager commented, "Looking at your test results, it seems you would make a damn good Indian scout, but I am not sure

supervision is for you." He continued, "Your individuality blew right off the chart. I am not sure that Standard
Register is ready for that much individuality."

His thoughts on this matter resulted from my answer
to one question on the test. The question was, "If you
were in the room with a conscientious objector, would
you feel uncomfortable?" The Vietnam War was in full
swing at this time. My answer was, "Absolutely not, for
I am a conscientious objector." Upon hearing this, the
interviewer completely changed his feelings on how
well I might manage at Standard Register. I was given
the position and promotions followed quickly and soon I
was supervising in one of their major production control
divisions.

Through exhaustive research and gnosis, that is, the
application of the mind to the truths uncovered in my
study of "The History of Marriage," I can absolutely say,
"Marriage is the first physical union between a man and
a woman for the purposes God had intended for this act."

This understanding governed all of my dating years
and was the major influence in my choice for a wife who
would be the mother of any children which would come
from this union.

Love of our enemies (peace) was also a primary consideration in the selection of a mate. The "end result" is
seen in our large family. We have seven children and many
of the extended family conform to the major tenets of my
faith position on peace. Four have served in Alternative
Service programs.

All who know our family will attest to the results
achieved as my wife and I applied the principals of "love
and peace" to the training of our family.

Over the years I have participated in numerous
peace meetings. I attended a march in Cincinnati, Ohio

and one to Washington D.C. in 2005. On these marches, I positioned myself in a location for optimum opportunities to personally present the "Gospel of Peace," brought to the world by Jesus Christ.

It is my goal to never pass up an opportunity to present those "truths," never fearing how those truths may be received or how my presentation may negatively impact my life and the life of my family.

I teach continually in a Church of the Brethren.[7] This is a church where 70% of the members do not agree with my peace position. This is also a church where our youngest daughter is the pastor's wife and six of our family members are very active in church polity. I dare not allow these circumstances to change or silence the presentation of the Gospel of Peace.

I definitely find pleasure in my family. I also find pleasure in the results of my continuing search for TRUTH. In this search I have produced

1) My autobiography
2) "String of Pearls" in which I share truths I have found like:
   • Nationalism is inherently evil and is indisputably the oldest religion in the world and frequently anti-Christ.
   • When Christianity unites with nationalism, an especially deadly religion results.
   • And the truth that pride is consistently shown to be sin. This is true in the entire Bible and most of religious history.
3) "The Continuity of Confusion" in which I retrace the history of the Christian religion, showing how nationalism and Biblicanism have subverted the "True Faith" down through the centuries.
4) "The Millennium Family" (a historic fiction)

I have very few regrets and none worth presenting in this book. I am eighty years old. Forty-seven of
those years the U.S. has been at war with some nation.
For the balance of my life this country and even some
of my root family have tried
to teach "hate." This truth is
especially sad when we commonly think of this nation as
a "Christian country."

I deal directly with the
temptation to become dis-
couraged by using what I
believe are Provable Truths.
These truths are:

- God is winning, not
  losing.
- The world is getting
  better.

To facilitate the finding of TRUTH, I suggest that
a detailed list be made of all those conditions which
would seem to suggest "the world is going to hell in a
hand basket," then make a chart of twelve hundred-year
increments. Using your list, glance back each hundred
years and carefully compare your entries on your present list with what history tells you of these problems
in the past. I believe you will find, just as I did, that the
world is getting better, not worse.

Lessons I've learned are recorded in my writings. I
find these writings to be unique and I hope one day they
will be published and shared with the world.

Henry Ormsby (1915)

"I said I did not want to go and fight, but I wanted to do a job of national importance."

I was a birthright member of the Society of Friends and normally would be opposed to any war or fighting. Probably at the age of ten, I became opposed to war and fighting and that sort of thing. This was basically because of my father and mother. Dad was a very kind and gentle person. I never remember him even striking me. When he spoke, you know that he meant to be obeyed and it was just that simple. He was opposed to going to war in the First World War. He did not have to go and I'm not sure why. I know he was a conscientious objector in his own way. I was very aware of that at the time. My brother and I both felt that he was a good example and followed him in a lot of things. He was a quiet person and not demanding in that sense. You wanted to do the things he wanted you to. This was different from many families where you got paddled for misbehaving. He had a strong effect on my direction as far as opposition to war.

I was probably about age ten when we went into how Quakers felt, going to Meetings. I have a brother who is two years younger than I am, and part of being the older brother was to stick up for him in the neighborhood. This was in Brookline, Pennsylvania, outside of Philadelphia. Of course there were always young men who were willing to challenge your ability to fight and become leaders of groups that hung together. We opposed that right from the beginning. They went to public school and we went to private school. As far as thinking, immediately we were on a different level than they were. Their parents had told them that we must be very rich to go to private school. Of course we weren't. We were there on scholarships.

Interviewed by Allan Brick and Mary R. Hopkins, transcribed by Terry Engeman

I went to Friends Select School. I lived at home then, and came into the city with my father when he worked at the Philadelphia City Hall. I came in on the train with him and then walked over to 17th and Parkway to the school. I made that trip from the first to fourth grade. The conductor knew me and would look out for me.

We had Walter Hamlin as the headmaster. He was another excellent teacher and an example for any of us who were leaning in the pacifist direction. My teachers all had a special effect on me. They were outstanding women and really dedicated teachers. I can still remember their names.

I started at Westtown School as a boarding student at age ten. My mother had a breakdown and had to go to a hospital for a while. The Meeting felt it would be good for me to go to boarding school, so that is why I started early. I was fortunate to have eight years of boarding school, which was very unusual.

One of the things I got into at Westtown was in the wood shop and building and repairing things. I got that from my father because he was very handy. He had tools and we used them at home, so I had ability to use my hands, to be constructive and make things. I got into sports at Westtown and played soccer, baseball and track. I got letters in three of them.

At Westtown we lived in the Stone House. We were not ready to go up to the big house and be teased. We were under a house mother, Jackie Woods. She ran it more like a family than anything else. This was a good experience. We did a lot of things together. We had our own bed and bedroom. We had Saturday entertainment and Sunday go to Meeting. We did homework every night and had Friday night projects. Actually, I was never a good student, never a very good reader. I read with a lot of problems. I was never good at reading aloud. Anything related to science was easy. Math was not difficult.

We had a lot of excellent teachers there, and some of them got interested in our leisure time. Albert Bailey taught botany and zoology there. He had a keen interest in boys and would give us Friday night entertainment, including being a ventriloquist and an amateur magician. He would build miniature stages and build dolls and marionettes. He had studied magic tricks and had a lot of his own. Both were ideal entertainment for boys.

I wanted to graduate and start to work. I was looking for work in 1935 during the Depression. When I went to places like Bell Telephone it was difficult to even get an application. One day I came home and mother said that Mabel Llewellyn called and said she had seen me at Midweek Meeting and wondered if I was working. Mother said I wasn't. Mabel said to have me call her brother. She was sure he would have a job for me. It turns out they could use me. I was riveting runners on Flexible Flyer sleds. My original salary was 28 cents an hour, but I refused to join the union. I was able to get another job. Dad had passed away and Mother needed my help, so they called me to come back home. I was moved to the engineering department. I got into photography there doing photos for the catalog. I worked there until I was drafted.

At the time of Pearl Harbor, Mother had died. I was rooming with a friend. My draft board refused to give me a conscientious objector classification. They just gave me a 1-A classification. They said the Army will work it out when they draft you. So I had to go to a federal hearing to get my classification changed. That was pretty unusual for a birthright Quaker not to get a CO classification. I think I was about 28 years old at that time.

What pleased me was that it got around the office that I was going to have a hearing to be a CO. The Vice President of the company, W. C. Warren, went to the hearing with me. It was very short, almost like an interview, and that was it. They asked if I was a member of Friends and how I had come to my feeling about being a CO. So then I got my classification.

Men that I worked with at Allens could not understand my view. Being in a Quaker family was an important part of it. One of the earliest books I read while I was at Westtown was, *The Power of Nonviolence*, by Richard Graves. That gave me a strong background. One of my most successful converts was Alec Wilson, who was a chief machinist at one of the shops. He wanted to try to understand me. I said I did not want to go and fight, but I wanted to do a job of national importance, things a pacifist could do rather than killing people. He said it was the first time he had heard anything like that. Then he handed me two dollars and told me he wanted me to use it wherever I needed to. He had come to this country from Scotland as a young man and become a machinist at Allens. He wanted to help the group that I was joining. There were a lot of people who didn't understand, but that was no problem for me. I had a lot of opposition anyway because I wouldn't join the union. They called me all kinds of names for that. I liked to think I was a free thinker.

I was sent to CPS[14] Camp in Royalston, Massachusetts. It was an old Civilian Conservation Corps[13] camp. We had about fifty men there. You can imagine a camp that was made up of all kinds of religions that were in CPS.[14] We had four or five who were followers of Father Divine.[24] When they joined the Father Divine group, they were fed and housed by him—they were taken care of. They were all renamed after they joined to show that they had been reborn. When they went up to the draft board, they said, "I'm not eligible. I'm only three years old. I'm not old enough to sign an application yet." But that didn't affect the draft board. They had them sign it anyway.

One was renamed Peaceful Brother. He was African American and he looked like anything but a peaceful brother. If you wanted to star him in a movie, he would be a perfect gangster's chauffeur. He was heavy and strong willed, but he was still a pacifist. We had open bedrooms with bunk beds along the walls. We all ate together, worked together, and lived together. We soon learned to forget about race—we were all part of the group.

We were digging water holes, little ponds to collect water for forest fire protection. They would bring in pumps to spray the water out, a quick water supply in wooded areas. After about a year some American Friends Service Committee[4] men came. One was a personnel man from one of the hospitals in New York City. They asked if anyone was interested in working in the hospital. It was work of national importance as far as the draft board was concerned. I thought about it for awhile. It was a difficult decision because I had a personal dislike of hospitals, but it seemed to me that working in a hospital was more important than digging water holes.

I would be working at Columbia Medical Center, right at 168th Street in Manhattan in New York City. Peggy and I were married about three months before I was called up and my wife was working for Bell Telephone in Philadelphia, a short distance away from New York. I could take an overnight and go down to Philadelphia to see her.

We were both members of Friends; in fact I met her at a meeting. She was a member of a meeting in Ohio. We realized that we couldn't have a Friends wedding because of the time involved to get approval, so we had a Friends wedding of our own type at her uncle's home there in Philadelphia.

I worked at Columbia Medical Center for a year and then found out they needed help at a mental hospital in

Vermont, where my wife could come with me. I talked it over with Peggy and we decided that it would be a good direction to try. We were both uncertain about what it would mean. Would they slam the gates behind us? We went up there and it wasn't like that at all. It was an open area. No gates at all. Brattleboro Retreat was a very unusual hospital. For one thing, it was located in Vermont. It was actually a private hospital, but they took in state patients. Vermont was not able to provide enough space for all their patients, so they paid a per diem amount for all the state patients they turned over to the Brattleboro Hospital. That made Brattleboro part of the state setup.

We were there until the end of the war, about three years. We had Peggy's money, for she was getting the regular salary for working there. She became pregnant, and we decided it would be a good thing for her to get a room in the town. She would be there and could go to the local hospital when the baby came along.

One of the important things, I thought, was the effect we had as pacifists on the individuals we met in Vermont, New York, and the other places, even in our own home town. When we went to Vermont, there had been a lot of violence used at that particular hospital. Taking care of the patients had really gone downhill. We came in as a group and established a new standard. There were a lot of things we wouldn't do. We were there to help the doctors and help the patients. We had a whole different style of handling the patients. The doctors became very friendly with us.

In Brattleboro the idea was that these conscientious objectors were going to take the work away from our employees. They didn't want to have anything to do with us. They thought we were just trying to get out of the war—that was their whole attitude. They didn't want us to even come into the restaurants in town. But it was only a matter of time before we broke that situation down and showed people that we were human.

One of the local hospitals had a doctor named Bob White who had a church program that he did at the hospital every third week. We were responsible to get the patients there who were able to go and stay with them for the service. He became very interested in us and tried to help out. He was a good contact in the town and helped people to know that we were doing a service, helping people out without killing. He was very much for us. We were able to go to his church if we wanted. We were accepted in the town much more freely because of his work.

When the war was over and after the baby came, we moved back to Philadelphia. We didn't have much money, and a young baby. Peggy went to her mother's with the baby for about three months while I stayed to get situated and try to get a job. I visited my aunt in Pitman and she said there were lots of houses available, so we saw a real estate agent. He had just had a call to sell a summer house for three thousand dollars. I looked at it and put money down on it. I called my wife, who was in Ohio with her parents and our daughter, and told her "We bought a house, but we need your $1,500. Bring the money and come on over." It was a lovely place for her and it worked out. You can imagine a summer house that people had come there from Philadelphia and just been down there for a month or so each year. They had it all furnished with china and a refrigerator, but no lighting in the house. There were four bedrooms and even the beds were there, it was furnished that way. It was just what we needed. I just had to do the insulation and get a heating system in by wintertime.

Allen's was no longer in existence, but I remembered one of the men I had worked with told me to look him up when I got out of CPS.[14] I found he had started a company in Philadelphia. When I called him, he said by all means, come. We'll find a job for you. They had a place down at 3rd and Chestnut Street. I worked as a design draftsman for them. At that time, companies would get a contract and sometimes they did not have enough men for work. So they would send out men for a short time. I would stay with them until they got situated, then I would come back to the main office and take another group out and do the same thing. We were doing a lot of work for General Electric. They were overwhelmed and we would send out a group of 25 or so men.

Pacifism certainly figured in what I decided to do. I wouldn't do any work related to any armed services or anything like that. Probably one of the closest ones I had was work for the Army. They had a canvas cover that was used for a gun cover that they had no drawings of. I did work on that.

I worked about four years with them. They were only be able to pay me when they had work, so I had a lot of time off. I found a friend that I went to Westtown with was working with American Viscous. They has a plant in Marcus Hook. It sounded awfully good to me. He had a kidney problem, so he had to go to the hospital for three months. They gave him his full pay for the time he was there. I thought that was wonderful—any company that would treat you like that. So I went to their office, which happened to be in Philadelphia, and was hired as a drafting engineer for American Viscous. I spent 25 years with them. They were bought out by FM Tool Machinery Corporation, but I stayed on with them.

We had two girls. They went to public school there in Pitman, New Jersey, because it was a very good school, and the nearest Friends school was not available to them because of distance involved. They both graduated from the school there in Pitman, and then went on with their work.

The nearest Friends Meeting was at Mullica Hill about five miles away. We went there instead of Philadelphia because it was closer. We kept our membership in Philadelphia but they had a First-day School at Mullica Hill, which was good for our girls. We had a lot of friends and family there.

I have tried to live a peaceful life. People have come to me to ask me about it, so I have done it by the way I've lived, more than going out and standing on a street corner and advertising.

I think I am proudest of my family, and what they've done, particularly the progress that they have made. I was pretty proud of the fact that after I got out of CPS[14] with basically no money, I was able to get a small house and completely rebuild it while I worked at a job at the same time.

I regret that more people are not interested in being pacifists and seeing that there are other ways to overcome the problems that we have in this world besides fighting and killing. I think that some of them are just not brought up right in the beginning. You can't start out teaching them to defend themselves and that the strongest is the best, rather than the thinking man. It's difficult to change them, although we have met a great many that have changed, simply through contact and seeing our example as pacifists.

Because it is my decision I like to feel that's the truth. I'm sure it has affected some of the people I've contacted, but it's a slow process that takes a long time. Being a pacifist is not a very popular thing to advertise, particularly at the time when there's a great deal of war stress going on. But there is another way to do it.

It is difficult for those who have not been brought up as Quakers, but a lot of Quakers are not pacifists. They don't normally have to be. But I think it's very important to realize that there is another way of living, and it affects your everyday life. It isn't just at one time when there's a draft, or a decision you make and hold to for the rest of your life. It is important to pass it along, which you do through example rather than through lecturing or preaching.

Warren D. Sawyer *(1920)*

"The real estate business is responsible, I think, for creating new ghettos."

A t the time I joined the Religious Society of Friends[52] in 1937, I accepted that I would be a pacifist, no matter what happened. I knew that if a war ever broke out, that would be my position, or, if it was not my position, I would immediately resign from the Religious Society of Friends. I was an idealist! It seems to me that pacifism automatically goes right along with "there is that of God in every man"[26] as a dual thing, so they're both tied together. If you're one, you should be the other.

I started going to Quaker church—pastor, minister, choir and all that stuff —in Poplar Ridge, New York, in 1933. I went there regularly, to young people's gatherings, Sunday school, sang in the choir and so on, but I didn't join until 1937. I read tremendous numbers of books on Quakerism. I think, as far as I was concerned, I got a very good picture of what it was all about, and a fairly good picture of how and what I should be.

I am the first Quaker in my family, and the only pacifist, also. When I was 13 years old, I left my mother in New York City and went to live on a farm in Poplar Ridge, an old Quaker community. Elroy Reynolds, the minister, was a pacifist in World War I, and had gone to Europe in relief work. He had a great deal of influence upon me, though I'm sure he didn't realize it. He was a very humble man. Another man, Frank Olmsted, was a pacifist—and a Socialist—and those two men influenced me greatly just by the way they lived. The minister, and the Socialist—it seemed to me that those two things went together, socialism as a good, Christian political set-up. So I've always had socialist feelings and attitudes in terms of

Interviewed by Priscilla Adams, transcribed and edited by Terry Engeman

development in the country, and I voted Socialist a number of times. I strongly believe, like Frank Olmsted did, that the natural resources of this country: coal, oil, minerals, all these sorts of things, should belong to the people, to the government, instead of companies taking advantage of them for their own profit and gain. And that's a much more Christian way of looking at economics than what we have. I think those two were the main influences in my life to become what I am.

Going to the farm after I left my mother in New York at age 13 was the best decision I ever made, to give me the kind of environment that I wanted, without the bigotry and anti-racial things that went on in New York, even in my family. They all used words like "niggers," "kikes" and "wops" and all that sort of thing. So, getting away from that, Quakerism appealed to me tremendously in terms of hoping to overcome words of that sort.

Poplar Ridge was a rural, country town, just 150 people, and we had a farm one mile away from there. I had two aunts—my mother's sister, and a courtesy aunt who owned the farm. So with farming, milking ten cows twice a day, getting up at 4 am, then school, I never had much time for any kind of athletics. We didn't do much in the Depression days. There was a basketball team and baseball team, but that was about it. I was not very good in either one. I didn't have much spare time on the farm—working when I got home until suppertime, then studying at night. All summer I worked in the fields, on the threshing machines, in the garden and all the rest. A hobby that I did follow for many years was collecting stamps from all over the world.

The school was small. Being in a small school and getting a lot of attention was a big benefit for me, because I'm a lousy student. There was a big centralized school that I could have gone to, but I was sent to this one instead, hoping that the smaller school would help me the most.

My favorite subject has always been History. I hate Math and Science. I always read. I read twenty and thirty books a year, beyond what was required. And I still read a great deal. I'm not a fast reader, but I love to read.

I finished high school in 13 years. Prior to the war, in 1940, I went to Madison College, a Seventh Day Adventist college in Nashville, Tennessee. I worked six hours a day, studied six hours a day, and did homework in the evening. I started work in the morning at 6:00 a.m., worked till 12 p.m., had classes in the afternoon, and so on. I hadn't been on campus an hour before my roommate was giving me the lecture on Seventh Day Adventism. I think I was the only Quaker that ever hit that school. I worked with foreign students there and one of my best friends there was a Japanese, Isiro Nakashima. On the morning of December the 8th I got up, and he was gone. I never saw him again. I don't know what happened to him. I suppose the FBI had all these guys lined up long before Pearl Harbor. That experience had a profound impression on me as far as international relations and interracial relations, so I've tried to work at this sort of thing most of my life.

After the war I went to William Penn College in Oskaloosa, Iowa, for a year. I was married then. It was a Quaker school, which I liked much better than Seventh Day Adventists. I took the basic courses, English, History, Math, Biology. I didn't graduate; I only had one year at each of those places, one before, and one after the war.

At the time of Pearl Harbor I had no problems whatsoever, being accepted as a conscience objector (CO).[17] I registered in Tennessee and got my draft card, and that was it. It was very simple. Since pacifism is a part of Quakerism, there were no second thoughts in my mind about making any other choice. I accepted whatever came my way. I never debated the idea of going to prison or not going to prison. That thought never occurred to me until

I got into CPS,[14] and then some of them were leaving CPS and going into prison. But I stayed in CPS the whole four years.

There was no backing from the family, of course. My youngest brother volunteered for the Marines on December 8th, 1941. My second brother waited until he was drafted into the Army. I was drafted February 5th, 1942. My dad was anti-everything—no Catholics, Jews, or Negroes. My mother was against pacifism. The two aunts were not against it, they just didn't understand it, even though one of them, my courtesy aunt, had been born and brought up a Quaker. They never made any remarks pro or con. I felt comfortable at the farm, with a Quaker church there, and with the people there. There were only two other fellows from that church that were COs beside myself. After the war one of the members of the church told me that she had a star put on the flag for all the veterans.

When I was 17 years old and was joining the Quakers, I hoped to find, some day, a woman who looked Quaker and also used the plain language. Ruth was a teacher at Westtown. She had come to Byberry before Thanksgiving, and I said to someone, the first time I met her that evening at Byberry, "That's the girl I'm going to marry." She used the plain language, which I liked. I shared her with an army Quaker doctor from Langhorne Meeting—he'd see her one-week, I'd see her the next. So beginning in March—we did that alternating business for dates. We'd both met her at the same time and we both proposed to her at the same time. Why she picked me over a doctor, when she wanted to be a nurse, I had no idea, but I got her.

In terms of our married life, it was very quiet, she wasn't an excitable person. She was a thoughtful person, generous in many ways, but she wasn't a rah rah rah kind of person. She was a teacher, but she didn't want to be a teacher all her life, she was going to go to nursing school. She was going to go to Columbia Nursing School, and was accepted, and I interfered with that, in terms of her career plans. We were married in 1945, in October, and I got discharged on her birthday, in January of 1946, so I didn't have much experience as a married man at CPS.[14]

I'm not so sure that she liked my activism attitude. I had a lot of things that came out of the CPS experience in terms of my feelings and attitudes, and things that I thought I should do. While we were at William Penn College, Ruth and I organized a demonstration against peacetime conscription from Oskaloosa. We had a truck, and we drove around to all the colleges in Iowa to let them know about this peace demonstration we were planning. We had about 150, maybe 200 people in the peace demonstration that we held in Des Moines at the public library, with an evening meeting for discussion and speakers. We felt it was pretty successful. We strung out in Des Moines about 25 feet apart, one, by one going down the main streets of Des Moines with banners. Then we assembled in front of the capitol building and had our picture taken. I've got that picture.

After the war I went to Poland in April, just after I was married, and took 800 horses to Danzig to help get the farms started again. It was a Brethren[7] project that later turned into the Heifer Project.[33] The great idea was to get animals to people who need them to sustain their lives. You give a calf to a family, and the first-born calf has to be given to someone else who doesn't have one. From the first litter of pigs, you give part of that litter to other families who don't have any and that's the way that the project grew. (*The photo on the next page was taken on a Heifer Project ship.*)

After CPS and the Heifer Project, my position as a CO was absolutely no problem. Back in my little village of 150 people I had a job assured to me at Simkins Hardware.

The Simkins were pacifists, longtime Quakers. Robert Simkin was an Elder, he had been a missionary in China for many years, and they were all COs. He took that position even though he was too old to be drafted. So I had this job, at any time I wanted, after the war. We bought a home and lived there for four years, but the pay was very

low. For the first two or three years I got $35 a week. It didn't go very far, as inflation was progressing. Besides, I didn't want to be a hardware person all my life. I had to think of something else.

I went to Delaware, Ohio, to a cooperative community with a farm and a print shop where we printed books, the songbooks that were given to CPS[14] camps. We did things for 4-H and Boy Scouts, plus making games to be sold—international game boards with directions. The presentation for me to come there was to sell these games. When I got there, I never had an opportunity to sell anything. They had me working in the print shop, folding the books and packaging them to be mailed. I got frustrated very quickly with that, because I wanted to be in the selling business, as it was originally presented to me. While we were there, the owner brought a family as refugees for the Rural Service from Danzig, Poland—Andrew Demidenko, who had two kids. He handed us the job of helping them get acquainted. We spent a lot of time with them. They worked with me planting trees.

Then I got a job selling products door-to-door, working with a man who was an Earlham graduate, a very devout Quaker. He offered me a job any time I wanted to come from Delaware, Ohio to Columbus, Ohio, a matter of thirty miles. We bought a house trailer and lived in it for a year while I was getting established, with the idea that after I'd worked with him for a year, selling door to door, I'd have a distributorship of my own. That ended up being in Wheeling, West Virginia, but it was not too successful because the ironworks and the coal miners were all on strike at the same time. You can't sell anything then! So we only stayed there a year and then went to Kansas City, Missouri, to manage the city distribution center.

From there I went to Philadelphia. We bought a house in Moorestown and I ran a distributorship in Philadelphia. Then we transferred to Memphis, Tennessee, and I had charge of sales for Arkansas, Oklahoma and Texas. I was away one or two weeks at a time, which was difficult on the family. I give my wife full, one-hundred percent credit for raising our kids to become what they are and who they are, because I wasn't there, except weekends.

Next we went to Lexington, Kentucky, where I was in charge of the eastern half of the state in sales. I had been an NAACP supporter for a long time. When we were in Lexington I carried a sandwich board on the street in front of the 5 & 10, to integrate that 5 & 10. It's the hardest job I ever had, because that's where I got the most antagonism, with people spitting at me and shouting at me. I hadn't experienced much of that in my life, but I did have it there.

We were in Kentucky for two years, and then decided we wanted to bring our kids back north to get their education, so we came back to Moorestown, New Jersey where my wife, a Quaker, was born and raised. The kids went to Moorestown Friends School. I looked for a job, got one at the *Burlington County Times* and worked there for a year, selling real estate advertising. Five different real estate brokers offered me jobs if I ever decided that I wanted to leave the paper, so I quit the paper and worked with a lady up in Mount Holly for seven years. At the end of seven years I came back to Moorestown. I've been there now for forty-two years in Moorestown selling real estate. I felt I had a mission, when I went into the real estate business, to get anybody, whoever they might be, a house that they could afford wherever they might choose to live, but I didn't have many opportunities. Moorestown being a fairly well off town, there weren't many blacks who had hopes of even living in Moorestown. But anyway, I helped a few people get houses where they wanted to live.

I had some interesting experiences in selling to blacks. Along with pacifism, the respect for other persons is equally important, and if you're a Quaker and believe that there is that of God in every person, you have to respect other people for who or what they are.[26] The real estate business is responsible, I think, for creating new ghettos. When I went into that I knew what my feelings would be.

A teacher at Friends School wanted to buy a house. He didn't have much money, but he could afford one in Riverside. I found a house, sold it to him, and he came back to the office. Then the broker for that house called me because I showed a black man a "white person's house." He said, "I want you to know the house is off the market." He warned me, "Don't ever try to show one of my houses again." That's against the law, so I reported that broker to the New Jersey Realtor Board. He could have lost his license, but he was also a lawyer. The state came down and talked to him. What they said I don't know, all

I know is he kept on working. But at least I reported him for illegal actions.

I went on to show a house of his in Rancocas Woods to a young woman with two kids, a veteran's widow. He was killed, and she had ten thousand dollars. She came into our office in Moorestown and told me she'd been to a lot of other brokers but nobody could help her. I knew why—because she was black. I told her that I would help her. Any place you can afford to buy, in any town, I'd be glad to help you. I found a house in Rancocas Woods, and she bought it. Of course he didn't want me to show it, because there were no blacks there at the time.

A teacher had been teaching French in high school in Mount Holly. He got a Ford Foundation grant to go to Africa for three years. The school had written to him saying that his job would still be available if he came back to Mount Holly. When he came back I told him, "I'll be glad to help you get a house, anywhere that you can afford. I will not let you dangle or pass you off."

Burlington County Trust Company had had $10,000 of his in a savings account for at least three years. Naturally I suggested he apply there for a mortgage. The house that he was looking at was in the most exclusive area in Mount Holly, Dawn Drive, the lakes area. The bank dilly-dallied around for several weeks. There was no excuse for those delays; there wasn't that much business activity. I went to them and said, "What's the matter here, what's taking you so long? I want a mortgage commitment within ten days for this gentleman. He's been banking with you all these years and you have ten thousand dollars of his money, or we'll go somewhere else." In no time I had a mortgage commitment for the man. The house he bought was right next door to the urban renewal guy working for the federal government. And was he mad because I put a black guy right next to him!

Any black person that came in, no other salesman would follow up on them, because they were afraid that they would get accused of integration. Real estate people never think about the fact that they are the ones that are creating new ghettos. When I was in Kansas City a real estate broker had sold to a black person, and in the yards all over the geographical area there were signs: "This House is Not for Sale," "Don't bother calling this house!" in people's front yards. They had accepted the black family. It was a demonstration of the wishes of the people. It was not so much in support of the black family, but to discourage real estate people from coming down and using the scare tactics, "There's a black family down the street! List your house and get out of here while you can get the top price!" But they put up all those signs, which I thought was quite interesting.

When we came back to Moorestown to live, we got involved in the Committee of International Visitors. We had people come for weekends and stay at our house from all around the world—Europe, Asia, Africa.

I worked with Global Volunteers, Global Citizens Network it's called now. It was set up whereby you go into a community with volunteers who would work along with the people in that community. We did not go there to do the work, but to help them improve to do the work. Through this organization I went to Tanzania, Indonesia, Belize, New Mexico, Cupa and Haiti. For Witness for Peace I went to Nicaragua.

I have been a financial contributor to peace organizations for a long time and have been involved in demonstrations in Washington for women's rights, blacks, and all kinds of things. I've been on the Peace and Social Order Committee for 33 years at Moorestown Meeting— not always an official member—but that's the committee I like.

My first wife, Ruth, started volunteering to read textbooks for the blind. Reading a textbook is very difficult; you have to put all the punctuation in when you're reading. When she died, I took up the case and I have been broadcasting to the blind every Wednesday morning for twenty years, reading the Philadelphia Inquirer.

Since I was in Philadelphia every Wednesday morning, I took on another job, so I am a guide in Arch Street Meeting House on Wednesday afternoons. I also haul clothing and food for our Meeting into Camden, approximately every ten days, for New Visions.

I volunteer for different things at Medford Leas, my retirement community. I like to work in the gardens. I try to give about eight hours a week to the landscaping department. I have a big flower garden and a big vegetable garden of my own. For a number of years now I've been taking people who are caregivers to the hospital, doctors' appointments, shopping, whatever it might be, one day a week. I worked in prisons for six years, helping to conduct Alternatives to Violence Program[2] workshops. It always takes two to conduct these workshops. One weekend a month we conduct these workshops to try to better the relationships between prisoners, to teach them to respect and listen to their fellow prisoners, to get along better. It's amazing to me, not that it happens overnight, not that the change is profound, but it's interesting to see the change in attitudes and feelings, the improvement in interracial problems.

I've enjoyed my life. I'm kind of a happy-go-lucky, un-philosophical individual. I do have some regrets, and one is that traveling kept me away from the family when the kids were growing up, when I should have been there. I also have regrets at the time I spent trying to support my family my first six years in real estate, which were formative years for the kids. I was working until nine or ten o'clock at night because the office in Mount

Holly was open that late. I would see them at breakfast, and I wouldn't see them again until the following morning. That's why I give all the credit to my wife for raising the kids and the fact that they turned out as well as they have. That's the main regret that I have.

As far as lessons for future generations, I'm mostly concerned about Quakerism. It seems to me to make our Religious Society of Friends stronger, that everybody who wants to join should attend for at least a year on a regular basis, and read plenty of material on Friends. Then they can express the interest in joining, accepting some of these things. They may have a vague idea of what we think, how we act, but to really get it within the person's spirit and mind takes more than two months, eight Sundays. We have a few people like that, who want to join right away. I think that is terribly wrong, as far as the good of the organization is concerned, as far as the spirituality is concerned.

What would I like people to know about CPS[14]? I think it's important that we should emphasize every time we have an opportunity, that there is a CO position, not only among the Quakers but among every other religion also. I don't hide the fact that I was a CO in World War II. People are sometimes reluctant to admit it, but I don't know why. They're not going to be ostracized by this time. They might have been during the war, but they're certainly not now. To me, it's a mainstay of being a Quaker. CPS matured me considerably. I enjoyed listening to these guys philosophizing over nothing—by the hour! I just sat there and listened. I had nothing to say. I wasn't in their league as far as intellectual abilities are concerned. But I had a good time and it was a very stimulating experience. I don't know that it made me any stronger a pacifist as a result of being in CPS, because I was in that position before I went.

Chapter Two
Social Workers

Chapter Two
Social Workers

S. Allen Bacon

Edwin P. Stephenson

F. Evert Bartholomew

John Bartholomew

Chosing Social Work as their profession, these social change agents absorbed their mother's gentle reminders, their Sunday School lessons or the customs of a segregated Southern United States. Then they set out for college. Here they were challenged to question all they had previously learned. Three graduated with Masters Degrees and one with a Doctorate. John Bartholomew taught social work and the others became powerful shining lights in depressed urban areas. Though they mention having to change jobs because the low pay did not cover the expenses of their growing families, they did not leave the field. They became Directors of very large and complicated social service agencies.

The Bartholomew brothers are the first of several pairs of siblings in this book who demonstrate the complexities and challenges that family life presented as they went into adulthood.

S. Allen Bacon (1919)

"I thought I was doing something to improve conditions in Philadelphia and cut down on violent crime."

After a couple of years of public school my parents sent me and my brothers and sister to what they called a progressive private school in Cleveland, which was not religious or pacifist in any way, but people were tolerant. It was a liberal influence, I would say.

Yes, I played competitive sports. We had a little football team and baseball. I don't think I was particularly competitive when I was at Park School and then I went to Westtown. That was before the Second World War. There were two German boys who came to Westtown. I think they were members of Hitler Youth! They thought Germany was a great nation, better than the rest of the world. There was a lot of good discussion in the dorm.

I would say on the whole it was a fairly happy and undisturbed childhood. I had conflicts with my older brother, who was stronger than me, and we sometimes fought, but on the whole we got along very well. We had an active neighborhood in Cleveland, and we had lots of kids to play with on our block. We "liberated" various pieces of wood so that we could build our clubhouses. I remember a rather upsetting experience. There was a kid who had some kind of chronic illness and so he was marginalized. He wasn't a member of our small neighborhood group. It got kind of nasty toward him. His father built a clubhouse for him, because we had built one. His parents were very indulgent. I played with him because I felt a little sorry for him. He had lots of toys and we made lead soldiers. But I was a member of the "opposition," so one night we went over and turned his clubhouse upside down. He knew that I had been a part of that.

Interviewed by Mary R. Hopkins and transcribed by Terry Engeman

At Westtown I especially liked English and History. I had a history teacher I didn't like, but I was interested in his classes. The English teacher was across the hall from him. The history teacher was a Republican and the English teacher was a Democrat. They were both named Brown, but the latter had a sense of humor. Of the students, I would say, the majority were Republican, as my father was. He voted for Hoover, the Quaker president who had also facilitated the child feeding in Germany. But my father converted to be a Democrat after 1936. I think my mother voted for Norman Thomas whenever she could.

I went on to Haverford College for my freshman year, but I wasn't too thrilled with Haverford. I thought it was kind of a continuation of Westtown, and I was beginning to get a little rebellious at Westtown. I thought Haverford wasn't going to offer me what I was looking for, which was something more liberal. My roommate at Westtown had gone to Antioch College so I took a year out and worked, partly to save up money for tuition and partly just to get my bearings, and then I transferred to Antioch. My major was Sociology and History. I didn't like the technical side of sociology so much as the philosophical side. I was appealed to by Dr. Manmatha Nath Chatterjee, who was an Indian professor of Brahmin background, very much a Gandhi follower, so I got pretty involved in that. He was the campus guru. He was quite popular with the students who were inclined in that direction. He was challenging, he used the Socratic method of teaching, and challenged even the more conservative people on campus.

We had some bad experiences with some of the Communists on campus. We were on campus when Stalin and Hitler arranged that pact in which Hitler agreed not to attack Russia if Russia would not join the alliance against Germany. The Communists on campus were in favor of peace until Hitler attacked Russia, when they switched from being so-called pacifists to being interventionists. They claimed that all pacifists should be, if not shot, at least disenfranchised. That kind of political switch was very destructive. The Communists also tried to infiltrate our interracial activities and manipulate them to support the Communist cause.

There were many active pacifists on campus at that time. Quite a number of my good friends were stalwart pacifists. Three of them went to jail for refusing to register for Selective Service. I think one of them registered, but then refused to go to CPS.[14] The others were not given their CO status and went to jail as a result. There were eight or nine of those pacifists on campus who were headed toward CPS.

When the draft act took effect, which was October 16, 1940, I registered. I had asked for a 4-E classification. With my Quaker background that wasn't hard to get. My father was well known in Cleveland. He was Dean of the School of Architecture and served on the Enemy Alien Hearing Board which was to detect what we would call terrorists today. In those days they were Japanese or German. So, it wasn't hard for me to get a 4-E classification. My brothers also went into CPS. My older brother was married by that time, and served for a while in the Quaker camps.

I went to a Brethren[7] camp in Walhalla, Michigan, because I was interested in the consumer cooperative movement. Morris Mitchell was the leader and was offering a course in the cooperative movement that I wanted to take, so I chose that instead of a Quaker camp. I was only there for three months. We planted trees, but when the local farmers were facing an emergency because of shortage of labor, we were asked to help. We were picking cherries and bringing in the corn harvest. I was almost discharged because I got asthma when we were putting up silage in the silos. So they took me to have a physical exam to see if I had too much asthma to continue work, but the asthma cleared up as soon as I saw the doctors!

Margaret[5] and I were married by that time also. Actually we were married before we graduated from Antioch and before I was drafted.

After those three months in camp, I had a chance to do mental hospital work, where my wife could also work. So I transferred and we spent the rest of the war in mental hospital work in Sykesville and Bowie, Maryland.

At the mental hospital there was a good deal of feeling against the conscientious objectors.[17] We were there as a unit, and there must have been 25 or 30 of us, including some wives. We replaced men who were drafted and women who got better paying war work. There were nurses whose husbands were in the Army and some of them were pretty nasty, calling us "yellow-bellies" and showing their disdain and dislike in various ways. But it wasn't devastating and we had our own group for support.

As the war was winding down, the Selective Service was beginning to discharge people who had been in for the required time, but I had not. The director of Camp Bowie in Maryland was discharged and they asked me to take his place for six months.

At the end of the war I decided I might want to teach history or go into academia rather than settlement house work or some other form of social work. So I went to Harvard and got my Master's degree in Education with a minor in History. I got a job at Friends Academy on Long Island and taught for three years there.

I was still interested in doing something more dramatic in the world when somebody called me from the American Friends Service Committee[4] to ask me to be the Director of the U. S. work camp program. Besides the experience as Director of a CPS[14] camp run by the Service Committee, I had worked for the Service Committee in the Student Peace Service in the summer of 1939. Through my father and all his Service Committee connections I guess they knew about me, and so they offered me the job.

I left teaching to direct the U. S. work camp program for three years. One of the work camps was in Philadelphia at a settlement house,[58] Friends Neighborhood Guild. I had known about a settlement house in Cleveland, and a member of our meeting there was the director of the settlement. The director of the Guild asked if I would like to come and work for him, saying he would pay me more than the Service Committee job. By that time we had all three of our children, so $4,000 wasn't much to live on, even in those days. The $5,000 at the settlement house looked great, so I switched jobs. Also it was an interesting field. So that is what I did pretty much for the rest of my career. My last job was at the Episcopal Community Services, directing their Center for Human Services. We had about 17 different social service programs.

I felt I was expressing my pacifism because I thought I was doing something to improve conditions in Philadelphia and cut down on violent crime. One of my major projects at Friends Neighborhood Guild was to develop a program called "Operation Poplar." We worked with the gangs in the Poplar area to cut down on the delinquency rate. We were working with gangs mainly from the public housing projects and addressing all the problems there. My chief activism was largely through my Meeting, being against the Vietnam War and working for reforms in the city.

I am proudest of my children and my grandchildren. Almost without exception they are into the same kind of work I was doing. My son built the house that we have in Maine, and his son is a builder, but they're into green, solar housing. Another grandson is working in Nicaragua and Latin America on free trade coffee and equal exchange and developing co-ops among the campesinos. He got his Ph.D. in Ecology. The youngest child, Annie, is running work camps in El Salvador, Nicaragua and Guatemala. Another grandson, my daughter's son is becoming a stock broker. So he is going to do very well! But he is also interested in reform and he's the only one who's specifically interested in going to Quaker Meeting. None of our children continued as active Quakers but they're all doing Quakerly kinds of things, and they all practice meditation. One is a clinical psychologist and with her husband is working with refugees on the Thai-Burma border. She still keeps her membership in Germantown Friends Meeting.

I regret that I struggled in actually making the decision to go into CPS.[14] I struggled with whether I should refuse to cooperate with the military system and go to jail to make a stronger witness. Looking back, I don't think that was so important a decision. In terms of alternatives to war, it wouldn't have that much meaning to the outside world. I do somewhat regret not pursuing the cooperative movement. The settlement movement, though it was very nitty gritty, and dealing with all of the cities' urban problems, wasn't so much about moving the world into an alternative direction; it was a little too much ameliorating the conditions, not changing them. I think that would be my major regret.

Even if we see all the terrible things that have been going on today, we have made a lot of progress in race relations, gender issues, and being more aware of the stupidity of war and its consequences. I'm impressed with how many of the Quaker values are espoused by other religious groups, which they were not when I was growing up. Discrimination against the Jews is not tolerated so much any more. The U.S. is doing its best to keep the Mexicans out, but also trying to do well for those that are here, even though there are conflicting paradoxes. I see things moving forward if we don't blow ourselves up.

When we were at Antioch, Bronson Clark, who was later the head of the American Friends Service Committee,[4] and other friends of mine, had this farm where we claimed to be training for nonviolence, searching for any alternative way to deal with Hitler. Dr. Chatterjee at Antioch, was pretty way out, but he put up $5,000 to help us start this training program on the farm near Cleveland. We called it "Ahimsa" and we had people from the Fellowship of Reconciliation[25] and from Congress on Racial Equality,[16]

James Farmer[23] and Bayard Rustin.[54] Bayard had come to Antioch and we were in communication with him. So we were doing a lot of studying about nonviolent resistance. I think that is what I would like to pass on. It's a growing concept now: the struggle in South Africa and revolutions in Poland and Serbia. Even in the Arab-Israeli conflict there are elements of nonviolence. We need alternatives to war and to reduce violence.

Edwin P. Stephenson *(1918)*

*I can't distinguish very clearly between violence and
social injustice. They go hand in hand.*

My mother was a Quaker but my father was not.
There was no Quaker meeting in the small eastern
North Carolina towns in which we lived. There was one
where my mother grew up, and we would oftentimes
go out and visit there. However, I identified as a Quaker
even in school. I was considered to be somewhat different from the rest because I liked my Quaker heritage. I
grew up recognizing that I would never fight, that is, I
would never carry arms, but I thought I would be a non-
combatant. That was my thinking in my youth, primarily because my mother's brother had been a 1-AO during
World War I. Men classified as 1-AO were drafted into
the military as a non-combatant, did not carry arms. The
4-E was for COs. In World War II they provided for what
they called "work of national importance under civilian
direction," but it was neither.

I grew up in eastern North Carolina as a very typical Southern white boy with all the prejudice about the
blacks that we now recognize. However, in those days
that's just the way things were. They were different from
us, and, therefore, they went to different schools, different churches, and different restaurants. If they came to
work at our home they came through the back door. They
would never sit down and eat with us, although they
would sit in the kitchen where we often ate, just not at the
same time as the blacks. My father owned a small lum-
ber business, which was really a family affair. My mother
kept the books and my older brother and I worked in
the plant, even as teenagers. I became a very good truck
driver and prided myself on being able to drive anything
with four wheels on the ground and one in my hands.

Interviewed and transcribed by Virginia Major Thomas

Going to high school, Guilford College would come to the local town of Wilson, N.C. to play the local college. I would root for the Quakers rather than for the local college, and had no questions in my mind but what I would be going to Guilford College. And I did.

However I was one of the most naïve freshmen that ever entered college. I felt hazing was part of the way in which the sophomores were welcoming the freshmen. I got exempted from most of the hazing because I went out for football for the first time in my life. My parents never would allow me to go out for football when I was in high school. So I got out of much of the hazing, but then one night the sophomores had us freshmen in a room. They wanted us to wipe off the smiles on our faces, but I was enjoying the thing so much it was difficult for me not to keep smiling. They kept insisting on my wiping off the smile and I'd do it but then I'd crack up again. Pretty soon they put me over a chair and beat the hell out of me. And I'm telling you, I realized, I mean, this was serious, and I went back to my room cursing like a sailor and threatening to sue them— it was not fun anymore.

I don't know that it necessarily had any effect on my feelings about violence, except I thought it was a horrible way to welcome young innocent boys out of the backwoods of North Carolina into college. So in the spring when we had the elections for the coming sophomore year, I campaigned for my roommate to be President of the class and we won. The next year we eliminated hazing in the college. That was my first attempt to do any kind of social change.

When I was at Guilford, we had a new sociology professor from New Jersey who made a fool of me when I defended the southern social mores in his classroom. So, when he and my roommate organized a tea one Sunday afternoon for black students from A&T College in a neighboring city, I organized a boycott. I was boycotting the tea where there were black people coming. They were trying to integrate the students. I was very much against that, saying, "That's not our way, that's importing these damn Yankee ideas down." In my early youth "damnyankee" was one word. So I grew up with that kind of background.

I had to quit school for a couple of years and worked at the plant because of the health of my father. When I went back, I took a major in Math, which is what I'd started off my freshman year with, but I didn't care for the math professor. So I went to the physics professor and said "Can I do my thesis under you?" And he said "Well you have to have a minor in physics" and so I took some courses in physics.

I loved it so much that I came out with a double major in Math and Physics and did research on the diffraction of light. That impressed my professor enough that he wanted to know if I would be interested in going to the University of Michigan to graduate school. I just couldn't perceive of myself, this little boy from the backwoods of North Carolina, being at the University of Michigan—forget it. About six weeks later he came to me and said, "Red, the University of Michigan has accepted you in the graduate school and they're expecting you there on

June 23rd." Well, I was riding on clouds! I didn't write to my parents, I waited until I got home to tell them that I'd been accepted. My father got up, turned on his heel and walked out saying "It's something that I have a son who, the state of North Carolina is not good enough for him." My mother quietly said to me, "Pack your bags, you're gonna be going. You may have to go by bus but you're gonna go." So I went to Michigan.

The draft came along in 1940 when I was a senior at Guilford. I was a couple of years older than my classmates because I had been out for two years. I was going to register as a 1AO but it was obvious that I was in a state of flux; I wasn't sure myself; I wasn't clear about anything. I was not thinking about social issues, whereas my roommate had been very much involved in following the civil war in Spain. I couldn't care less. I thought, "that's overseas, somewhere else—that's not me." But Dr. Emil Garness Purdom, the Physics professor, then not a pacifist himself, and Dr. Milner, the President, for whom I drove quite a bit, raised questions with me as to whether in my uncertainty it wouldn't be better to register as a 4E, because it would be easier to go from 4E to 1AO than it would be to get out of the military if I went as 1AO. So in 1940 I registered as 4E. Only my mother was against violence, against war. My father was very embarrassed when I registered as a 4-E. I was the only 4-E in Wilson Country. So I graduated in 1941 with a double major in Math and Physics, and I was in the first batch to be called up.

There were 125 young men called up in the first draft. I always remember my number was 120. I got deferred until after I was out of college. I knew I could get into summer school before I was drafted, so I went to Michigan for the summer and had a fabulous time! I took 3 units more than you were allowed, because I didn't know which two courses I wanted to take. I thought I would drop one of them, and never did, but I made A's and B's. Some of the guys there talking with me saying, "Look, you don't have to go into the draft, why don't you join the Navy? They have a program in which they'll send you to MIT and in two years you'll have your master's degree and be an ensign." That way I could continue with what I wanted to do, so I went in and talked with them. I asked what we would be working on. They said that ships will no longer set off magnetic mines because they had developed something around the ship to keep it from detonating magnetic mines. So they are trying to find other ways to detonate a mine when a ship comes close to it. I said, that sounds too much like a Charles Addams cartoon. If I'm going to do any killing I'm going to do it on the front lines, and not in a lab." I thought they were going to throw me out of the office. But then I was more convinced than ever that I couldn't be part of the military.

Then I was told that I could get exempted because I was in Physics. I thought I would only be in for one year. I could take a year out and get it over with. That was in the summer of 1941. So I went back home and got drafted in October. I was called in and went to Buck Creek, North Carolina, to work on the Blue Ridge Parkway. I was driving dump trucks and having a great time on the weekends. I had friends who had cars and we'd go to Asheville or Greensboro where I had friends and spend the weekend. As long as we were ready to go to work on Monday morning, they didn't care. So I was having a ball.

Then one Sunday morning we got news that Pearl Harbor had been bombed, and all of a sudden I woke up and realized, this is serious. Chances are that they will not allow this kind of camp to continue. I was going to have to make a choice between going to the military or going to prison, and I wasn't ready for either of them. So I had to do a lot of soul-searching. The more I did, the more I was convinced that pacifism was my way. It was not necessarily the way for everybody, but certainly was for me. And then I got deeper into what this meant, and realized there are ways in which you can harm people other than killing them. The Southern mores toward the blacks was a way of damaging people. Intellectually I was able to reject Southern mores but it was still in my gut and I had to work through it. I applied to MIT and they offered me an opportunity to do some non-military scientific research, but General Hershey[34] didn't want the COs to be doing things that would bring honor to them.

I did get an opportunity to go to a research station in Coshocton, Ohio, where a lot of CCC[13] boys had been, so they had the barracks and the place for it. Several of us had degrees. I was able to work on moisture evaporation from the soil and wrote a paper for the Department of Agriculture. The first day a black man was assigned to the cot next to me. He was very sensitive, he never intruded on me, and any time I'd reach out he was available. I got to know him as a person and on an equal basis. He helped me a great deal in those early days of my conversion. This is where I started to know the emotional impact of the Southern mores.

In November, the congressman was elected on the basis that he was going to get the yellow-bellies out of his district. Before the end of the month we had orders to go to Oregon because there was such a high fire danger. They wanted us there right then and wouldn't even let us go on furlough to see our families. When we got to Elkton, Oregon, we saw the sun five times in 50 days.

That was the winter of 1942-43. They were building a road into an area that had been burned by a lightning strike and burned an area that was sort of inaccessible, so you had all these dead trees back in there, and it meant that if the lightning struck again it would be tinder. Except I went to the foreman and said, "Look, I thought we were going to build a road to get in to fight the forest fires. All of the grades going in are much steeper than the grades coming out, and all the curves are wide enough for a trailer and the biggest thing that we have is a ton and a half flat-bed truck, so obviously we are building a logging road." He said, "Well, we're not going to build two roads." And I said, "My brother has an exemption to work with my father to cut timber for the shipyards in Portsmouth, Virginia, so what am I doing out here building a road so you can cut more timber when I could be back there with my father?"

So I refused to work. They threatened me with prison, and I said "that's what it will have to be then." But instead of doing that, they assigned me to pull weeds in a forest nursery, and it was one of the most monotonous, miserable jobs I have ever had. The next summer we fought forest fires, and the next winter we planted trees in the snow in the Siskiyou National Forest and the Tillamook Burn. Dr. Farquhar of the University of Washington invited me to come and work for him because he had a wind tunnel and was studying suspension bridges. I told him I'd be very happy to work for him, but once again General Hershey would not allow me to go.

Next I got assigned to Orlando, Florida, where the Quakers had established a camp of 25 men under the Health Department for hookworm control, which meant building outdoor privies in rural areas and destroying the old ones. In those days the headquarters for the state Ku Klux Klan was in Orlando. I went to Orlando where the Quakers hoped that a group of us would study Gunnar Myrdal's book which had just come out, *The American Dilemma*. But before I got there I helped a couple of the men with some drama who had been working in a black school. Some of the white people took offense and they had to spirit the two COs out of the city. We never did study Myrdal.

I was interested in knowing more about blacks, so I went to NAACP meetings and other places where I would meet blacks. I was invited to go to a political meeting one Sunday night at a black Baptist church. All the white politicians had been invited, but none came. Many sent telegrams that were read at the meeting. Two of us from the CPS[14] camp were there and as we came out, we got arrested. We went to the police station and they were having us put things out of our pockets on a shelf, and I said I wanted to use the telephone. And they said, "put your stuff on the shelf." And I said, "I want to use the telephone." And they said, "Do you want to use the sweat room?" Well, I knew they had a sweat room and I knew they would use it. In Orlando, Florida, I was not about to get into a sweat room. So I went to jail.

They were charging us with recruiting labor to go out of the state without a license. To do that you needed a license from the state which cost $1000 and $500 additional for each county from which you were recruiting. The next morning I was able to give the drunk who had sobered up in my cell a telephone number and he called the camp. Pretty soon my buddy and I were invited to the Chief of Detectives' office and there was the Director of the camp and a visitor from Philadelphia, who just happened to be in town. The Chief of Detectives told us what our charges were and that they had people who were ready to swear to this. Well, that frightened me, because I had lived in the South long enough to know that if you want an affidavit against somebody there are ways in which you can get it, so if this is what they wanted they could do it, they could frame us. Nevertheless, they released us in the care of the camp with the understanding we were not to leave town without notifying them. But we never heard from them, and that was the end of that.

One of the people who helped me through my conversion was Wayne Jones. He and I met in camp in Coshocton, Ohio. Along with Al Johnson and Don Powell, Wayne and I often walked in the woods after dinner and talked. That was when I was first introduced to Huxley and read his writing. Philosophy and Sociology had never concerned me, because I was a Math major and a truck driver—a practical man. Wayne was the one who raised questions about what some of the psychological effects could be of Gandhi's work, if he wasn't careful of possible damaging effects on people. We had some very good arguments, discussions and readings, so I became much more sensitive to the underdog. Conversion has a lot of strength to it. That's what has driven me for most of my life.

All the camps I was in were run by the Quakers. They were set up under the pressure from the pacifist churches—the Mennonites, the Brethren[7] and the Quakers who had lobbied for some difference for the COs. They thought they were getting a good deal by having the COs to do work of "national importance under civilian direction," only to find out that General Hershey[34] would not allow the churches to find work for us. When camp was over, we got released but I was not satisfied with what I had done for four years.

When the war ended, the boys overseas were being brought back and released, and then we were being released according to whether or not you had a family and how long you had been in. I had been in well over four years by this time, so I was one of the first to get released. I had written to the Quakers and asked if there was something I could do in relief work.

The American Friends Service Committee4 asked me to come as a truck driver mechanic saying they would send me overseas. I stayed at Pendle Hill until I got my passport. That is where I first saw Madeleine, but she doesn't remember that. She was madly in love with a doctor in Philadelphia at that time. Her love for him actually extended as long as she lived. But he did not wish to get married. She said to him, if you don't want to get married, I'm going to go overseas. And she did. We met on the boat going over in 1946, but she was 5'2" and I don't look romantically at women 5'2." I'm 6'4." There's a little difference. So, this was a safe one for me.

We stayed in Paris for six weeks waiting for an assignment. We saw each other but we also saw other people of the opposite sex. Her job was to write publicity to raise more money. My first assignment was to go to Marseilles to haul food materials to orphanages along the Riviera — not a bad job! An eighteen-year-old was driving a second truck down along with me, and I invited her to go in the cab with me and start a story on the trip down, so she did. Then we had a week together in Marseilles.

Before we left Paris there was obviously a drawing together of the two of us, no question about that. Then we had the trip and the week in Marseilles when we didn't see anyone except each other, so we had every evening together for a week. She went back to Paris and then she was reassigned to southern France to work with Spanish refugees who had been there since the Civil War.

After I was in Marseilles for about 6 weeks, they asked me if I'd come back to Paris to help with the leadership of the transport team to go to Poland. I wanted to go as far east as possible. Russia had been devastated and I wanted to do something there.

Madeleine got into a truck accident and had a concussion; it was a miracle that she was alive. In my book[61] I tell about trying to get from Poland to her bedside. She lay in a British army hospital, in the British zone of Germany, for two months. When she was released, she went to her mother's home town, Neuchatel, Switzerland, where she had visited her mother's brother. I spent a month with her in the hospital, and then when it looked as if she was going to survive I went back to Poland to clear up my work. Then I met her in Neuchatel and we got married there in her mother's home town before we sailed back to the U.S.

When we got back to the U.S. we went to a neurosurgeon, who said that he would give Madeleine six months to live without an operation. But there had never been a successful operation of this sort. So that's how we started our married life. And I could not hold a job. I couldn't even think about a job. But fortunately friends of hers took us in and I did the cooking for the four of us. Both of them were working. Madeleine had her operation, which was successful.

We felt that we should wait to have children because of Madeleine's illness. When she had the operation the doctor said we wouldn't know for 10 years whether or not it was successful. But in a year's time when she was recovering so well, we thought that we could get on with our life. But when we tried to have children we found we couldn't. This was before there were a great many fertility clinics.

We went to see a lawyer in San Francisco who specialized in independent adoptions. Madeleine and I talked about what we wanted. A red-headed child was what we most wanted, but that would be the least available. We had decided that we could not handle a black child because of our families, but we could have any other racial group. We learned before she was born of a child who was half Japanese, half Caucasian, and made an application for her.

We got Anne when she was about seven months old. Although she was half Japanese, when she went to junior college she started identifying with Mexicans primarily because she has olive skin and black hair. She prided herself on being able to pass in Mexico City as a Mexican because of her looks and her speech. Her Spanish was that good, even in high school. She married two Mexicans, had a child by each one of them, and raised both of them single-handedly. One is now teaching school in the same school she's in, and the other one will be graduating from college in December. She's done very well. As an adult she found her natural mother, and all of a sudden we acquired an in-law family. She had a brother, a sister and a mother, and their families. They accepted Madeleine and myself right in, as we did them.

One day, when Anne was four, I was in Toronto at a conference, and got a call from my wife saying, "would you like to have a boy?" The lawyer had called her and said that there was a boy available. So then we got a boy named Robert who was part Indian, part Hawaiian, part Caucasian. He grew to be over 6 feet tall.

When I returned from Europe I found out that I liked working with people. I loved physics, but being out of the physics field for six years, there was no way I could go back into it at that point. Steve Thierman at the San Francisco American Friends Service Committee[4] office wrote to ask if I would be interested in coming out to California to help with the self-help housing project in the little community of North Richmond. It was an all-black shanty town on the edge of Richmond, California.

Madeleine and I went out and six weeks later wrote a paper saying that this is not the time or place for Quakers to do this, because it was across the railroad tracks and the area should be zoned industrial. You could build beautiful homes out there but you're never going to be able to integrate it. I wasn't interested in building a seg-regated community, so I said that is not the place for me. They asked me to stay on and be community relations secretary for this area, so I did.

We ran weekend work camps in this small black com-munity, recruiting students to spend the weekend and do physical work. In addition to the weekend work camps in Richmond, in the Fillmore district of San Francisco, and in a mental hospital, we had volunteers in the San Francisco county jails. We had one summer project where students lived in Sunday school rooms in Pacifica and went to work every day in the San Francisco County jail. We worked with Hopi Indians to bring young children from the Hopis and match them up with families in the Bay area with similar-aged children. All those families got together once or twice during the time they were here. From that we created the Inter-Tribal Friendship house which is still running, now being run by the Indians.

I was very much involved in advocating for the blacks in the redevelopment of the Fillmore district. I remember going to Dr. Carlton Goodlet, a fiery black doctor who challenged me to my core. I am a rather naïve guy, very much motivated to do something, and fumbling all over the place. He challenged me about where I was, what I was doing, and what I thought I was doing. He didn't feel as if it was very significant. Maybe it wasn't, but at least I had the motivation to get out there and try, even if I didn't know what to do and where to go.

Bill, a black man that I was working with at Neighborhood House, came to me with the announcement of a conference on Negro leadership in Fresno, California and said he thought we ought to go. I wasn't sure we could afford it, but if we went early in the morning on Saturday morning so we wouldn't have to pay for two nights, I could get it out of the budget.

So Saturday morning we were in line for the registration and I knew three-quarters of the people there because I'd been working in the state for various racial kinds of things. All of a sudden I realized we had not moved very far and I said to Bill, "I think something's happening to me that's happened to you on a million occasions." He said, "I was wondering how long before you'd catch on."

One of the people in charge of the conference came up and pulled me aside, saying they had met the night before and had made the decision that in the workshops only blacks would be allowed in, no whites. Bill was ready to leave. He was having none of it. But I said that we needed to stay. Bill could go to the workshop and I would find something to do. I could go to the dinner meeting because it was an open plenary session.

I never had so many drinks paid for in my life as I did that weekend. But nobody ever offered to walk into the dining room with me, or offered me a seat. I just went in on my own. In the last session, eight or nine people sitting up there on the podium and making little short speeches. Before they called an end, I got up and started to walk up the steps at which point the guards grabbed me. Dr. Goodlet said, "let him come, I know that man. If he has anything to say, let him say it." So they gave me the microphone and I said, "There is one thing that bugs me. If you want to have a meeting with just blacks that's all right with me, but you knew that I had registered last night. You could have called me and saved me the trip. I have been taking a leadership role in interracial activities for a good many years now, and have gone to jail as a result of my interest, but if this is the time that I need to take a back seat, I hope I can do it gracefully." I got a standing ovation, and people came up to me afterwards and said, "have you been feeling the daggers I've been sending your way?" It was amazing the turn-around.

Madeleine knew I was very deeply concerned about the blacks and she was awfully afraid I would try to take a job in the South. She was from Rochester, New York. She was very much accepted by my immediate family, but she did not wish to live in the South. In addition, North Carolina was not large enough for both my brother and myself. He was very active politically and I wanted to be active politically. We would have clashed. We were not on the same wave length. He was a very generous and compassionate person but he was a right-wing Republican.

After I had worked with the Quakers for three years in California, some of them, like Josephine Duveneck and others put enough money together for me to go back to college for two years. There were no scholarships in those days. After I got my Master of Social Work, I was appointed by the Quakers to go back to North Richmond full time. In 1953 they gave me a budget of $7200, including my salary. I left at the end of 1969 with a budget of three quarters of a million dollars and a staff of 70. We really turned west Contra Costa County upside down. I left my heart there, there's just no question about it.

And after that I went to work for Planned Parenthood in Alameda and then in San Francisco and merged the two to become at that time the 3rd largest affiliate in America. I was the first male executive. I was there six and a half years. They had already started teen clinics without parental consent, which was still highly controversial. I often got calls from parents saying they had found pills in their daughter's purse. People I knew said, "Why didn't you call me?"

My answer was "That's exactly what I would like to have done, but can you imagine what would happen in Berkeley High if word got out that if you went to Planned Parenthood they would call your parents? I think you're very fortunate that there's an organization that can talk sympathetically with your daughter when she obviously did not feel free to come to you?" Pretty soon I'd have them on board. We continued with that and expanded it to do some research and develop human sexuality courses. We started an abortion clinic before the Roe-Wade decision. We were out front on that one.

A group of us bought 400 acres east of Santa Rosa at Monan's Rill for a community, knowing that was where we wanted to go for retirement. We bought the land in 1973. In 1975 Madeleine was getting a Master's in the Kodaly method and was planning to teach music. I said, "I've had a very full satisfying professional life. If you start to teach in Berkeley now, about the time you get established I'm going to be ready to retire and go to Sonoma  County and you'll have to start all over again. Why don't we go now?" She wondered how we would live. I said that I had an MSW and an active real estate license, so we would find something. She agreed, so I resigned and started looking for a job in Sonoma County. I could not find anything in the social work field that was anywhere comparable to what I'd been doing. I could have gotten a job in the welfare department or with a family service agency, but neither of those turned me on. So, I hung up my real estate license. Madeleine and I had put aside enough money to live on for six months, to see how I did. The first 5 months I grossed $100, but then I got one referral and the next 3 years I was the top salesman in the office. I put 25 years into the Monan's Rill community, and once again I left my heart there. I've had a good life!

I can't distinguish very clearly between violence and social injustice. They go hand in hand. I was encouraged in the 1960s by what was happening in this country, but I have been so terribly disappointed in what has happening since. Now we're in a situation where the gulf between the rich and the poor is getting wider. I worked hoping I could leave the world a better place for my children than the one in which I was born, and now I think it's getting worse. War is certainly part of that. We have not learned anything about diplomacy as a way of international negotiations. We still have to resolve things with force. Very little can get accomplished with force that damages other people. Whenever you do that, there's going to be repercussions. They may be unanticipated, but war usually comes out of injustice.

F. Evert Bartholomew *(1919)*

"I entered (CPS) as an orthodox religious Christian pacifist, I left as a secular humanist."

Ihave wondered how and when I became aware that
I am a pacifist. There wasn't a time when suddenly
I realized that I was a pacifist. I grew up in a very religious family and was very religious myself all through
my growing up years. I went to a Methodist University,
DePauw. In the late 1930s when I was an undergraduate
there was a very strong peace movement in the Methodist
church. This permeated into the college campus, especially the youth program, called the Epworth League,
where I was very active. We had social activities and discussions. There were visitors from the church hierarchy
who talked about pacifism.

When it became apparent that there was going to be
a draft, I was strongly influenced by the question, "What
would Jesus Do?" What about this teaching about loving
your enemies and doing good to those that hurt you? I
talked it over with my Sociology professor, my advisor.
He saw my point but did not encourage me. The Director
of Religious Education knew me well and he was very
neutral, he didn't want to discourage me or encourage
me. I graduated in 1941, before Pearl Harbor. By then I
knew that I was going to be a CO[17] and I didn't have any
trouble getting a CO classification because the Minister
of the church supported me, the Director of Religious
Education supported me, and my own advisor supported
me, not that they necessarily agreed with me. As far as I
know, I was the only person in my graduating class who
was a pacifist and a CO.

My father died when I was 12 years old. He had been
a soldier in World War I, a second lieutenant. Although he
was church-going and a Sunday school superintendent

Interviewed by Neil H. Hartman

in Terre Haute, Indiana, where we grew up, I'm almost sure he would not have been a pacifist. He died in 1931, long before Hitler. My mother was extremely religious and, while she didn't fully understand the pacifist decision, she supported me all the way.

My father was making a good living, but his sudden death during the Depression left my mother unable to support three children. Since my dad was a Mason, she put us into the Illinois Masonic Orphans Home in LaGrange, Illinois, a suburb of Chicago. So we left Terre Haute, Indiana and went to the Home where we all three stayed until we graduated from high school. I was the oldest. We enjoyed living in this children's home. The kids were all children of Masons from middle class families and we had a good time together. The public schools in LaGrange were excellent, too. We "Home kids" kept in touch with each other for years and every year there was an "Old Times Day" where alumni would gather and reminisce.

I was not an athlete. I participated in intramural athletics a little bit in high school, but I was more interested in music. I played the trumpet and was in a little jazz band in high school, played in the college band, and sang a little bit. I had a mentor in high school, my History teacher and debate coach. But it had nothing to do with religion. Of course, my dad was already dead five years. I didn't know any one person who was a pacifist that I remember.

I liked being able to go to DePauw, located in Greencastle, Indiana, because my mother had gone there and her brother and sister also. DePauw had very neat scholarship program for men only, full tuition for four years, and they gave about 100 of them a year. I got one of those scholarships and the fact that it was a school that my family had gone to made it even better.

I had one very important mentor in college, my advisor in my major, which was sociology. He was really a father figure. He encouraged me to work with him. I got paid 35 cents an hour and he would let me grade some papers when I was an upper classman. I don't remember talking pacifism with him, but he knew I was very religious.

My major was Sociology. I knew even then that I wanted to be a Social Worker and would have gone on to Western Reserve University on a semi-scholarship after college if the draft hadn't come along. I read a lot, just ordinary textbooks. I enjoyed my Philosophy and Psychology courses.

I got an A.B. with honors in Sociology. After the war I got an MSW from the New York School of Social Work, a part of Columbia University. For the last 28 years of my career I worked as a social worker in Montclair Public Schools in New Jersey. After I got my doctorate I also worked as a part-time Adjunct Professor at Montclair State College.

In 1940, as we were leading up to the war, discussion of pacifism was at the church and among the students – not much with the professors. I was 22 years old at the time of Pearl Harbor. By then I had been introduced to this idea that pacifism was the Christian way. I didn't have any choice.

I didn't have any detractors within the college. In early 1942 I got a job as a Case Worker in the Putnam County Welfare Department in Greencastle. I enjoyed that work and they liked me, but the local American Legion found out that there was a CO working for the county and they put pressure on the department, so they fired me. I found out many years later, that my brother, who was still at DePauw, was working for the same Psychology professor I had. He told the Psychology professor about my experience of getting fired from my job and the Psychology professor resigned from the American Legion because of what they did to me.

I got quite a bit of derision from some of my fraternity brothers. One of my closest friends, who had been a friend with me through grammar and high school, came to DePauw partly because of me, never forgave me. Our friendship ended.

When I was drafted in June, 1942, I was first sent to a camp in Ohio that was run by the Soil Conservation Service. I very quickly gravitated to working in the kitchen. In the late fall they sent 40 of us out to Oregon to help fight fires. I stayed for two and a half years working in the kitchen and learning how to cook. I went to a cooking school run for CPS[14] by the AFSC[4] at another CPS camp in Maryland and became the Chief Dietitian of the camp in Oregon.

I heard about a unit that was looking for volunteers to be guinea pigs of malaria in New York City at Welfare Island. About 15 of us in Oregon volunteered for that. We got malaria the old-fashioned way. They had mosquitoes in little round things with gauze on each end and the mosquitoes would bite us right through the gauze. After we got our mosquito bites, we all got sick with malaria after a few days. They let it run for three to four days, very painful too, so they could be clinically certain that we had the disease. This project was part of research trying to find a more effective medicine to subdue, and hopefully cure, malaria. They would give us this drug, I think it was called Plasmoquine, and see what happened with relapses. After this first time when we had relapses we were treated immediately, which squelched the worst of the symptoms. That was my last assignment.

The summer after I got out, I went to Mexico with AFSC[4] as the head of a little side camp in the mountains. Then I was accepted at the New York School of Social

Work. I started there in the fall of 1946. The school helped me financially, the AFSC helped me financially, and I always worked part-time somewhere. So being a CO really helped me. Of course, not the way the GIs received help, but I had a little help.

Five years later I started going to a young people's group run by AFSC and met a girl who emigrated from France after the war. She was born in Germany, but her family left Germany in 1933 when she was about seven years old. She stayed in France during the war and came here at the age of 22 after the war in 1946. Eventually we married in 1951, the first child was born in 1954, and the second one in 1957.

I entered CPS[14] as an orthodox religious Christian pacifist and I left as a secular humanist because I met men who were intellectually wonderful people. My wife is Jewish. Neither of us were orthodox religious so we joined the Ethical Society Fellowship,[22] which was a good mix of humanist and ethical principles, and our two boys joined their Sunday school. They also attended a secular Jewish school and are both pacifists. One registered as a CO in the Vietnam War, but was never called. The other one never had to sign for the draft.

Since being released from CPS, besides raising our children as pacifists, my other activism has just been participating in marches and demonstrations, joining the Fellowship of Reconciliation[25] and staying very active in the Peace Movement.

I have one achievement I'm very proud of. I was able to get into a doctorate program and actually get my doctorate. I learned that you don't have to be brilliant to get a doctorate. It was hard, but I enjoyed it thoroughly. I liked my work as a School Social Worker in Montclair, New Jersey. And raising two great kids, I guess that's pretty much what I'm proud of.

If I had to do it over again, I would still take the same pacifist position. Even though I met some **very** close friends who still argue with me, how could I possibly still be a pacifist when I married a woman who is a Holocaust survivor?

I would like to pass on to future generations that human nature is very slow at changing, but it can change. War is not inevitable. Just think of the fact that France and Germany used to fight every generation, and now they are allies. If it can happen in Europe, it can happen some day in Africa and maybe in the Middle East—I hope so.

John Bartholomew (1921)

"I'd just like to say that my experience—standing up for something that I thought was important—was never a drawback in anything that I wanted to do."

I became aware that I was a pacifist when I was a sophomore in college. I became involved with the Methodist Student Movement[20] which met at the Golden Memorial Church at DePauw. It was a little bit different in those days. The Methodist Student Movement was run by a guy named Ernschberger, who also put out the Motive Magazine and he was a pacifist. It was several years later when the Methodist Church men at their semi-annual convention they discredited Ernschberger and stopped the Motive Magazine. But I got involved with the Methodist student movement because I had been interested in church work and it so happened that there were a number of pacifists. We talked a lot about pacifism and by the end of my sophomore year I had decided to register as a pacifist.

We were very active in the Methodist church in Terre Haute, Indiana. My father was the Superintendent of the Sunday School and my mother was the lead soprano singer in the choir. She was very interested in religion and wanted her three children to take an active part in the church and in religious activities. She was not a pacifist. At first my mother was somewhat skeptical, but my brother who was two years older was also a pacifist. So by the time I came along, she was actively supportive.

My father died when I was about ten years old, so I went to the Illinois Masonic Orphans Home in LaGrange, Illinois. They had a library and it wasn't long before I had read most of the books there in the library. I was very interested in reading. In high school I was very active in sports and played on the varsity baseball, football and basketball teams. I made most of my letters in baseball. The coach of the baseball team at DePauw University was very active in the Methodist church. He was disappointed in my CO decision because he felt that as a pacifist I would have difficulty getting jobs and being accepted. He didn't put any real pressure on me one way or the other, because he was one of my good coaches and he liked the way I played baseball.

Despite the Methodist student movement at DePauw, pacifists were not very accepted. Several times the Dean of Men tried to convince me that I should be a 1AO. I looked into it, but the guy I talked to said, "Well, sure you can be in the medical corps, but if push comes to shove, we're going to give you a gun and you're supposed to use it." So I turned it down. The Quakers wanted a little bit of financial support from the church or from the CO. I didn't have any money—I grew up in an orphan's home and I was working my way through college—so I wrote to the minister of the Methodist church and he wrote me a very angry letter back saying that I was a disgrace to the church and they certainly were not going to give me anything. At the time of Pearl Harbor in 1941, I was 20 years old.

So my major influences were the emphasis on religion that came from my mother as a child, the fact that at DePauw I lived with my brother who was involved with the Methodist Student Movement, and then there were two or three of those men that I was very close to. I would say that it was my peers mostly. There was very little interest on the part of the faculty at DePauw to push pacifism in those days. My major detractors included the minister of the church.

I never had any problem one way or the other with my teammates. I got my greetings and was supposed to report on the first anniversary of Pearl Harbor. At that time I was living in the Sigma Nu fraternity at DePauw. I got all of my clothes together in a small bag—I didn't have very much and it was snowing a little. I went outside to wait for the taxicab and the whole fraternity came out, surrounded me, and sang our fraternity song. I really was touched. I'm sure that they wondered about me being a CO, but at the last moment they all supported me, shook my hand, and wished me the best.

My first assignment in CPS[14] was in a Brethren[7] camp in Kane, Pennsylvania. I showed up at Kane and all I had were my corduroys, which we wore in college in those days, moccasins and my letter sweater. That was it. They were building a road. Kane was known as the icebox of Pennsylvania. It had been an old CCC[13] camp and when they closed it and heard that the Quakers were coming in, they burned all of the equipment and all of the clothes and everything. I was having a real tough time because I didn't have any clothes and I had to go out on the gang.

My brother called to say that they were planning to start a camp in Elkton, Oregon because they thought that the Japanese were going to send over some balloons and set the thing afire. So I called the organization that was running the program and they said of course I could go to Oregon. I had been in Kane only two months. I went to Oregon stayed there until February of 1945. Then I transferred to Byberry Hospital in Philadelphia. I spent 1942 to 1946 in CPS,[14] almost four years, until I got released from the draft at Byberry.

My wife and I decided to get married in December of 1945 because we were told that I would be out in the fall. But one of the southern senators said that no COs could be released until every soldier was back. So I was still in CPS. The nurse at Byberry would not let me off so I had to go AWOL to get married. I took three days off on a three-day honeymoon and then went back to work. They were glad to have me, but that's what happened.

When I got out in 1946, my wife worked while I got my Master's in Social Work at Western Reserve. She was very good as a medical technician. I didn't have any money to begin with. The American Friends Service Committee[4] gave me a small stipend, but that was all that I had. I think I made about $3,000 a year in my first job as a social worker, which was in 1948. She was still working, of course. We adopted two children. Our first child came five years after we were married.

By this time I had joined Friends. We were married in the meeting house here in Medford. She was very interested in Quaker ideals and Quaker practices and Medford was her meeting. She grew up right here in Medford. We didn't have a whole lot of discussion about it, we just decided we were going to do the best by our kids that we could. My daughter is a pacifist. She is still very active in Quaker things. My son was very interested in Quakers and was very supportive of me, but he was not a pacifist.

When I was in Detroit, I was clerk of the Detroit Friends Meeting, and used to hold sessions for young men and women in meeting who were getting ready to register for the draft. Outside of doing things in the Meeting, that is the only other pacifist activity I have undertaken.

When you get a Master's in Social Work, you go half-time to school and halftime to the field and my fieldwork was in a settlement in Cleveland. I became very interested in the settlement movement because it was social work but they were interested in social change and in doing something for the community. I had my first year in one settlement and my second year at another settlement. The director of that settlement wanted me to work there so I continued to work at the East End Neighborhood House in Cleveland until 1955 at which time I became the executive of another settlement in Detroit. I stayed there until 1965 when I moved to Boston to be the director of a group of four settlements in Boston. I stayed in settlements my whole career.

There were never any roadblocks that the CO decision put up for me. Any job that I ever applied for I received. Everyone knew that I was a CO. When I got to Boston two of the four settlements were in black areas and two were in white Irish Catholic areas. Some of the people in the community made remarks that we were doing such a good job that maybe this Quaker CO is not so bad after all.

I am pleased that all three agencies that I directed did a lot. Being successful at each of them was why I was able to get a better job the next time around. When I went to Boston the four agencies had a budget of about $185,000; when I left the total budget was about 12 million. It was the biggest agency in Boston, even bigger than the Y. I think I can say that it accomplished a lot in the area of Dorchester.

I have no regrets about being a pacifist. My only regrets are that I could have been a little bit more aggressive on my various jobs. Being a pacifist, I think sometimes I was a little too pacifist with people who weren't doing their jobs. I should have gotten rid of them faster, which was hard to do, particularly if I had to fire some black people in the 1970s and 1980s. I don't have any real regrets about my marriage, my kids, my job, or about being a pacifist.

I have thought a lot about why I was a pacifist. I realized that the world was going on and we were not going to stop the war. But I hoped that not only was I acting out my own principles, but that society in general was going to look at some of us who were trying to do something differently. I am disappointed that our country and things generally are still pretty much war-like and that the defense budget is bigger than ever as a percent of the national budget. I think that some of us have done some good. On the first Saturday some of us have been standing out in front of the meeting house in Medford with big signs "War is Bad." We started this two months before the war and in those days we used to get a lot of thumbs down. Now, three years later, we're getting thumbs up and "'Atta a boy!" So maybe we're making a little change by doing things like that.

My experience of standing up for something that I thought was important was never a drawback in anything that I wanted to do. It wasn't a drawback in marrying the woman that I loved, it wasn't a drawback in any of the jobs that I had. In all three towns where we have lived Ann and I have had a very rich social life. It is important to do things that you think are right and just. That is the first important thing that I would like to pass on. Whether or not any of us are able to make big changes in what goes on in the world, we have to start small and make sure that we do what we want to do right. Making changes with our family and friends is important.

Chapter Three
In the Ministry

Chapter Three
In the Ministry

Marshall O. Sutton

T. Canby Jones

Charles F. Cooley

Leonard A. Stark

Walter W. Stark

Charles R. Lord

Over and over again the men in this book begin their interviews with, "I always knew I was a pacifist." As inner-directed adults, the men in this chapter led consciously Christian lives using theological guidance to lead their parishes. T. Canby Jones peppers his story with scriptural references and Charles R. Lord tells us to "follow one's conscience wherever it leads one and to persevere." They ministered in a variety of religious settings as administrator, teacher, preacher and missionary, exemplifying ecumenical and inclusive leadership.

The mainstream Protestant churches of the United States were in a state of flux. Within denominations the pacifist pastor could be an uncomfortable fit for his pulpit. But regardless of the setting or the role, the acceptance or dismissal of the congregation, the primary measure of success was their personal feeling of inner peace.

Marshall O. Sutton (1918)

"Deciding to become a CO had been a gradual process of becoming acquainted with the Quaker peace testimony. I could not kill. The decision really started me on a spiritual journey and meetings for worship took on more depth for me."

I became aware that I am a pacifist with my grandfather when I was five or six years old. I didn't recognize it as pacifism, and thinking about things deeply, but my grandfather Sutton was a prayerful person who went on his knees at night before he got in bed. He read the Bible. He was not talkative, but I remember as a child sitting with him on the porch of his home and long periods of silence in which I felt very comfortable because I loved him so much. I was introduced to loving silence then and to Friends Meeting.[52] I grew up in a Friends Meeting in Clintondale, New York. My parents were active Quakers. I stopped regular attendance at the Meeting when I was 13 and entered the Quaker boarding school at Oakwood Friends School in Poughkeepsie NY. I was the only pacifist at the Clintondale Friends meeting. The Meeting as a whole was not sympathetic with my stand. There was one family in the meeting that gave me a good deal of support. My mother was a great support to me. My father was wondering what it was all about as he did not have a Quaker background, but my mother did.

I went to a two-room schoolhouse. It was a very caring school. I skipped a grade so I was one year younger than my classmates at Oakwood, but I made the varsity baseball team my freshman year. I felt the support of the community. My parents were so worried about me over there, but I never got homesick. It was a very positive experience at Oakwood. I played on all the varsity teams, I was active in student government, and I was a proctor

---

Interviewed by Edith Ballard and Beth Edelstein, transcribed by Beth Edelstein

in the dormitory. I seemed to take on responsibilities both as a student and otherwise.

There were two members of the faculty at Oakwood School who mentored me. The principal of Oakwood School, William Reagan, and a history teacher, Curtis Newlin, particularly influenced me. William Reagan told stories about Rufus Jones. As a student at Oakwood, I dipped into two books by Rufus Jones, *A Small town Boy* and *Finding the Trail of Life*. My favorite subject in school was history. I had little instruction in Bible or Friends journals but I experienced a supportive community. My grandfather on my mother's side of the family was a country lawyer and he was always writing historical articles and talking about the history of the local area. I became interested in that, and I began to read. My hobbies as a child were fishing, hiking, swimming, camping, all sports, and reading. I graduated from Oakwood in 1935.

At Colgate Kenneth Boulding[6] was teaching economics. He had a work camp there, so I was aware of pacifism and nonviolence resistance. At the undergraduate level in college I remember studying war and peace and western civilization and sensing how easily we as a nation get into wars and that the avenues to work out foreign policy and prevent war are sidetracked. I began to lose confidence in the power of reason to solve conflicts. I became aware of a religious context to hope for the future.

I graduated in 1940 from Colgate University with a major in History. Also, I have a Masters from Columbia University Teachers College; and I matriculated for a doctorate at Columbia University Teachers College later. My pacifism began in a focused way in 1941 when I was an intern teacher at Oakwood. I was a teacher of history and assistant to the Dean in the dormitory. I was finding some difficulty with the Bible early on, and my own religious growth began when I started reading the

Friends' journals, particularly John Woolman and George
Fox. I read a lot of Quaker history, the works of Howard
Brinton, Douglas Steere,[60] and Henry Cadbury, which
helped me with the Bible. At graduate school I read Paul
Tillich, Richard Gregg, Henry Thoreau, Emerson and
Rufus Jones.[38]

I was 23 years old at the time of Pearl Harbor. The
decision to become a CO[17] was not a surprise to me when
I submitted to conscription as a CO in 1941. I was busy
at Oakwood School when I received the notice. I immediately asked my draft board for instructions to become
a CO. Deciding to become a CO had been a gradual process of becoming acquainted with the Quaker peace testimony. I could not kill. The decision really started me on a
spiritual journey and meetings for worship took on more
depth for me.

I have a lot of inner strength; I don't know how I got
it; I must have gotten it very young. I was much loved
in the family, and had a good upbringing, a wonderful childhood. I was so insulated and supported by the
school community. I've always had a great deal of inner
security. It begins with early childhood. My mother and
my father really supported me. I would not have been
able to make the baseball team at the age of 13 if not
for my father. He played pitch and catch with me until
I got to throw a ball well. But I alienated my father the
first year in CPS[14] when I wrote a letter to my hometown
newspaper against a renewal of the conscription bill and
they published it. He really loved me, I knew that, but he
was very upset about the publication of the letter. We had
reconciliation.

My major supporters in my decision to become a
CO were Jerry and Elizabeth Herd, who were members
of the Clintondale Friends Meeting and very active in
New York Yearly Meeting, and William Reagan, who was
the Principal of Oakwood School. When I got to CPS[14] I

found a whole new world. I found that I was not alone. CPS was a good experience for me. It changed my life; it culminated in the starvation experience at the University of Minnesota.

I had four government assignments. I began at Ashburnham, Massachusetts, at CPS 11, supported by the American Friends Service Committee,[4] clearing up hurricane timber from the hurricane of 1938. Roger Dury was the Director of the camp there, and I got along very well with him. When he had to be away, I temporarily took on more responsibility. There were a lot of people from Philadelphia coming out so I met Philadelphia Quakerism in Ashburnham, but I was there less than a year.

We were looking for more important work. They needed firefighters in California, so I went to Coleville, California to CPS 37. The cook they assigned us was inept and no one volunteered to replace him so I said I would try. Then there was an opportunity to join CPS unit 101 doing relief work abroad. I was sent to Earlham College and from Earlham to New Lisbon, New Jersey, working in an AFSC[4] unit with the mentally handicapped at a state institution. The superintendent had a son flying planes for the Air Force in the South Pacific. He took us on as COs only because he really needed some help. I was the AFSC Assistant Director of the CPS unit there and met with the superintendent regularly.

I corresponded with AFSC in Philadelphia and got acquainted with the young adult Friends group in the Philadelphia area. Sam Legg was in that same unit. I got acquainted with Douglas Steere[60] and began reading Thomas Kelly.[39] And that is when I really began to reflect on my own religious journey, who I was, and what I was doing on this earth. I attended a Pendle Hill[50] retreat held in Bernardsville, New Jersey, where I met Virginia Rice, now Virginia Sutton. She worked for the New York Times.

When they asked her to sell war bonds she refused. She knew A. J. Muste[43] in New York and was a pacifist. She began working for the AFSC[4] in the personnel office. As the Assistant Director at the CPS camp, I was receiving a lot of mailings including an invitation to join the semi-starvation experiment in Minneapolis at the University of Minnesota. I showed it to Sam Legg, and we both decided to go. Before we left, there was a second retreat sponsored by Pendle Hill, held in Bernardsville. The week that we left for Minneapolis, Ginny and I attended the retreat together, and that was in many ways a turning point for me. I began keeping a journal.

My conscious spiritual journey began at New Lisbon in a more deliberate way and was a steadying force for me during the stress of the starvation experiment, which was a disciplinary exercise. I met some people teaching at the University of Minnesota who were members of a Friends Meeting. We had meetings in their home and I attended regularly. I was reading Thomas Kelly, re-reading Woolman's journal; I selected four books to read in depth: William James' *Variety of Religious Experience*, St Augustine's *Confessions*, *Theologia Germanica*, and *Journal of John Woolman*. I looked at these rather thoroughly as you can see from the brown paper covers on them. During the experiment, I copied quotations. I kept a daily journal of my weight with some comments, which I turned over to Todd Tucker who wrote a book on the starvation experiment for Simon and Schuster.[64] I was there a year and took some courses at the University. I entered CPS[14] November 8, 1941, and left CPS December 11, 1945, receiving a formal honorary discharge from the Selective Service.

Virginia Rice and I got married and moved into the Boys Dormitory at Oakwood School where I was Dean of Boys. I also taught a class in Social Studies and assisted the coach in the three major sports. I was still recovering from the experiment. I was feeling the joy of gaining my weight back. What we should have done was take a six-month honeymoon. My CPS experience was a real part of our attraction to one another. Our life together was the way to keep it alive. We had two children, Lisa, a natural child, and we adopted Peter. We raised the children in the pacifist tradition.

We were there at Oakwood two years when we moved to Germantown, Pennsylvania. I took an interim job in the office of the Friends World Committee for Consultation as Secretary of the Young Friends Committee of North America planning a national conference. I applied to go to the Gaza Strip with the American Friends Service Committee[4] relief effort in 1949. Ginny was just recovering from rheumatic fever, so she stayed in Germantown with a Friends family. She joined me in Gaza later.

When we came back from the Middle East, Virginia's mother was not well. We moved in to care for her in Ossining, New York, where our daughter Lisa was born in 1952.

I got my Masters degree in 1950 and continued on after the Master's and matriculated for a doctorate. Instead of going for an interview for a job in San Francisco, I came to Stony Run Meeting in Baltimore as Executive Secretary. I was more interested in service than an academic life. I am sure the relief work in Gaza influenced my decision and the Quaker community tended to open itself up to me.

I continued with graduate work at Columbia University and Union Theological Seminary and passed the matriculation exam for a Doctorate in Education while I worked part time as Meeting Secretary for the Lafayette Avenue Friends Meeting in Brooklyn, New York. I have worked for Friends organizations all my life.

I don't know of any one thing I'm proud of. I've had a very blessed time so far and it's still continuing. I have followed a "leading" and I feel much peace within.

I enjoyed being Secretary of Stony Run Meeting, but it wasn't just Stony Run; it was half-time with Baltimore Unity Meeting. When I left the job to work for the World Committee, they hired two people to take my place. It was during those years that the camping program was starting in the Yearly Meeting and Friends purchased Catoctin Camp in Thurmond, Maryland. I was very active in all of that and thrived on it. It was fulfilling.

My leading to help Friends communicate with each other led me to serve as Associate Executive Secretary of the Friends World Committee for Consultation with an office at Wilmington College, Wilmington, Ohio, in 1958. I visited widely among Friends and traveled abroad. We wanted to return east after six years with FWCC. Later I accepted an invitation to serve as Executive Secretary of the Friends Meeting of Washington. A Meeting in the nation's capitol provided many unique opportunities. My deepest regret is not spending more time with our children. I traveled a lot and often had evening meetings. I left Ginny alone with the children.

It is very hard for us right now. We are reading about the Middle East every day in the newspaper. Since we both have lived in Gaza, we feel very close to the struggle there. Ginny and I sit down after breakfast to think of the day that's coming up, the dates we have, the obligations and responsibilities. We meditate awhile and read something from a book. We are quiet awhile to gather ourselves before taking up tasks.

We value deeply our participation in the Gunpowder Friends' Meeting. We go regularly, we participate in the committee work, and we know everyone in the Meeting. This has been just a lifesaver. We also have close friends here at Broadmead who come and read to Ginny who has lost most of her sight. Every day we have an opportunity here to converse and interact with wonderful people.

The spiritual growth of Friends in this area is a great joy for us. It is growing numerically and in spirit because of two things going on. The Young Friends program is very healthy, with the camping program. The other is the spiritual formation program that started in 1983 and is still going. There are a lot of people in our Meetings who want to be a little more deliberate in what's going on in their own spiritual lives and in the Meeting. We still give time and attention to it.

I would advise the next generations, don't neglect the scripture. I did in the beginning; I was turned off and read journals more, but I've come back to the scripture. There is a tendency with the present fundamentalist temper of our times to neglect the scripture and that vocabulary, but it's important not to do that. I'm grateful we have a successful Bible study at Gunpowder. We enjoy getting together and reading the Bible. It is important to share our Truths with others and to seek God's Will for ourselves and for our religious community. It is not easy for us to speak of our faith. We also need to have fun together.

T. Canby Jones (1921)

"A pacifist is defined as a person who is committed to the use of complete nonviolence in actual or potentially violent situations."

The one real test of my pacifism occurred in CPS[14] Camp 94 in Trenton, North Dakota, in 1944. Every Saturday night we put on a dance in the camp barracks dining hall. We invited the young people of Trenton to attend. We especially hoped the handful of Lakota Indian girls who lived there would come. Often a brother or other male relative of the girls would also attend. At one of these dances I noticed a young man from town standing by the opposite wall of the hall kept eyeing me as the evening wore on. Finally he came over and asked me if I was a conscientious objector and a pacifist, which I said I was. He asked if I would strike back if I were hit. I responded, "I don't think so, since it's against my principles."

Later in the evening, he invited me outdoors and started swinging at me. Little did he realize that when I was a youngster I used to fight frequently with my older brother. Our dear mother would step in and try to stop us, Quaker that she was. Several times we drove her almost to distraction by our continual conflict. Through all that fighting I became expert at ducking blows. When this young man in North Dakota started throwing punches at me, I simply ducked. Before he could really land a telling blow, another CPS man from the camp, a Roman Catholic CO who was not a pacifist, saw me being attacked, intervened and knocked my attacker flat, who immediately left the premises. That was my one personal test of responding with nonviolence when attacked. Since he left, I had no opportunity to seek reconciliation with him. I wonder whether I would have?

Assisted by Linda and Mike Sears

My brother was older, bigger, and stronger than me. In our fights I once got so frustrated that I threatened him with a kitchen butcher knife thinking that was the only way I could even the odds. Someone intervened and grabbed the knife. Afterwards I felt very remorseful that I had threatened him with the knife. I knew it was wrong and must never do it again! I can't remember my mother spanking me but I'm pretty sure that she did. But it was my father who was given that "honor." He much preferred severe verbal admonishment, but I remember several spankings especially the one whipping that I "earned."

Our family lived in North Nashville Tennessee on the campus of Fisk University where my father, Thomas Elsa Jones, served as president. My brother and I, along with other Fisk faculty children, attended George Peabody Demonstration School two-and-a-half miles across town in south Nashville. Our mothers took turns driving us to school in the mornings but it was up to us to walk home after school activities terminated. One morning as mother let me out of the car at the door of the school she did not have the customary five cents for my bottle of milk in the lunchroom. Having no change she trusted me with what she had, a five dollar bill. After lunch I had $4.95 in my pocket. My walk home took me past three drugstores. As I approached the first one I succumbed to the temptation to stop and spend five cents of the $4.95 to buy my favorite candy bar, a caramel filled "Milky Way" chocolate bar. It tasted so good! I did the same at the next two drug stores arriving home with $4.80 change. After my mother had shared her consternation with my Dad, he decided I deserved a whipping for my embezzlement. We went to the basement. He sent me out to cut my own green switch, crying my eyes out as I went. I believe he swatted several times. My remorse was overwhelming. I have been careful with other people's money ever since! That was the only time I earned a whipping.

My mother was brought up in Philadelphia Yearly Meeting of Friends (Orthodox) and my father was an Evangelical Friend from Indiana Yearly Meeting of Friends (Five Years Meeting).[52] Both grew up with the Peace Testimony. My father was not as deeply committed to it as I came to be, but my mother was strongly committed to it. When my brother and I fought, she would weep as she threatened us with her hairbrush, because it was against her faith to use it. Both of us boys knew that too!

There were no other Quakers in Nashville in 1926-36 so our family attended Collegeside Congregational Church. The most formative experience for my brother and me in attending that church was our male Sunday school teacher who was a World War I veteran. Regardless of the printed Sunday school lesson, we always got him to share his war experiences with us. That was important background later for our pacifist convictions.

Other than through annual or semi-annual visits to my Quaker grandparents and cousins in Indiana and Delaware, as a boy I did not have much experience with silent Quaker worship or with the major Quaker testimonies. I wasn't much of a pacifist until age 13 when I went for four years to Westtown Friends Boarding School. The atmosphere and convictions of both my teachers and fellow students were heavily colored by all the Friends testimonies. They are Simplicity, Peace, Integrity, Community and Equality. As a school community we went to Silent Meeting for Worship twice a week, on Thursdays and Sundays. At age 14 I had my first experience of being moved to rise and speak in one of those meetings for worship. I said something to the effect that we had to "be and become the faith that we professed." I was thrilled to learn from one of her classmates that my mother, who graduated from Westtown in the class of 1908, also had her first experience of being moved to share a message in Meeting when she was a student there. That event led to my life as a Quaker minister.

My favorite teacher at Westtown was Albert L. Baily Jr., who taught Botany and gave me my love for trees and the Bible. I have grown to have a great love for both subjects during the rest of my life. It was fantastic that his wife, Helen S. Baily had been Esther Balderston's (my mother) roommate when they both were Westtown students. Because of my personal relationship with the Bailys, I was invited to join a Bible study group that met at their home down the lane from the meetinghouse after Sunday worship. We engaged in an intensive study of the Gospel of John—the most spiritual of the four Gospels. In the spring of our senior year, 1938, the Bailys invited me and many others in our class to a weekend retreat at their farm near West Chester, Pennsylvania. They invited one of two philosophy professors from Haverford College to lead the retreat. The one who could come was Thomas R. Kelly, now well known as the author of the widely read, *A Testament of Devotion.*[39] In the retreat Tom kept challenging us to a life of unconditional commitment to God. Although I was impressed by his infectious enthusiasm, I felt that Tom's appeal was too emotional and not intellectual enough. His statement that "the price of a God-given life was entrance into suffering" stunned me. I left the retreat shaking my head. Nevertheless, the next autumn when I entered Haverford College as a freshman I went round to Tom and Lael Kelly's apartment on the campus and inquired whether I and some other students might meet at their home to share religious and Biblical insights as we had done at Westtown with the Bailys. Both Lael and Tom were enthused by my proposal and thus began the worship-sharing group that met regularly at Tom and Lael's home for the next two years until Tom's untimely death in January 1941.

Four or five of us, including one Bryn Mawr College student, met every Wednesday evening at the Kelly's on which occasions Tom would share with us Scripture and Christian Devotional Classics, which inspired him.

He also shared manuscripts of lectures on the Inner Life, which he had been invited to give at various Friends Meetings in the Philadelphia area.

Douglas V. Steere,[60] Haverford's other Professor of Philosophy, gathered a group of us concerned students at 6:30 AM each Tuesday to study pacifism and peace-making around the world. He called our group "The Peace Cell." He invited both Peter Maurin and Dorothy Day, the founders and leaders of the Catholic Worker Movement,[10] a strictly pacifist group, to lecture on campus and to meet with us. Maurin's famous aphorism was: "I don't want pie in the sky when I die; I want pie here and now." When World War II became imminent, Douglas founded the "Haverford College Service Project." It was a program of community service and improvement in which we painted and repaired run-down homes in the area and received Physical Education credit at the college for participating, fantastic! Of course I never made better than Junior Varsity on the college soccer team, but what a wonderful alternative, Wow!

Participation in the Peace Cell was an important preparation for our registration as conscientious objectors[17] when the United States Selective Service Draft became law in 1940.[57] Rufus Jones,[38] Clarence Pickett[51] and leaders of the Mennonite[42] and Church of the Brethren[7] had persuaded the framers of the Draft Law to include a classification for religious conscientious objectors. It was called 4E. Such persons had to fill out a difficult application form and were expected, as an alternative to military service to do "work of national importance under civilian direction." I spent an agonizing three weeks as a senior at Haverford formulating my answer to question number four on that application. It read, "To what extent do you believe in the use of force?" In subsequent years I have heard of, read about, and participated in "non-violent direct action," but I knew nothing of such at the time. I had heard something of Mahatma Gandhi and his Satyagraha movement, but he was way off in India.

My father was the first appointed Director of Friends CPS,[14] organized in the summer of 1941. It was a national body with similar directors appointed by the Mennonites and the Church of the Brethren. CPS was dedicated to providing alternative community service for pacifist men of draft age.

On December 7, 1941, the day the Japanese attacked Pearl Harbor, I was on my way with my father to attend Quaker Quarterly Meeting in West Chester PA. That afternoon as we walked by a drugstore on the way to the meetinghouse, we heard a radio blaring the news that Pearl Harbor had been attacked. My father and I were totally shocked. The news was particularly hard on my father since he had spent seven years as a Quaker Missionary to Japan and both my older brother and I had been born there. Obviously, we spent the whole Quarterly Meeting discussing the bombing and what the response of Friends should be.

To use a Quaker phrase, I felt very "low in my mind." The whole world was on the point of going up in flames, but still I felt totally confirmed in my decision to be a CO.[17] The sinking of the Arizona and other events showed the absolute insanity of war. Supporters of America's entrance into the war, who attacked me because of my pacifism, knew nothing about the "Peace Testimony." They would ask, "Are you just going to sit there and do nothing?" Most people felt this was a "just war." But I felt that even if humanity had gone insane and gone to war, I was going to stick to Jesus' commandments to "love our enemies" and to "overcome evil with good."

I graduated from college the next spring, 1942, with a B.A. in History and promptly received from my draft board a card notifying me that I was "IA to be inducted into the army." In consternation I met with the Board, told them my father was the Director of Friends Civilian Public Service (CPS).[14] They were surprised and immediately granted my 4E CO status. Disillusioned with the control of CPS by Col. Lewis F. Koch and the Selective Service System, my Dad resigned from CPS and returned to Nashville, Tennessee, and his job at Fisk University. This meant a transfer to a Nashville draft board. They, however, accepted my 4E status and saw to it that I was assigned to CPS 14 at Merom, Indiana, in January, 1943. Thus began my CPS camp experience, which lasted until my discharge on April 16, 1946.

Towards the Japanese I felt pity. I felt the Japanese people had no voice in the military-industrial complex that had led their country into war. Their culture demanded that they show reverence for their Emperor but they had no reason to hate America. After the attack on Pearl Harbor, America's reasons for going to war with Japan were obvious but such reasons were not clear at all to Japanese people. Moved by the idea of fate, they felt they were "fated" to obey their "divinely appointed Emperor" and serve in their nation's armed forces.

The Germans had suffered under Hitler and his megalomaniac ideas and had seen their society transformed into a military machine to establish "The Thousand Year Reich." The determination to persecute Jews and stamp out all opposition became obvious after the "Day of Broken Glass," in November 1938 in which all the shops and businesses run by Jews were destroyed. The German people had no voice in the decisions made by their "Fuhrer" or his underlings. I felt sorrow for the German people. I had no patience with their leadership. Their leader and his ideology were lunatic!

During the war, because I was a well known Quaker and had traveled widely among Friends, I was twice released from CPS 94 in Trenton, North Dakota, to visit Quaker Meetings in Illinois and Indiana to raise money to support the Quaker CPS camps and the men in them. The historic peace churches, the Mennonites, Church of the Brethren and Quakers, were expected by the U.S. Selective Service System to raise enough money, at $1.00 a day, to pay the entire support of the men in the camps. It was on one of those fund-raising trips to Danville, Indiana, where I met H. Eunice Meeks at the home of two of her friends who had hosted me. On my return to camp in North Dakota, Eunice added a $5.00 check to the amount her friends, Lillie and Philip Shaw, had collected to send to the camp. So I make a joke of her contribution and say, "She bought me for $5!" She was an active ecumenical Christian, had a degree in Latin, Music and English, and taught high school in Rolling Prairie, Indiana.

We started a spiritual correspondence. She was a Christian minister's daughter and relished our exchange of letters. She came to visit the camp in Trenton twice. We maintained a close relationship by letter between visits. On her second visit in December 1944 we took a walk in the moonlight. There was snow on the ground and the thermometer read twenty-five below zero! We decided it was the Lord's will that we should be married while I was still in the CPS camp in Trenton. It was a Quaker ceremony with my father, T. E. Jones, presiding in her home church, Danville Christian Church, on 19 August 1945. She got a job teaching in the school in Trenton. We lived in a small house in town while I continued my duties at the CPS camp, where I served as foreman of the construction crew. The camp at Trenton was closed in January 1946 and I was transferred to another camp in Gatlinburg Tennessee. Eunice followed me there. With rejoicing we both returned to my parent's home at Fisk University in Nashville when I was released from CPS April 16, 1946.

The AFSC[4] then invited us to become members of an international work camp to do reconstruction work in northern Norway, which the retreating Germans had totally destroyed. The headquarters of the camp was in

Hammerfest, 200 miles north of the Arctic Circle. Eunice and I were assigned to a side camp in Talvik which was about a day's walk south on Altafjord. We helped rebuild a school and its playground. We had seen the midnight sun in the summer. Now we experienced "the mid-day night." The sun does not rise from November until February! In that winter darkness I contracted bacterial pneumonia. They sent me to the barrack, which served as a hospital in Hammerfest. My temperature reached 106 until I was given penicillin, then a rare, brand new medi-cation. Immediately my temperature came down into the high nineties and Eunice and I were evacuated to a rest home in southern Norway at Drammen. We were very impressed that the priest in the Drammen Church was committed to nonviolence as a Christian and had been faithful to that conviction during the German occupa-tion. His name was Eystein Paulsen. His daughter was a member of our Finnmark work camp. As I recovered we were offered the opportunity by the AFSC to continue our international service in France. We declined and were flown back to the U.S. in January 1947.

Back in Philadelphia I was offered a job with the AFSC to become Associate Secretary of Friends Peace Service with Harold F. Chance as the Director. My job was to restore the commitment of Friends to the Peace Testimony. Considering the fact that only about 1400 Quaker men out of 10 or 12,000 took the CO stand and went to camp or into detached service, the job was quite challenging! As I traveled and witnessed, I found that "there is no limit to the love of Christ." This basic con-viction leads me to know that I should not judge other Christians whom I deem to be in error. In addition I have come to celebrate Christ's promise, "And I, if I be lifted up, will draw all men to myself." These convictions have led me to visit and participate in Quaker meetings and activities of all flavors and types and find acceptance among them. I am also very interested in ecumenical contacts and experiences of other religious groups including Jews, Hindus, Shintoists, Buddhists, Muslims and others. In my forty years of college teaching in Religion and Philosophy, Bible, and Classics of Christian Devotion classes, Comparative Religions classes were among my favorites to teach. I remember opening several of them with the announcement that "This class will inspire you to practice "Much ado about Nothing!"

My main mentors at Yale Divinity and Yale Graduate Schools were professors Roland H. Bainton, Kenneth Scott Latourette and H. Richard Niebuhr.[47] Many of my close friends at Yale were pacifists like myself and took courses that would teach us how to promote pacifism and prevent future wars. We dialogued with each other and with WWII veterans in a very constructive manner. Those who had been in the armed forces were eager to find peaceful alternatives. There were 104 in my Divinity class of 1952, including a few women.

I picked George Fox[26] as my thesis subject because, as a person who loved and majored in History, and as a Quaker, the travels, ministry and exploits of George Fox had intrigued me for years. There was and is a regularly published journal, *The New Foundation Fellowship*,[46] that was first published by the Call Group in Philadelphia. As a person concerned to see a revival of early Quaker vision, I was active in the group under the leadership of Lewis and Sarah Benson, and John and Barbara Curtis. While I delighted at Yale Divinity School in the study of the religious leaders of Christianity throughout its history, I was especially keen to make an intensive study of George Fox, the founder of Friends. Lewis Benson had a burning concern to recapture the vision and universal Christian message of George Fox and to spread it today.

Obviously my active participation in the Call Group was formative in my decision to do my Ph.D. thesis on George Fox. The Call Group helped a great deal financially in the year, 1953–54, which I spent in Britain with my wife and five-year-old son, Timothy. I served as a Fellow at Woodbrooke College in Birmingham and had many trips to Friends House Library in London where George Fox's manuscripts are kept, most of which have never been published.

I had earned my Bachelor of Divinity degree at Yale Divinity School and back in New Haven had a fellowship to study George Fox in Yale Graduate School with the aim of earning a Ph.D. degree in the process. By April 1955 I had completed my thesis, *The Christology of George Fox*, and turned it in to my Committee of three who would read and decide whether it would be accepted for the degree. Alas, one of the readers was Professor of Historical Theology at Yale and strictly defined the term "Christology." He rejected my thesis on the grounds that George Fox had virtually nothing to say about "the nature of the person of Christ," which is the definition of Christology. Fox's whole concern was with Soteriology, the saving work of Christ! My six-year-old son, Timothy, burst out crying at the news. Another of my thesis advisors Roland Bainton and his wife Ruth stepped into the breach and offered us their home in Woodbridge CT as a haven where we could spend the summer as I rewrote and my wife Eunice retyped my thesis as *George Fox's Teaching on Redemption and Salvation*. It was accepted in November 1955 for my Ph.D.

In the meantime I had been appointed as Assistant Professor of Religion and Philosophy at Wilmington College, a Quaker College in southwestern Ohio. Samuel D. Marble, the President, had invited me to visit the campus earlier. My small family moved there and I began teaching Autumn 1955. Sam had known me well when I worked with AFSC[4] in Philadelphia after World War II. I received a beginning salary of $4,000 a year and my wife Eunice taught part-time in the Music Department.

Besides some part-time teaching at Earlham School of Religion, I spent my whole teaching career 1955–1996 at Wilmington College.

My greatest accomplishments included inspiring so many students in Bible and Philosophy. My enthusiasm transmits in my teaching. In 1984 I had a class of eight in Classics of Christian Devotion. I asked that the class write a paper relating to all the classics we had been studying. As I asked each of them what topic they had chosen, I was overwhelmed. Thomas Kelly[39] himself would have been inspired by each choice because each topic showed such depth of Christian vision and understanding. They had picked topics that could have come right out of my heart. I was so touched that I sat there and wept tears of joy. I taught many other classes that produced the same sort of inspiration.

The other major contribution I made was to join with Hugh Barbour of Earlham College in preaching, publishing and proclaiming "The Lamb's War" as an alternative to international war and conflict. James Naylor, a prominent early Quaker, had written an essay entitled "The Lamb's War and the Man of Sin." After studying Naylor's essay, Hugh Barbour and I thought it an ideal scriptural way to describe Christian nonviolence as an alternative to war.

In Ephesians 6:11-17 we are instructed in the kind of weapons we will use in this God-inspired conflict of overcoming evil with good. "Put on the whole armor of God … For our struggle is not against enemies of blood and flesh … against the cosmic powers of this present darkness, against the spiritual forces of evil … Stand therefore, and fasten the belt of truth around your waist, and put on the breastplate of righteousness. As shoes for your feet put on whatever will make you ready to proclaim the gospel of peace. With all of these take the shield of faith, with which you will be able to quench all the flaming arrows of the evil one. Take the helmet of salvation, and the sword of the Spirit, which is the word of God." NRSV

Of all the weapons here mentioned the most important is the last, "the Sword of the Spirit," which is the Word of God. That Word is both Jesus himself and the judgment and mercy coming out of his mouth. In Rev. 19:11-16 Jesus is depicted as riding a white horse with a sword coming out of his mouth. Make no mistake that is not a sword of ferrous metal, but the living, transforming Word of God, which is incarnate in Jesus (Rev. 1:13-16)

Committed to Jesus not only as Lord, but also as Prince of Peace and peacemaking as his warriors, we eschew anything to do with war and the things that make for war. He commands us to love our enemies to return good for evil and to pray for those who despitefully use us. I see his command to love our enemies as binding on all Christians. No exceptions! Do you? Paul in Romans 12: 17-21 challenges us: "Do not repay anyone evil for evil … live peaceably with all … Never avenge yourselves … for it is written, "Vengeance is mine, I will repay, says the Lord … No, if your enemies are hungry feed them, if they are thirsty give them something to drink … Don't be overcome by evil, but overcome evil with good" Despite my struggles to control my anger, I freely confess that what Paul has just required, I must do.

As a writer I have some regrets. Even though my bibliography includes dozens of short articles I have only written two books, one for a class in Military History at the U.S. Naval Academy entitled *George Fox's Attitude toward War* which was later republished by Friends United Press. The other book, *The Power of the Lord is Over All: The Pastoral Epistles of George Fox* was published by Friends United Press and is still in print. I also wrote a pamphlet called *The Lamb's Peacemakers*, first published by Baptist Peacemakers International Spirituality and reprinted later by Wilmington College Peace Resource Center.

Upon my full retirement from teaching in 1994 I was honored by the publication of a Festschrift, seventeen essays in my honor by my friends and colleagues across the country, *Practiced in the Presence: Essays in Honor of T. Canby Jones.* It has a marvelous bibliography that includes just about all the articles I ever had published. Two of my colleagues at Wilmington sparked the effort. I was invited to give the Commencement address in 1995 at Wilmington College and was there honored with the degree, Doctor of Humane Letters.

From 1961 until 1980 I participated fully in the joint efforts of Mennonites,[42] Church of the Brethren[7] and Friends[52] in what we called "A New Call to Peacemaking." We published a journal, held joint conferences by turns at the several participating institutions. My little book, *George Fox's Attitude toward War,* got republished twice chiefly because of its use by Mennonite and Brethren institutions, who learned of it through those contacts.

I think there is more awareness now of the cost and suffering of making war than at any other time since the Vietnam War. Many more people are now aware that there is another way to ultimately solve international problems besides that of international violent conflict. I firmly and fervently hope that humanity will wake up to the vicious absurdity of believing that "kill or be killed" is the ultimate resource in solving international problems

I find my inspiration from Scripture. "He who is faithful unto death shall receive the crown of life!" (Rev. 2:10) This line of Scripture is so precious to me because it came alive for me upon the sudden death on January 17, 1941 of my teacher and spiritual mentor, Thomas R. Kelly,[39] author of the now widely known book, *A Testament of Devotion.* At age 46 he died suddenly of a heart attack

while washing dishes. I was a sophomore at Haverford College at the time. Suddenly my overwhelming grief was transmuted into a vision of the glorious life of total commitment to God which Tom had both shared and exemplified in our worship-sharing group that met in his home. I freely confess that I have had no problem with believing in the Resurrection of Jesus since that night.

Charles F. Cooley (1918)

I cannot recall a time when I was not a Christian and a pacifist.

I cannot recall a time when I was not a Christian and a pacifist. To be the one was to be the other. Jesus said we were supposed to love everyone, even our enemies. I not only learned this in Sunday school, but from my parents as well. And in a real sense the concept was taught by my public school teachers. When altar calls were given at summer camps, I did not go forward until one call combined believing in Jesus with care and concern for all God's people. That afternoon, I responded with enthusiasm.

I was deeply stirred by three accounts from World War I. *All Quiet on the Western Front* by Erich Maria Remarque told about the suffering of German soldiers in their trenches. And I came across a novel, *The Woman of Knockaloe* by Hal Caine. In it a maiden on the Isle of Man fell in love with a German prisoner of war. They planned to be married at war's end, but after an apparently endless agony resulting from not being accepted on the Isle or in Germany, they strapped themselves together in a final embrace and hurled themselves off a high cliff into the sea. The other book, *Character "Bad,"* was based on letters CO[17] Harold Gray wrote to his parents. Whether he was forced to live in prison filth, or was standing before a Court Martial and hearing a demand he be given the death sentence, Gray maintained a kindness and composure that could only have come from his allegiance to God.

Soon after graduation from high school, I entered an Ohio Council of Churches Prince of Peace Declamation Contest, for youth 18 and under. I took first place in the

Interviewed by the Reverend Deb Oskin, Church of the Brethren Peace Minister and President of Central Ohioans for Peace

local church, and received a bronze medal in the district round. A principal idea of the speech was that we "should teach not what to think but how to think." Publicly proclaiming these ideas probably gave them a solidity they may not have if I had kept them quietly to myself.

Then it was necessary to earn some money. I got a clerk's job at the Republic Steel Company, first in their hospital and later in the billing office. While I was there, the Little Steel Strike took place. About half of the workers went on strike while the rest of us stayed inside the plant. Carpenters made bunk beds, food was flown in by airplane, and we insiders did not get home for over a month. Though I was an office worker and not a target of the Congress of Industrial Organizations (CIO), the experience of living through that strike was an important part of my education. Also, the time-and-a-half I was paid was a great boost. My year's income paid for three years at Kent State University.

While a freshman, I participated in John Galsworthy's stage play, *Strife*. It depicts the struggle between an English industrial chairman and the laborers who suffered under his iron fist. Clearly, Galsworthy wanted his audiences to realize the value of give-and-take bargaining as opposed to rigid defiance. The play was a virtual reenactment of what I had just experienced at Republic Steel.

Charles Rann Kennedy was so eager for people to understand that each of us is responsible for the actions we take, and we cannot blame them on centurions, kings, generals or presidents, that he produced a non-royalty play, *The Terrible Meek*. The play, which I saw at a Methodist student event, surely made the desired impression on me. It was given in almost total darkness, with just three characters, Mary, the mother of Jesus, the centurion, and a soldier. Suddenly the centurion realizes the majesty of the One they have killed. Grieved, he chastises the soldier for his involvement in the awful deed and asks, "Why?!' "Duty, sir, it was my duty," the soldier replies, "Twas you told me to do it!"

And I will never forget a Memorial Day service at Kent's Unitarian Church, where the speaker told about a dying World War I soldier telling the fellow who was holding his head, "It's all right, because I know my son will never have to go to war." Also about this time a friend loaned me a book, *Preachers Present Arms* by Ray H. Abrams. In it Abrams took to task the thousands of clergy who had literally turned their pulpits into recruiting stations during WW I. Then I learned about an opening for a boys worker at the Rebecca Williams Community House in Warren. It was operated by the Woman's Division of the Methodist Board of Missions. Group social work was really what I wanted to do and here was the opportunity to get started.

But something relating to my pacifism happened after I had been there awhile. I led one of our two scout troops. A letter came telling about an aluminum drive. Boy Scouts were supposed to canvas neighborhoods collecting old pots, pans and other things made of aluminum, with the idea they could be melted and used in war planes. I informed the members of our Scout Committee that I could not in good conscience participate, but said I'd call a meeting so one of them could tell the troop about the project and then escort them on the appointed date. Nothing was done. But days later, when I went to the county scout office for a camping permit, the Scout Chief hailed me and said there was a rumor he knew could not possibly be true, that I was claiming to be a conscientious objector. I told him it was no rumor, I was a CO. Chief Olds was noticeably angry. In a few days, I received word that he had contacted the national office suggesting my lack of patriotism and unfitness to be a scout leader. I gave up the troop without protest. But looking back, I

think that was a mistake. I should have taken the matter to my scout committee, the community house board,
and to Methodist authorities. I'm sure they would have
backed me. I once said that I had become a "fighting pacifist," just not going quietly into the night, but struggling
for what I think is right.

During 1941, I met Louise Knipper at a YM-YWCA[74]
co-ed club. As we dated and began thinking of marriage,
I spelled out at length about my pacifist commitment.
Her brother was waiting for a call up to join the Navy,
and I wanted Louise to consider how he and their parents
might handle having a pacifist in the family.

I belonged to one of many YMCA clubs, the Squires
Club. We were a close-knit comradeship of men in our
early twenties. While many topics were discussed, we
often got into animated debates on the war that was raging and the draft. I was totally alone. No one agreed with
my pacifism though, fortunately, that did not damage
our friendship.

Because my thinking placed me in a distinctly minority status, it seemed wise to do some double-checking with persons I had come to admire. However, most of this exercise just proved how really alone I was. Only one person told me he was glad to know I was a pacifist. A former minister told me he had become a dualist, meaning he had come to hold completely contrary beliefs in tension. Some said the Hitler regime simply had to be stopped and going to war was the only way it could be done. My grandfather, the teacher of a huge men's Bible class, urged me to enlist. As for my parents, they agreed with me but were afraid what going against the crowd would do to me on down the road.

Then one evening, the great Methodist missionary to India, E. Stanley Jones, spoke at Warren's First Methodist Church and, after the service, I walked with him about two blocks to his hotel. When I told him how I felt, he simply replied that he thought a person should do what he thinks he should do. It was then I knew I would not turn back. Jones had become a great friend of Gandhi, and his excellent books, *Christ of the Indian Road* and *Christ of the American Road* were widely read.

About a month after Louise and I were married in February of 1942, I received a 1A from the Selective Service.[57] Responding by letter, I indicated that on my registration card I had said I was a conscientious objector (CO).[17] Months later, I was told to report to a hearing officer, James Logue, in Cleveland. I was determined to stay calm, cool and collected, but when Logue said he could not understand why a "red-blooded American lad" would not fight for his country, I launched into a virtual sermon about Jesus' teaching and demonstrating nonviolence as the way of God. Almost immediately Mr. Logue changed into a warm conversational manner and, within days, I received a notice that as a CO, I should report for a physical exam. And in short order I was on my way to a CPS[14] camp in Pennsylvania, the only person granted CO status by that draft board, and one of only two in all of Trumbull County, Ohio.

I was in four different camps, all operated by the Church of the Brethren and all doing work for the U.S. Forest Service. Two of these were in Marienville and Kane, Pennsylvania and two in Waldport and Casccade Locks, Oregon. In one camp I became education director which meant I had to 1) establish a range of educational classes which campers themselves could teach, like insurance, woodworking, photography, literature, etc.; 2) be sure every camper had an outlet for his religious life, which was no small task considering the many faiths represented, including followers of Father Divine,[24] Jehovah's Witnesses,[37] Catholics, Adventists, and Christadelphians; and 3) line up a full schedule of recreational activities.

In another camp I became the Assistant Director, which helped me learn some administrative skills. While in the Oregon camps, I was able to take courses for my senior year at the University of Oregon, and received my sheepskin just days before being discharged from CPS. I became acquainted with the Wesley Foundation on the campus, and was encouraged by the minister of Eugene's First Methodist Church to apply for its directorship. For the last three months, Louise and I were able to live just outside of camp in the back room of an abandoned eatery. I left CPS in June of 1946 after three years and a month, all without pay.

A professor from Garrett Biblical Institute in Evanston, Illinois, had visited me in camp and encouraged me, upon my release, to enroll at the seminary. I told him that would have to wait until I found employment and an income. To my surprise, he gave my name to the Executive Vice-President of the Wisconsin Council of Churches, Ellis Dana, about the possibility of my becoming a counselor for a large group of GIs and their families living in a University of Wisconsin compound called Badger Village. Before getting back to Ohio, Louise and I spent a full afternoon with Mr. Dana, visiting the Village and talking about the job. However, we were not surprised when word came they were going to seek an ordained minister. But the fact they did not indicate my CO position was a problem was a real boost for our morale.

Shortly I was back at the Community House but, because I hoped for a campus ministry post, it was on a temporary basis until they found a permanent worker. When one was secured, I made a mistake, and wanted to register as a CO. I was permitted to appear before an appeal officer and give testimony regarding the young man's character and sincerity. After graduation that student went on to a full career as a seminary professor.

On the other side of the ledger were several occasions when I probably helped students realize they were not pacifists. Fellows, knowing where I stood, wanted to talk about not joining the military. Yet, as we talked, it became pretty clear they were just looking for a way out. So, by playing the role of a draft board or appeal officer, I'd ask probing questions to help them discover their true selves and, hopefully, save them from probable later embarrassment.

At Western Michigan our Methodist fraternity decided one of their programs should be a debate between a pacifist and someone who took a strong military position, but I was informed they did not want me because they already knew what I thought. So I gave them a challenge: find a speaker for the pacifist position and let me argue as if I were a militarist. While the debate may have been a draw, it became clear that I understood the military mind. I think that helped to win a new openness to nonviolence as a tactic.

I was in the Freedom March when Martin Luther King spoke from the steps of the Lincoln Memorial. I was able to ride on one of the two long overnight trains from Chicago to Washington. Together they carried 1,700 passengers, mostly black, and every one so friendly and optimistic about what the March could mean. This so impressed me that, when we arrived in Union Station, I phoned a firsthand report about the ride to the Kalamazoo Gazette, and closed with these words from a letter handed to us shortly before leaving the train:

"We are about to embark on one of the momentous events in history. If we preach the ideals of brotherhood of all men and the concept of equality and justice to the rest of the world then we must practice them at home..... Let each of us conduct ourselves with solemnity and dignity, and act with firmness of purpose that will leave no doubt to anyone what our purpose is." The report was printed in full and on the streets of Kalamazoo before the Washington March ended.

During my years at Western, I was active in the Kalamazoo Peace Council that had many visiting speakers, Norman Thomas being one of the more memorable. Articles in area newspapers and literature booths at county fair time were means we used to urge peace thinking. From 1964 through 1969 I was president of the Council.

An important part of my campus ministry involved our students in give and take sessions with international students, many of whom became active in our program. We often spoke of them as "unofficial ambassadors." Every summer Wesley students participated in mission projects and work camps. Some graduates put off planned careers to spend three years of service overseas or two years stateside. I'll never forget the fellow serving at a Mennonite hospice in Eastern Europe who said he asked himself one day, "Why did I come way over here to change the diapers of grown men?" But when it came time to leave he could hardly pull himself away from those very men who had come to depend on him so very much.

I think this is particularly true when we seek no reward and are outgoing just because we want to be that way.

Prior to retirement, I spent four years as the pastor of Columbus' Westgate United Methodist Church. One summer, Westgate hosted an inter-church Children's Peace School. When some of the teachers learned Louise and I were planning a trip to Russia, they asked the children if they would like to make "God's eyes" and bookmarks with short messages of peace for us to give to people we met. The kids were enthusiastic, and they attached slips of paper explaining, in Russian, that they were gifts from American children. Our trip was during the period of Glasnost engineered by Gorbachev, but before the Baltic areas had gained their independence. The day we arrived at our hotel in Tallinn, Estonia, the pastor of the local Methodist Church asked if there were any Methodist ministers he might invite to speak to his congregation that night. There were two of us and, though it was a week night, the church was packed.

The things we said were translated. I decided to speak about the Prince of Peace, and said I did not think the peace Jesus sought was just peace of heart and mind. Nor did I believe it was just peace within the family, nor did I think it was just for others within one's own country. I expressed the belief that Jesus meant all of these, and that he also meant peace should exist among the nations of the world. Then I told about the children's Peace School back in Columbus, and about the gifts they had made, which I had brought with me. Moments later the District Superintendent suggested that Louise and I distribute the gifts while the congregation sang. And did they sing! We did not know the words but we knew the music, "How Great Thou Art." We went up the aisles and handed the tokens to eagerly outstretched hands. One elderly lady, held Louise' hand and said in very understandable English, "God bless you."

We began attending a church in the suburb of Westerville, Ohio, where I accepted the chairmanship of its Peace Advocacy Committee. One of the projects we were involved in was Westerville's interdenominational Peace School for children, similar to the one on Columbus' west side. A teaching staff of approximately fifteen adults worked with upwards of a hundred children. Art work, singing, and storytelling surrounded a brief snack period. I enjoyed telling my class about some of history's amazing nonviolent successes, in which very few people lost their lives even as they overthrew despotic regimes. In my third year with the Committee, I served as Director for the Peace School which was held in our church.

Retirement has given time and freedom to share with friends made decades earlier. We have enjoyed five large reunions of COs, meeting in Pennsylvania, Indiana, Wisconsin and Oregon. In addition, we've had numerous get-togethers with Northeast Ohio CPS families.

Around 1995, Louise and I learned about and joined some Brethren CPSers who were meeting annually in Southwest Ohio for fellowship, serious discussion, worship and a carry-in meal. One discussion included the fact that we were "a dying breed" and wondering if there might be some way to involve younger persons who would carry on ideals that might bring peace. This led to the formation of Midwest Peacemakers which had its first meeting under that name in 2002, the year I became chairman.

Above all else, I am pleased that Louise and I have been a two-person team, so that most everything we have done has had the strength of two. We have been cheerleaders for each other, and whatever major decisions either has made, has had the advantage of our thinking things through together. Louise died in 2009. Close behind, is the fact that I followed through on the advice given by E. Stanley Jones who said a person ought to do what he thinks he ought to do.

I regret that my efforts, along with those of almost every other CO, toward ending conscription have not brought the desired result. Today's all volunteer military groups are at the beck and call of the Commander-in-Chief and the invasion of Iraq was made easier than if he had to get more of the citizenry on board.

While still in grade school I often heard America described as a melting pot in which people of widely different backgrounds were getting along together. Then the civil rights movement helped us further this reality. But, today, in all too many quarters, there is great unrest about ethnic, racial, national and religious differences that is cause for considerable regret.

Yet, how often God uses a remnant to keep alive the things He wills. So it is that when warring is at its height, a faithful minority refuses violence, loving, caring for, feeding and clothing the victims in ways made possible only by His grace.

I have saved something for the last, a poem written by a CO in 1944. In only eight lines it spells out the problem and offers a solution that could bring peace to the world.

Come forth and fight for peace! The bugle cries;

Drums call; there is a mustering of men;

The cannons speak. And other armies rise.

To fight for peace again.

So shall it be until, with flags furled,

The nations forge at last for their defense

The only weapons that can save our world

Tolerance and common sense.

Leonard A. Stark (1922)

"That night I felt as free and unafraid as I have ever felt.
I had lived up to my convictions."

In high school days we attended the Methodist Church in Springport with about 500 residents, because my father became upset with our church, the Salem Evangelical and Reformed (E. and R.). Salem Church was in Albion, which has a big Methodist College. He wouldn't drive us and we couldn't drive, so my brothers and I walked to the Methodist Church where some of our school friends attended. During those years while attending Epworth League I thought about being a pacifist and even before that when I was confirmed at 13 years old at the Albion Evangelical and Reformed Church. The Methodist Epworth League[20] studied and discussed various religious and social issues and there were pacifist sessions. The youth were very positive during the late thirties. However, when the war started, my brother Walter (*see next interview*) and I were the only ones from the Epworth League who continued as conscientious objectors.

My mother grew up in a very religious family. They came from Germany in 1850 and settled in southwestern Indiana. They moved to Chelsea, Michigan, in 1912 and became active members of the E. and R. Church, now the United Church of Christ. It was not a pacifist church.

My mother came from such a peaceful family, but my father was very judgmental and sometimes wouldn't even talk with neighbors, had fence-row conflicts and wouldn't talk with them for years. That was something I felt was so wrong. So growing up with Mother who was so different than my father, I think had a lot to do with the feelings of my brother, Walter, and me. Mother's family was such a caring family. For instance, when her parents died and they had few resources, each one felt the other

---

Interviewed and transcribed by Melba C. Gulick

needed it more. There was no conflict in her family. Growing up with a
father and mother who were so different in spirit made a very deep impact in
my life.

My father's grandparents brought their family from Germany because they did not
want their children to be in Bismarck's
army. I doubt it was because they were
pacifists. Many German people came at that time, but not because of
pacifism.

I was born in 1922, so I was in high school from 1936
to 1940. This was in southern Michigan, a hundred miles
west of Detroit and thirty miles south of Lansing. My first
eight grades were in a one-room school with eight grades
and 20 students. In our one-room school we went barefoot
as long as weather permitted and in high school we wore
shoes and overalls. I went to high school in Springport.
Ours was the largest class with 31. My brother Walter's,
two years earlier, had 24. I did well and was valedictorian
of my class, graduating in 1940.

We had very few books at home. Math was my easiest subject all through school. When I took algebra as a
freshman in high school, the teacher wanted us to write
each step, but I knew the answer and didn't want to write
it all. She finally gave up on me and let me do it my way.

When my father took grain to the elevator to sell, he could figure it out in his head before they could add it on paper. If they were wrong he told them.

As for sports, my father was a work person and we had to get home from school as fast as possible to work. If we didn't, we were punished, so we were not permitted to take part in sports. In the one-room school when we played at noon, my brother and I were chosen last because we were not skilled. My childhood was work, school, and church.

My father was negative toward education and almost made us drop out of high school. After graduation Walter worked on the farm, but did not really enjoy it. He decided to go to college, so I stayed on the farm. I worked there for three years after high school. Some of my friends went to Albion College. Often they had outstanding speakers like Muriel Lester and Kirby Page. Whenever possible I went to hear them. During the depression years my Albion Church could not afford a pastor, so pastors from Dexter and Jackson came every other Sunday afternoon. One was O. Walter Wagner from Jackson. He was a pacifist and became one of my closest friends and supporters. When I came home from CPS[14] on furlough I always stopped to visit him. We talked about pacifism in the family and Dad knew I was a CO.[17] There were no detractors.

I had one brother in college preparing for the ministry, and a younger brother on the farm. I could have been deferred as a farmer, but I didn't want my younger brother to face the draft, so I decided not to ask for deferment as a farmer. Walter went to Elmhurst College west of Chicago. First he was deferred as a pre-ministerial student. In the summer between his sophomore and junior years he worked in a school for troubled youth. As a result the draft board changed his status. He decided he would have nothing to do with the draft and didn't respond. For me, there never was, and never has been, any ambivalence about any of this.

On the Registration Form there was a place you could check if you were a conscientious objector, so I checked that. There were two choices, you could go into the military as a noncombatant in the medical corps, or you would not serve in the military. Of course, that was my choice, to go into alternative service.

Many people had a really tough time with the draft board, with all kinds of pressure and refusal. My draft board was reasonably accepting. We had to write statements as to why we were pacifists and why we would not serve in the military. We were interviewed and finally were given the choice whether we wanted to work with the American Friends Service Committee (AFSC),[4] the Church of the Brethren[7] or Mennonites.[42] When the war started the people from these three peace churches worked very hard to get choices for COs. During the First World War there were men who were unwilling to be in the military and they were imprisoned, tortured and some killed. For this reason the three peace churches worked so this would not happen again.

I was drafted in May of 1943 and was sent to New York State to a camp at Big Flats, a former CCC[13] Nursery Camp. The CCC Camps were empty after the war started, so they decided this would be a place for us. There were different camps, soil conservation, forestry, etc. I left Jackson on my first train ride on May 15, across Canada to Buffalo and then to Corning, New York. When I arrived, the spirit was under the floor. That morning a group was ordered to go to a camp in northern North Dakota. Most did not want to go, so they told us when we arrived that we would only be there for a few weeks and then would go to Oregon.

This was a totally new experience for me. I had no college and many of my co-workers had college degrees. Much of our work was with the seed beds on our knees. One day I would be across from a theologically fundamentalist person who wanted to convert me and the next day across from an atheist, who questioned everything. I had never had the chance to search through what I believed and thought. It was a very growing experience. Many youth experience this in college if they take Bible or other courses, but I went through this long before I went to college while I was in CPS.[14] I did not need to rethink my faith in college or seminary. We made some of our best lifelong friends while in CPS.

We were sent to Oregon to fight forest fires. At the end of June they gave us a short furlough. I went to Michigan to visit family and then to Chicago for a train ride to Oregon. There were about 35 of us in a train car and the black porter said this was the first time he was with a train-load of preachers. It was a great experience going through the Rockies to Spokane and then to Portland, Oregon. We went about 100 miles south to Elkton—in the Oregon Coastal Range.

Some CPS men thought we needed to do more important and needed work. Many of the camps were make work. Sometimes a bulldozer would be left standing while we slowly did the work by hand. They wanted us to work. As a result the three peace churches began other service projects. Some wanted to go abroad and a few left by boat for Asia, but they were returned. Many went to serve in mental and children's hospitals, dairy inspection, and other services. In the winter Jack Corbett left for Byberry, Philadelphia State Hospital, and I finally followed him there in May, 1944. Soon after arriving I met Charlie Lord. We have often been mistaken for each other ever since. Their wedding in 1945 was the first Quaker wedding I attended. It was in northern Delaware.

The war was over but Congress was considering whether to continue the draft. I was so against the draft that I spent most of my time off visiting the pastors of the Evangelical and Reformed Church informing them about the draft and urging them to have their congregations contact their congressmen. Finally I hitchhiked to area churches and even to the Allentown/Bethlehem churches. This way I made some long-term friends.

A number of us said that if the draft was extended we would walk out of CPS.[14] The government was very slow in discharging us from CPS, even when most of the drafted soldiers were discharged. In mid-May, 1946, Congress extended the draft, so a group of us sent our draft cards to General Hershey[34] telling him where they could contact us, but that we would have nothing more to do with the draft numbers. Numbers of us did it, and said we would have nothing more to do with a draft. We just left. Ten or fifteen years ago, before the hospital closed, it was learned that a patient had gone into the building where we lived and destroyed papers including our records.

After two years there, on May 15, 1946, I left Byberry with my few possessions and spent the night with my cousins west of Philadelphia. That night I felt as free and unafraid as I have ever felt. I had lived up to my convictions. The next day I hitchhiked to Durham, New Hampshire, to visit a CPS friend who had contracted polio in Ohio. Then I hitched to Michigan, worked on the farm and counseled at a church camp in Wisconsin for two weeks.

I was thinking of Walter wanting to go to seminary and my wanting to go to college. About this time I decided I also wanted to be a pastor—go to college and then seminary. I started at Heidelberg College. Then I began thinking about going to a different college. I had learned about Olivet College in the summer of 1945 when

I took a furlough to work on the farm. This is where I met Betty who knew some of my Youth Fellowship friends. In the summer of 1946 I again went to Olivet to see friends at the Conference/Camp. There I met Betty again and she introduced me to some of her friends and faculty. During my year at Heidelberg I hitchhiked up to visit Betty and attend various school functions. The next year I switched to Olivet. I did my college work in three years and one summer, 1947 to 1949.

I cannot recall any negative responses to my having been a CO.[17] The college gave me all kinds of routine work—picking up paper, cigarette butts, cleaning the art studio, snow shoveling, etc. They estimated the time and paid me 20 cents an hour, but I worked so fast it was nearly a dollar an hour. During Betty's first year at Olivet she worked in the Business Office and for the other three years she managed the cooperative bookstore. Whenever I had time I helped her.

The college had outstanding faculty members. It was the first Michigan college to have black professors. A third of the students were Jews from the New York City area because it was the only Midwestern school to accept Jewish students. Some professors dressed differently, one man wore ear rings. In this small Michigan town of about 800 residents it was hard to accept, so there were town and gown problems. For the 1948 Presidential election our Economics Professor, Tucker Smith, was the Vice Presidential candidate with Norman Thomas, the Socialist. At least a third of the Olivet faculty members were pacifists, so it was accepted. Another one of the professors, Paul Leser, an anthropologist, came from Germany. He opposed Hitler strongly.

We were still students when we married in March of 1948. Betty was one of those in charge at the women's dormitory. When we were married we rented a small upstairs apartment in a house at the edge of campus. A single woman owned the house and we had a stairway by the front door. We had three former bedrooms and a half bath. In May, 1949, after graduation, we wanted to go to Eden Seminary in St. Louis. We found a 1931 Model A Ford for sale down the street. It cost $100 and we borrowed a trailer and hauled our furniture to Eden Seminary, took the trailer back to Olivet, reloaded the car with a floor lamp on each back bumper and a table, a bicycle, etc. on the roof. We drove the Ford for almost three years at Eden and sold it for $90.

Here, about half of the faculty members were pacifists. The first year at Eden we worked as youth pastors in Christ E. and R. Church, Belleville, Illinois. The first summer the Mission Board employed me to do survey work for a new church in Fairview Heights east of East St. Louis. That summer we also served a tiny church every other Sunday and began a church school. We served that church for almost two years until graduation. It grew from 30 to 120 members.

We thought we couldn't afford to have children while we were at college and seminary, otherwise we couldn't continue. We wanted to have a child when I was near graduating from seminary, but were unable to have one. While serving our first church in San Pierre, Indiana, we learned there was an adoption agency between South Bend and Mishawaka. We scheduled an interview with director of the agency in September of 1953. We met with a staff member on Monday and I had an appointment for the removal of an impacted wisdom tooth on Wednesday. The Agency phoned and asked Betty to come for another interview on Wednesday. Betty left me at the dentist and drove to the agency. They told her they had a girl they were considering giving us for adoption. When Betty picked me up, I was telling her what they had done to my jaw and she was telling me we had a baby, six months and three days old. We went to see her in Michigan where she was in a foster home and they told us we could we pick her up on Friday. When we left home on Wednesday we had no baby, but when we returned on Friday we had a baby. On Sunday when we went to church and the children saw the baby, some ran home to tell their parents. I always said I was more pregnant the day after she came. My jaw was really swollen and very sore from leading worship and greeting people.

We were living in Colorado when we adopted John. When we were in California we wanted to adopt a child, but they wouldn't place a child in a pastor's home because he might move. They thought it was not good for adopted children to move. John was almost three when he came to our home.

I served churches across the country from Indiana to California, Colorado, Iowa, Minnesota, Ohio, and Pennsylvania. All my life I've been involved in social issues. We began a mission church in Garden Grove, Orange County—a very right-wing county southeast of Los Angeles. Almost no blacks lived there, only three or four servant families who didn't own property. We arrived in September of 1955 and the following summer I learned that a Black family had bought a house some eight miles east of Garden Grove. Before they moved in people broke in and poured cement in the plumbing, slashed doors, etc. The family moved in and the first night someone threw a Molotov cocktail bomb in the bedroom where the children slept. Fortunately they weren't injured. I heard about it and arranged for a few of us to take turns standing in the front and back yards until it stabilized.

In mid-January Bob Schuller Sr.,[56] founder of the Crystal Cathedral, phoned me to have a meeting of the pastors in his office that Saturday afternoon. I was president of the ministers' group. We lived about a half mile apart and I had a sermon at the dedication of his first building.

At the meeting Bob Schuller reported that on Friday night he was driving about three blocks from his home and a crowd filled the yard around a house. He stopped to inquire and was told a black couple had bought the house and they didn't want them to live there. Bob said that he went in the house and told them that if they weren't wanted they surely would not want to live there. He wanted us to agree with him, but I told him I couldn't do that. I would tell them that it was up to them, but if they would live there we would do all we could to help them feel welcome.

We learned that the man was a graduate of the Annapolis Naval Academy and his wife of Sarah Lawrence. He was stationed between Garden Grove and Long Beach. Sunday morning there was a meeting at the Women's Civic Club, a half mile from our home. Four of us pastors went and a few Jewish mothers of the daily nursery school in our church. About 150 people gathered plus an attorney from Whittier. Their goal was to raise money to buy the house, so that realtors would need the approval of a committee for the sale of any house. They wanted to prevent blacks from moving into Orange County. We raised many questions and opposed their plans and were called negative names. However, the meeting did not achieve its goal.

Perhaps unfortunately we had train tickets to go to Michigan so our four year old daughter, Susan, could see her grandparents. We had been away a year and a half. While we were gone the situation boiled and a few members joined Schuller's church. I received angry phone calls from two members, so I called the church president to discuss the situation. This was a new church and he had joined the church in December. He said he would contact members to see what their feelings were. Every few days he reported their negative comments—not wanting me to visit them, my poor sermons, etc. In a meeting with our

Synod President I finally decided to resign and search for a new call. I didn't want this small mission church to fall apart—there were only about 70 members and our new building was badly in debt. I finally received a call to a mission church in Lakewood, Colorado. I soon found that over half of the members had supported me and indirectly that had something to do with conscientious objection because both were matters of principle with me.

All my life I have tried to be involved with peace issues. One of our churches was in Duluth, Minnesota. I was so active opposing our participation in the Vietnam War that our church became somewhat divided. It was badly in debt and I didn't want to divide it. I had planted the seeds and now it is one of the most anti-war peace churches in Duluth. A woman is a fabulous pastor there. I had difficulty getting a new call, so went to Indiana to check on a job with CROP.[18]

In Duluth we had the fourth U.S. CROP walk with four to five thousand walkers for 29 miles, and the next year we walked 30 miles. In my CROP interview I was told I'd be away about three-fourth of the nights. Because of the ages of our children I decided not to accept. Then he said, "We need a pastor of my church. Would you be our pastor?" It was a Church of the Brethren in Nappanee, Indiana, so we went there. I was too liberal theologically for some non-Brethren members so I stayed a little less than three years. Some members became lifelong friends. While there I became involved in marriage enrichment, bringing couples together for a weekend sharing experiences and helping their marriages grow.

I received a call to a United Church of Christ (UCC) in Lima, Ohio, in 1975. In Lima there had been serious racial conflict. blacks lived in south Lima in shacks like in the South, so the churches—Methodist, Catholic, UCC, etc. worked together beginning a program called, "Churchmen for Change and Reconciliation" with the goal of building bridges between the blacks and whites. Later we changed it to "Churchpeople." Soon they started other ministries, including a jail ministry. The county had four cell blocks for men, with twelve in each. There was a small meeting room with a long metal table and toilet stool. There were two tiny rooms with double-decker bunks for six. We went into the jail three days a week, being locked a half hour in each of the men's cell blocks. We purchased TVs for each block, placed card and other games, reading material, etc. for those confined in jail. I soon became one of the volunteer chaplains. We went in, not to convert them, just to be there and be a friend. We made contacts with their families, arranged for Christmas and birthday gifts, etc. They had begun other programs, and then the Catholic priest who headed the program resigned and I was asked to head the program for the next four years. We did varied ministries in Lima—renewing rundown neighborhoods, building apartments for low income elderly, etc.

The more I was in charge of the jail ministry the more I felt that somehow you need to keep people out of jail and also give them a chance when they leave jail or prison. Half-way houses transform lives. I learned about half-way houses, visited several in Ohio, and then started a halfway house in Lima in 1980. We found an old house, no longer livable, in a poor neighborhood. We restored it for men and employed a man as Director. He still leads the program. That building is now for 19 women and they built a new building for 39 men north of Lima at Bluffton, which is a Mennonite college.

I heard they were having a speaker on justice, so I went to hear him. He was Howard Zehr and he was speaking about Victim-Offender Reconciliation Programs (VORP).[66] VORP began in Canada in 1970 and Howard learned about it and began the first U.S. VORP in Elkhart County, Indiana, in 1975. That was the year we left that county for Lima. His talk turned me on and I began the second U.S. VORP program. In 1981 I received a call to serve a church in Coopersburg, Pennsylvania. I hoped to start VORP there in the Allentown/Bethlehem area, but didn't make it. The church asked me to lead them in a church building program which was seriously needed. I was so involved in that and other ecumenical programs that I had no time.

I feel pacifism is a way of life and must be lived out in creative ways. I had begun the VORP program in Ohio and when I retired here at Uplands Retirement Village, I began the VORP program in our county in 1989. Due to my stroke in 1995 I can't go to big demonstrations in Oak Ridge, but I do go there most months to demonstrate. Going to the School of Americas demonstration is too difficult for me. I have some limitations but I do what I can.

My brother Walter and I have been members since 1941 of the Fellowship of Reconciliation,[25] a peace organization begun in Britain during World War I. We have attended some of their national meetings. When Betty and I were dating we went to one in Evanston, Illinois. During our early life together our travel was by hitchhiking. I think VORP, halfway houses and all these things put my pacifism into practice.

There are two things I am proudest of: starting VORP here and starting the Half-way House. I am also proud of being able to welcome the black family into Orange County. And Susan, our daughter, has become a very active pacifist. Her songs and all she does is related to peace and justice. No regrets. I guess we all hope for change, but I have learned that you work for justice and peace no matter what, whether the world changes because of it or not. That is life. That is what my faith as a Christian and my philosophy of life is all about.

Walter W. Stark

"Martin Luther King was a student there at Crozer at that time so I was a fellow student there with him for two years. He was a couple of rooms down the hall from me, so we had lots of discussions. He wasn't convinced about nonviolence yet then."

I was born in 1920, and when I was seven years old I became aware I was a pacifist. George Betz and his wife had been teachers in the Philippines before he became a teacher in our school. When I was in first grade in our one-room country school, he took us to a movie in the county seat, Jackson, Michigan. It was a war movie, probably about the First World War. I felt I could never participate in inflicting such death and destruction.

My father was a very violent man, and I seldom could do anything to please him. He always told me that I would never amount to anything. My mother and her family were very religious people. I don't know whether to call them pacifists, but they weren't really supportive of war. One of my mother's brothers was in the army. He was drafted in World War I.

We went to an Evangelical and Reformed Church of the Evangelical Synod of North America in Albion, Michigan. Once in awhile we went to the Methodist Church in Springport. It was two miles from where we lived on the farm. Then my father had an argument with some of the people in the church in Albion, and we quit going there. So then we went to the Springport church. Lots of the time my brothers and I walked there. We were very active in the Epworth League[20] which was the Methodist youth group. We started going there when I was about sixteen. I had been confirmed already in the other church. We had a pastor at that time who took a year off from Eden Theological Seminary to pastor the

Interviewed and transcribed by Melba C. Gulick

church in Albion. The pastor of the Methodist Church, Chauncy Green, was very much opposed to war. He had been in the air corps in the First World War.

As children we had to get home and do chores. My father wasn't interested much in our even going to high school. We had to do chores before we went to school in the morning, and we had to get home and do chores after school, and other work on the farm. I liked science and math. When I was in the country school, I read *All Quiet on the Western Front* and *The Three Musketeers*. I read those before I completed the eighth grade. When you are in a one-room country school you hear all the classes, the recitations before and after you. In town they had an elementary school with three grades in one room so the first six grades were in two groups and the seventh and eighth grades had the high school teachers. It seemed like some of us who went to these one-room country schools did better in high school than the ones who had gone to school in town.

I went to high school in Springport, Michigan. We started out with forty-one in our class when we were in the ninth grade, but when we graduated there were only twenty-four, five boys and nineteen girls. Most everything was required. One thing that wasn't required was Latin, so I didn't take Latin. That was the only foreign language they taught. I guess you didn't have to take all the science courses, but I took them all. They just had biology, chemistry and physics and as far as math was concerned they just had plain geometry and algebra.

I didn't know how I could go to college because I knew my father wouldn't pay any of my expenses. He didn't want us to go to high school very much. He thought we should become farmers, and you didn't need to go to high school for that. He had kept me out sometimes to work on the farm, like for three weeks or so.

After finishing high school in 1938, I was working on the farm some, but he didn't really need me too much, so then I helped my uncle, Albert Pielemeier, in his orchard near Chelsea, Michigan. After that I got other work in the Fram Oil Filter factory in Ann Arbor. I worked there for awhile and then I got a job at the Methodist Old People's Home in Chelsea.

When it came time to register for the draft, there was a supportive pastor in the church in Jackson named O. Walter Wagner who I talked to and the Methodist pastor in Springport, Chauncey Green, who said that was what everybody ought to do. I talked with Harold Gray who had refused to cooperate or to go into the army or anything during the First World War. He lived in Ann Arbor and he had been sent to Alcatraz during World War I. I knew that he had written a book called *Character "Bad."* I wasn't sure whether I could go through with going to prison. I also talked with Kenneth Morgan, Director of Religious Activities at the University of Michigan

I had wanted to go to college to begin pre-theological education because I had been active in the Methodist Church, and held different offices in the youth group. I thought about going into the Methodist ministry, but I knew that my mother's family would like for somebody to go into the ministry of the Evangelical and Reformed Church. I knew they were interested in that and that is the reason I went to Elmhurst College in 1941.

Just about the time I signed up with the draft board, I decided to apply for being a

conscientious objector. Timothy Lehman, the President of the Elmhurst College, was on a draft board, so, I went to see him. He said he would be willing to tell the draft board that I was a pre-theological student, even though I was only there for orientation week at that time. So he did and right away they classified me 4-D, which was for pastors and theological students. I think they knew that I had enough backing and people supporting me that they would have to classify me as a conscientious objector if they didn't do that. So that is what they classified me as. It was the easiest way out.

I didn't do anything about it although at Elmhurst College I was part of a group who were followers of Reinhold Niebuhr.[48] Reinhold and Richard Niebuhr[47] had both graduated from Elmhurst College. Later Richard was President of Elmhurst. They felt that you shouldn't take deferment for being a theological student. So I was sort of the leader of the other side. I was active in the Chicago Fellowship of Reconciliation (FOR).[25] *The Epworth Herald*, the magazine for the Methodist youth organization, was pacifistic, and I used that and read *The Christian Century* and other magazines like that. George Houser was one of those from Union Theological Seminary who refused to register. He was Executive Secretary of the Chicago area FOR. Bayard Rustin[54] was there. He was active in FOR and James Farmer[23] was also.

I was at Elmhurst almost two and one-half years, starting in 1941 and until Christmas of 1943. During that time, I started a FOR group at Elmhurst College. We gave blood at a black hospital in Chicago instead of giving it to the Red Cross. Some of the students called me "Abe," and they asked me to represent Abraham Lincoln standing on a pedestal while the band played "The Star Spangled Banner" for the homecoming musical. I refused to do that, and some of us did not stand when "The Star Spangled Banner" was played. It was done every time when there was a student assembly. This brought forth an exchange of letters to the editor of the student newspaper.

In the summer of 1943, I guess the draft board was scraping the bottom of the barrel, but anyhow they reopened my case. I didn't go to college in the summer so they classified me 1-A and told me I had ten days to appeal my classification. I sent my draft cards back to them with the statement that I couldn't accept registration status as a theological student. When the ten days were over they sent me an induction notice right away. I wrote another statement telling them that I wouldn't be reporting for induction.

The Evangelical and Reformed Church had an unofficial social action group called The Council for Social Reconstruction of which Edward Schlingman was the leader. He had asked me to get a group of pastors from the Chicago area together to plan a conference. We were having that meeting when the FBI came to Elmhurst College to get me so they didn't know where I was. When my former roommate, Eugene Schneider, told them where I was, they called the church. I said if they wanted to come and get me they could come to the church and get me. The pastor said, "We need to teach these fellows a lesson," so they put on the outside of the door a picture of a Christian flag flying over an American flag. I doubt that they even noticed it, but they got me in the car and told me that the air I breathed was too good for me.

They set $1500 bond on me, and George Houser let my parents know. My dad blew his stack, but he sent the $1500 for the bond so I got out of jail. I was over the weekend in the Cook County jail and then I got out and went back to college until Christmas vacation. I sent them a notice that I was going home to Michigan over Christmas vacation, but they didn't get it in time. They had sent me a notice to appear in court in Detroit and I didn't get that, so the Deputy U. S. Marshals came to get me at home. My dad, Leonard, and I were in Springport shutting off the water and electricity in my grandparents' house when they came. My mother told them where we were. They came there and took me in my old farm clothes to Detroit. They took me before the judge and he sentenced me to five years in a federal correctional institution.

It was all in one day, the sentencing and everything. I was in the Wayne County jail over Christmas. Detroit is in Wayne County. Then I was taken to the Federal Correctional Institution at Milan, Michigan. I was there for two years. About thirty COs[17] were there for reasons similar to mine, some because their draft board didn't consider them sincere, like a couple of Roman Catholics. The draft board told them no Roman Catholics could be conscientious objectors. Some Jehovah's Witnesses were there because they said they were all ministers and they should be deferred for being ministers. The draft board wouldn't do that. One man didn't have religious reasons for being a CO, and you had to have religious reasons if you wanted to be considered a CO.

They weren't all COs. Most of the people in the federal correctional institution were there for narcotics violations. Some were doctors. There were German-American Bund[31] members. There were very few others, like for taking stolen cars across a state line and other things like that. The population grew a lot during the time I was there.

We were in a dormitory that had about forty men. We each had a metal desk beside our cot. I became a vegetarian while I was there. Lee Stern was Jewish, but he had become a Quaker,[52] and he had a degree in engineering from Case Western in Cleveland. He was a vegetarian, and he convinced me that you could be healthy; you didn't need to eat meat or any animal products at all. It takes a lot less land to produce the food. I had to help with butchering at home and I had always thought that you needed to eat meat and eggs, and to drink milk in order to be healthy.

I was paroled at the end of two years. You are supposed to be eligible for parole after one-third of your term, but that was a little more than a third. They released me just before Christmas in 1945 and gave me a bus ticket to get home. I got paroled to work in a church in Philadelphia. My brother, Leonard, was there in CPS[14] at Philadelphia State Mental Hospital, and he got this worked out. It was an interracial church, a few black people, but mostly white people. I was working with young people and some senior citizens there for six months. Harry Truman decided to pardon two thousand COs. I objected because I did not know why the others were not pardoned.

In a Methodist student magazine they had something about Berea College. So I got literature and decided that was where I would go if they would accept me. Berea College didn't charge any tuition. Instead of majoring in one area I had an area major with Sociology and Religion being the core subjects. I had drama, agriculture and music courses, and so on. A lot more hours were required than majoring in just one subject. I was at Berea two years and then graduated. In 1948 I went to Chicago Theological Seminary and the Federated Theological Schools of the University of Chicago.

I was at Chicago Theological Seminary only one year because it was very expensive, and I had to pay my own way. Rueben Harkness, a church history professor from Crozer Theological Seminary in Chester, Pennsylvania, was teaching there that year. Also Jack Corbett, who was with Leonard at Byberry Mental Hospital, was going to Crozer Seminary. I decided to transfer to Crozer because it was very inexpensive and had courses in which I was interested.

Martin Luther King, Jr., was a student there at Crozer at that time so I was a fellow student with him for two years. He was a couple of rooms down the hall from me, so we had lots of discussions. He wasn't convinced about nonviolence then yet. While I was there at Crozer, I was the manager of their cooperative bookstore and the chairman of the Philadelphia Area Inter-Seminary Movement. I graduated in 1952.

Dorothy was a student at The Baptist Institute for Christian Workers. They invited seminary students to parties there, so that is where I met Dorothy. We were married one year before I finished at Crozer. After finishing theological school, my father was sick and needed help on the farm, so I went home and helped on the farm. We had a new baby then, too.

I took a church in the autumn of 1952 in New Palestine, Indiana. If they asked us once, they asked us a thousand times, "Oh, isn't this a wonderful place, no poolrooms, taverns or Negroes?" I wasn't particularly happy about that. After two years we went to southeastern Ohio where I had three churches that were part of the Pioneer Larger Parish of fourteen churches with six pastors. In one I only conducted worship services every other Sunday There were a lot of people who were of Swiss background. In 1957 we went to Belvidere, Tennessee. I had about two hundred fifty members in one church there. I was asked to leave there after three years because I did not use the Heidelberg Catechism for confirmation instruction and because I tried to show the students how we could see God's purposes working out through evolution.

About 1960 we went to Hayden, Colorado, about two hundred miles west of Denver with seven hundred people in one church. We were there for just one year and then we went to the Fort Berthold Indian Reservation. We were in North Dakota from 1961 to 1965. We had one congregation that was Indian on the reservation and one congregation not Indian in the town. That was Halliday. In Colorado it was kind of different. It was a shock because we hadn't been used to people being divorced and still being in the same congregation, women smoking, and so on. At some women's meetings the smoke was thick enough to cut. Then we went to the western part of Iowa where I was pastor at Mapleton, Iowa. There was another church in a neighboring town that asked me to come and serve them too, which was of Congregational background. We were in Iowa for three years. In my career there was one place where I went to have an interview I mentioned about my conscientious objection to war and it resulted in their not asking me to be their pastor. It was an issue just that one time.

Then we went to the University of South Dakota for me to get a Master's degree and secondary school certification. I went there one year and two summers. Among others, I took courses in counseling and theater, got a Master's degree in Speech and Dramatic Arts and a Teacher's Certificate. The second summer was being at the Black Hills Playhouse.

That lead to a teaching position in Latimer, Iowa, in north central Iowa, near Mason City. The Superintendent hired me to be the School Counselor and the Drama Director. This Superintendent was really a progressive guy. So, he made the job for me to be Counselor and Drama Director because the fellow, who taught what he called American Studies, a combination of American History and American Literature, was the Drama Director before and he had him be the Technical Director. So I was directing the plays, but he was doing the technical work.

Our third and fourth daughters took so many courses that they almost fulfilled requirements for graduating. They didn't finish high school at all, but just went on to college. Of our six daughters, we had four with us when we went to an intentional community in 1973. It was called Plow Creek Fellowship at Tiskilway Illinois, near Princeton and it was related to Reba Place Fellowship in Evanston, Illinois. They did gardening and construction work on houses. I helped some with some of the construction work and then I got a job driving a school bus.

We stayed there four years, 1973 to 1977. We weren't members, but the members shared their incomes and we had Sunday worship together which they planned themselves. They had sharing groups where they talked about their spiritual journeys and if they had problems, concerns, or joys to share. We didn't put our income into the common pot. That went on for four years when we moved to Philadelphia. One of the reasons I was looking around for other place was because they had livestock and I am vegetarian. I didn't want to deal with that.

The two youngest ones were with us when we moved to Philadelphia and bought a house. Dorothy worked for *The Other Side* magazine in the subscription department. She did that until she got a full-time job at the Philadelphia Geriatric Center. I had a part-time job with *The Other Side* in the Book Service that they had. A couple of years after that I got a full-time job at the Free Library of Philadelphia as a library assistant at a branch library in Mount Airy, called Lovett Memorial Library. I was there for eight years. Dorothy worked for ten years as an "in-home service worker." This brings you up to our arrival in Pleasant Hill in 1990.

Other pacifist activities have been a part of my life here. I've gone every year for about eight years to the School of the Americas to demonstrate at Fort Benning, in Columbus, Georgia. I went to Washington to a rally before the present war in Iraq. I go to Oak Ridge about once a month.

I have been involved with local organizations, also. I was Chairperson of the Church Library Committee for about five years, then I was Chairperson of the Peace Committee of the church for a couple of years, and I have been the coordinator of the Sunday Morning Adult Study Group for many years.

I was the secretary of Cumberland Countians for Peace and Justice for quite a long time. I was the first chairperson of the Cumberland County chapter of Save Our Cumberland Mountains (SOCM) for five years. I was invited to participate in a conference in New Orleans on "Keeping the Earth: Environmental Ethics, Global Warming and the South" in early December, 1998. As a result I wrote a series of six articles on global warming for the *Crossville Chronicle*, our county newspaper. I wrote a nine-page article on "Human Responsibility to Other Creatures from a Biblical Perspective" which I used for a workshop at an Earth Care conference at Chattanooga and for another workshop at a Roman Catholic Justice Day in Knoxville.

Well, I think there are three achievements that I am proudest of. They are directing those plays in CAL Community High School in Iowa, getting people in Uplands Retirement Village to respect and accept vegetarianism as being a responsible form of diet, and getting the church library started in Pleasant Hill Community Church. I guess I have no regrets even though I've gone to Oak Ridge quite a few times to testify against nuclear weapons, but I don't know that anything has changed. In the biography of me that my granddaughter wrote when she was nine years old, she wrote, "My grandfather's advice for the youth of today is to remember that the earth does not belong to us human beings to exploit, pollute, and destroy as we please without regard for others and for future generations. We need to remember that we are a part of the total community of life and to live that way."

Charles R. Lord *(1920-2010)*

"There was no ambivalence at all in my mind. If I had known fully the horror of the Jewish pogrom and the gas chambers and so forth, I might have had some ambivalence, but I put reports of that as lies and propaganda to get us into the war and to support the war because the government was lying about a lot of other things."

I became aware that I was a pacifist by the time I was aware of anything because my father and his father-in-law were ardent pacifists. My maternal grandfather was a Quaker preacher in Iowa and he took the teachings of George Fox,[26] John Woolman, and William Penn very seriously. Dad was a Methodist, but under the influence of my Grandfather he became a Quaker, so with my early milk I took in pacificism.

This all took place at Grinnell, Iowa. I grew up on a farm four or five miles from school. There were Quaker meetings or churches in Grinnell and Oak Grove where my grandfather had lived on a farm and preached. I'm not sure where this Quakerism came from that came into Iowa. Most of the Friends Meetings were not pacifist in the same way. They were more nationalist, but he was really a strong pacifist. My mother was of the same mind with her father and Dad. They were definitely my mentors.

I was born in 1920 so it was taking place before, during and after the Great Depression. Pacifism gave me a little trouble in school because the other boys sometimes would try to start a fight and I wouldn't fight. So they would gang up

Interviewed and transcribed by Melba C. Gulick

on me and one time they tied me up to a post and pelted me with snowballs to make me give up but I wouldn't. So I tried to return blows with the other cheek whenever possible. In grade school in those days we had no sports except throwing a ball back and forth or once over a roof, Fox and Geese, childhood games. In high school I was either riding a horse or hiking five and a half miles to school, so I could not stay for football. I didn't really like football, but I went out for wrestling. We had wrestling practice during school hours, so I became a pretty good wrestler. I won eight out of nine matches my last year in high school. One guy was determined to get the same weight I was in. He had been to reform school and we were both in manual training class. One day he hit me on the back of the head with a chisel. He thought that would frighten me so that I would let him win in wrestling, but it didn't. I still went ahead and won.

I liked English, History and Geography and most subjects. I wasn't so keen on Math. However, I did all right in Math. I went to college at Berea College, Kentucky. The college was not a peace-church school. It wasn't Quaker, Mennonite or Brethren, but it was very tolerant of pacifism. We had a very small Fellowship of Reconciliation group at Berea to which I belonged and we had one or two professors who were pacifists out of the twenty or thirty in the college. Their main emphasis was on educating youths from the seven states of Southern Appalachia and they restricted people from outside. I went there because my cousin taught there and I am sure she had some influence in my getting in, even though I had good grades that helped. In college I took mandatory English and History and different things. Then I began to take Music, Art, Philosophy, Religion, and Agriculture. Everyone usually got a Bachelor of Science degree in Agriculture but I got a Bachelor of Arts which required a lot less hours of Agriculture so I could take other subjects I was more interested in.

During my senior semester and after Pearl Harbor, Dr. Frank Laubach came to speak at Berea and I had breakfast with him. He challenged me to go into the mission field. I was very impressed by him and decided to change my career and go as a missionary. I took as much Bible and Philosophy as I could the last semester and went to Garrett Theological Seminary in the summer of 1942. I registered as a 4-E when I first registered but the draft board called me in. The fellows knew Dad. He had a reputation all over the county. He would argue with the oil delivery man or anybody about pacifism. They would have been much happier to give me a 4-D, which would have meant I could go on to theological seminary and then be exempt from the draft. But I did not do that because I did not want to be sitting in class just studying when my friends were in front lines getting shot at overseas, so I stuck to 4-E and they approved.

My major supporters were my father—my mother was dead by that time—and my grandfather. His brothers were not COs. His children, my three uncles, were not COs, although they knew Grandpa's position very well and respected him. They were my mother's brothers. The Friends Church[52] supported me but some of the guys at the local little non-denominational church we attended Sunday mornings looked quite askance at me. There was opposition. I was engaged to a girl from the eastern mountains of Kentucky at that time and her family was not pacifist. She sort of was, at least she understood very well.

There was no ambivalence at all in my mind. If I had known fully the horror of the Jewish pogrom and the gas chambers and so forth, I might have had some ambivalence, but I put reports of that as lies and propaganda to get us into the war and to support the war because the government was lying about a lot of other things. They talked about the allies would have forty-five losses and the enemies two thousand or something like that—just great big differences which I did not believe was really going on in that war over there. I didn't really know how bad Hitler's pogrom against Jews was until later.

They assigned me to a government forestry-project in Big Flats, New York, where I worked in the woods and in a plant nursery. Then in the Spring they sent a bunch of us to Trenton, North Dakota, to a land leveling project with the Bureau of Reclamation and Land Development. There I drove a big D-8 caterpillar digging out earth for a canal and leveling the land for irrigation. They wanted to level some 15,000 acres of this river bottom of the Missouri River. We made a lot of progress, got a lot done.

In the Fall I heard that the government was inviting volunteers for a jaundice experiment at the University of Pennsylvania Hospital in Philadelphia. I thought that I would like to go and take part in that because many people were dying of jaundice in Italy and other places. They said more U. S. soldiers died of jaundice than of fighting in Italy at that point. So many friends were facing possible death in the army and I was very happy to offer myself as a guinea pig to help in the struggle to understand hepatitis. They accepted me for the unit. At the same time we were working half-time at Byberry, the common name for Philadelphia State Hospital for the Mentally Ill, which is 18 miles out of Philadelphia. We traveled by subway, elevated and bus to get there. And so three times a week we volunteers went in to the hospital in Philadelphia and were given all kinds of tests. They checked several chemicals in our body. They took blood samples three times a week. Our veins got so punctured that they could hardly find a place to puncture to draw blood at the end.

They gave me first the endemic jaundice which was from the blood serum of Fort Bragg, North Carolina, where many soldiers had gotten sick with jaundice. I got sick with that. I felt like a horse had its foot in my stomach and wouldn't move for two days. Later they gave me the infectious kind that came from infected water from a children's camp in Pennsylvania and I got sick again with that. Some people thought that we were going to have slow and inevitable destruction of the liver because of these experiments but they did a biopsy on me two years later and my liver seemed to be healthy. At the same time we worked at the state mental hospital where conditions were so terrible.

The patients had very little clothing. Many in one building were naked. If a visitor came we had to quickly grab trousers and shirt from another patient and a pair of shoes and stick them on so they could see their visitors. And at night the beds, some of them had no blankets; sheets and mattresses were torn; they were sleeping practically on the springs. It was cold at night there and they just didn't have enough blankets and sheets were non-existent. I became so concerned about this that I snuck a camera in and took pictures of these conditions and we started using the pictures in our little mental health publication that we organized there among the COs. And *Life Magazine* heard about it and sent down a man and I was taking pictures for them. Then another guy was in competition with them. He lied to the Director of the hospital and to me, and scooped the story in *Phildelphia Magazine*. That made *Life* so mad that they transferred their story to the Cleveland hospital, but he still used three of my pictures. I think my pictures helped in the national effort to improve conditions.

I started CPS[14] in October or November of 1942 and was discharged April of 1946, four and a half years later. During that time I met Joy Swift. She was working for the American Friends Service Committee[4] in downtown Philadelphia. She came out and visited our unit, as other young Friends women did. I hoped, when I married, that I would find a Quaker and I certainly would not have married anyone who was not sympathetic to conscientious objection. Joy was determined to marry a Quaker, so we were very happy to find each other. We fell in love.

I did some photography as a sideline and worked in the settlement house in South Philadelphia where we lived and then volunteered to help take cattle and horses to Europe under the Brethren Service Committee and United Nations Relief and Rehabilitation Administration (UNRRA).[65] That was the beginning of the Heifer Project.[33] They celebrated fifty years just two years ago. I went with horses to a little town, Kavalla, Greece. That was supposed to be it—one trip—but then our captain got a message to go to Durban, South Africa and get a load of horses. So, we had to take on oil at Haifa; we also loaded phosphate and wine and took them to Mozambique. Then we went to Durban, came back, and then made another trip, so I was gone five months instead of a month and a half.

I wanted to do work which would help humanity and follow Jesus Christ. I wasn't necessarily going to be in a field where I would teach pacifism all the time but I definitely had my conscientious objection in mind when I thought of my career. I lost one job working for a professional photographer when he found out I was a pacifist, a CO. He fired me.

I worked one year as a professional photographer in Philadelphia and then began this weekend work camp program under the Friends Social Order Committee of Philadelphia. While doing that in 1948 our daughter Beth was born in Philadelphia's Lying In Hospital. I felt that Dad really needed help on the farm as he was in his seventies. My brother, who had been helping Dad, got married and left to study for the ministry, so Dad was alone. Joy and I moved out with him on the farm for five years. Our second and third children, Donna and Ron, were born on the farm.

A short time after moving back to Iowa, I felt a call to the mission field, so I studied at Grinnell College for five years. I was working full time on the farm and going to Grinnell part time. I had gotten a B.A. at Berea, and then I got a Teacher's Certificate at Grinnell. Then we went under the Congregational Christian Church Board of Commissioners to Southern Rhodesia, Africa.

I became an educational missionary and Superintendent of Schools, joint government and mission primary schools. These were scattered over an area almost the size of Rhode Island. Our mission had the only schools in that area when I started out. We had forty schools. I was the educator for a big area, two thousand children, later up to four thousand children. The teachers were indigenous people. They were all black. Toward the end we got permission to start an interracial school on our station at Chikore. It got started in time for our son to attend it for about two years before he finished elementary and went to a boys' high school in Umtali

Later we had a boarding school there and then a high school. I was chairman of the Educational Council which ran all the educational institutions; teacher training college, a building and joinery school, two primary schools on the two stations, and the out schools. As Chairman I had something to do with all of them. We were there from 1955 to 1966, when we came back to the States and had a year of furlough or "home assignment." During that time I did quite a bit of speaking. The church was trying to educate people about the work of the mission and the importance of that work. We were just starting to pack all our goods into drums and boxes to go back when we got the letter from Ian Smith, the Prime Minister, saying we were prohibited immigrants, we could not return. The local farmers had put enough pressure on the government that they kept us from coming back. They eventually expelled all the missionaries, even the ones who had been born in the country and were citizens. They were determined to get these white people out who were spoiling the Africans by giving them education and letting them eat in their homes, sleep in their homes. That was just too much.

We were living in Wilmington, Ohio. Joy's sister's husband was a professor at Earlham College. They lived in Richmond, Indiana, and had a big barn so they had plenty of room to store our drums and boxes for a whole year. I taught a little bit and then got a little United Church of Christ church out in the country—Cove Springs near Troy, Ohio. I was there a year and a half and then we had planned to go back to Africa as missionaries, going to Zambia this time but our oldest daughter became mentally ill—manic depression or bi-polar. We just couldn't go away. So I got a church in Pennsylvania as Minister of Christian Education and studied for five years at Moravian Theological Seminary while I was working full time again. After five years I got a Masters of Divinity and was called, in 1976, to the mission field in Tanzania and we served there two terms.

The Moravian Church was paying us, but we were still associate missionaries of the United Church Board of World Ministries. That time Joy and I both taught in a theological college. We started out with a small school, only about twenty to thirty students. Joy taught English and I taught Bible, philosophy, world history, church history—almost everything except politics. I didn't touch politics and I had to teach in the local language, Swahili. We had six months training in language school before we started. The first few months preparing lessons was very difficult. I had to write every word, look up what the meaning should be and translate it using a dictionary. It was tedious work, especially since I was teaching theology. Theology is bad enough in English. Anyhow, we enjoyed it. We liked the people. We had been there only six months when the German Moravian and Lutherans together built a brand new campus down at Mbeya, just four miles from the center of a fairly good-sized city. So we moved from an old mining camp and very old buildings with rats and white ants and all kinds of stuff to the new campus where we had a new house to live in, new classrooms, and a new library. Joy was also the librarian and we had more fun getting books and putting them on these new bookshelves. Then we had a beginning class of fifteen a second year and we kept adding and we had a third year and we had a fourth year and in the end they could speak some English.

I was almost sixty-five years old and I figured if I was going to get any church in America and keep on working, I had better do it before I got over sixty-five or no one would want me. So I resigned from the mission field and took a little church in Wisconsin to be near our son and his two children, our only grandchildren. We were there three years and then he moved to Oklahoma to work on a doctorate, and so I looked around and got a little church at Carrier, Oklahoma, and preached there three years. Then, at the age of sixty-nine, I retired.

I didn't push pacifism very much in Rhodesia although we had other Quakers on our missionary fellowship. We had almost as many Quakers as Congregationalists, three couples, members of the Society of Friends, and in Tanzania I didn't push pacifism but they could tell that I was. I preached pacifism in my churches. The Sunday school superintendent at the large church, the 15,000 member church in Pennsylvania, said he was going to get me fired because of my pacifism and liberal social views, but he didn't.

I marched against the Vietnam War in Dayton, Ohio, and have taken part in vigils against getting into the war in Iraq and then pursuing it in front of the courthouse here in Crossville. I've also shared in Sunday evening prayer vigils against the nuclear bomb plant near Oak Ridge, Tennessee, and have gone eight or nine times to protest against the School of Americas (School of Assassins) at Fort Benning, Georgia each November.

I guess I am proudest of my photographs which drew the attention of the American Public to the terrible conditions in mental hospitals and helped bring change and improvements in that situation. I regret that I was such a workaholic all the time and didn't give the time that I should have to Joy and especially the children while they were young. I should either have delegated the answering some of the 250 teachers' letters to my clerk, or let them go unanswered.

I don't think I ever had illusions that things would change because of my decision. And during the last six years things have become worse, not better. The short advice I can give is to follow one's conscience where it leads one, and to persevere.

Chapter Four
Academics

Chapter Four
Academics

Harlan Smith

Reed M. Smith

Neil H. Hartman

Kenneth D. Roose

Samuel P. Hays

D. Thurston Griggs

Roger D. Way

In high schools, colleges and universities, men who learn and lecture find solid ground in concrete facts and data. Once those are mastered, the meaning and experience of wisdom often emerge. Their knowledge was put to use influencing high school students, finding economic systems which do not generate wars, and providing more jobs and adequate incomes. Not only did one invent "Environmental History," another invented new varieties of fruit.

"Know what you believe and act on it," one advises. Another knows of an immeasurable power in the universe always tempered by the power of human choice. None here regretted their decision to become a CO.

161

Harlan Smith *(1914)*

"War is the most inefficient activity people can possibly engage in"

I was born in 1914, which is an important year, the start of World War I, but the first time I had the opportunity to take a pacifist stand was in 1932 when I refused to take ROTC (Reserve Officer Training Corps)[53] at Pennsylvania State University (Penn State). What I later realized was that, growing inside me from early childhood, was a belief that I should not harm anyone. But it was just a belief.

Personally, I inherited from my dad a bad temper, which I never learned to control completely, despite all my mother's efforts, so I'm not a personal pacifist by nature at all, even though I know I should be. I was the oldest of three children in the family, and we all lived in constant terror of doing something that would trigger my dad's temper. I would fly off the handle for no reason at all. My folks told me that whenever I didn't get my way, even as a baby, I would bang my head on the floor and this scared the life out of my mother. I don't know where she learned it, but somebody must have told her, "if you want to control that kid, tell him to go on banging his head so he learns that this doesn't get him what he wants." Apparently that worked.

I found later that most people who are COs[17] are temperamentally very pacifistic people, but I'm just not— I wish I were, but I'm not. I just had the teaching that I should not harm anybody because I did not want to be harmed myself.

It was a very religious family. They were all Lutherans, and we went to church quite regularly. They were not pacifists. My dad gave me toy soldiers to play with whenever I was sick, which, as I child, I was very

---

Interviewed and transcribed by Duane L. Cady

frequently, so in bed I played war with these toy soldiers. I realized that my mother didn't like that but she didn't try to stop it. She said it wasn't good to play war so I knew that was her feeling.

As I grew up dad gave me more guns—water pistols, cap guns and other toy guns. I did what other kids do, I played with them. My mother told me, "Now Harlan, you should never point a gun at anybody. You should never pretend in play that you want to hurt somebody. You don't want to be hurt, so you should not even play that you want to hurt others." But I'm sure I didn't obey her. I pointed guns at people, but her teachings stuck with me and grew on me. I believed she was right. I had no right to hurt anybody and I shouldn't even play that I'm hurting anybody. I think this is what made a pacifist out of me.

I don't know whether my mother considered herself a pacifist or not. She never said anything to me that I would now think of as a pacifist teaching. She never told me that I should never fight in a war.

When I announced my resistance, I was away at Penn State, and whatever the reaction was at home I don't know. I never had any discussion at all with my dad about it. I'm sure he was very dissatisfied, but mother must have told him not to say anything. When my brother later took a pacifist stand, partly because I did, Dad was reconciled because he said, "he might want to become a minister." I never had any excuse, but I never had to answer to him for it.

The minister in my Lutheran church in my growing up years, from as early as I remember until sometime after I was in college, was himself one of the main Christian ministers who was so disillusioned after World War I that he essentially became a pacifist. Whether he had been in the war or not I don't know, but his preaching, while not explicitly pacifist, certainly made me lean in that direction.

When I was in elementary school, seventh or eighth grade, my history teacher had a small bookshelf and invited all her pupils to help themselves to any books that interested them. I saw a book on World War I, so I read it. It opened my eyes because it said WWI was not caused entirely by that wicked German Kaiser but that it was the result of a whole series of international treaties that brought countries together when any one of them was attacked. It was very hard to determine whether any one country like Germany was more responsible than France or Russia. This was an eye opener to me; it told me that what you're taught in school is not always the whole story. This was the start of my intellectual career I guess.

At the University of Chicago, where I took all my degrees, the intellectual atmosphere was absolutely wonderful. Actually, I started my study at Penn State where, like many others, I didn't know what I wanted to study. After two years I had decided on Sociology. Penn State had only one Sociology professor and he said "if you want to study Sociology, go to the University of Chicago." How I convinced my dad I don't know, but with mother's help I did, so I was allowed to go. Chicago was wonderful, partly because of the influence of Bob Hutchins and Mortimer Adler, who were both Thomists.[63] That created tremendous furor because most of the faculty were scientists and wouldn't stand for Thomism, so everybody at that school was debating all sorts of questions. It was just wonderful. The political science professor tried to convince me that pacifism was impossible, but I was never convinced.

I joined FOR[25] when I went to Chicago. I worked with Homer Jack[36] and got to know - and some of the Union Seminary guys. We studied pacifist literature that I had never read before. I was active with FOR from Chicago days on and got to know a very important group of pacifists in the CPS[14] camps. I knew A. J. Muste[43] very well. I met him when he visited the camp. I met other famous people at the camp, like Ray Wilson.[70] Both of them took an interest in me.

I majored in Sociology at Chicago for the Bachelor's and got a Masters in Social Science. Then I took a year of independent study on my own, which was the most valuable year of my education. During that year of independent study, I read everything I wanted to and audited all sorts of courses—Chicago allowed free audits. Once I had my masters, I had to start earning a living because my sister wanted to go to college and I had to get off the family budget. I took all sorts of campus jobs to keep myself afloat and I earned my own way from then on.

After that I went on for a Ph.D. in Economics. The night before I took my preliminary exams in theory—a real obstacle to getting a Ph.D.—as I was reviewing my stuff for the last time, I turned on the radio and heard about Pearl Harbor. I wrote that prelim knowing that it was not the world-shaking event that it might have been; it didn't even matter. That helped me a great deal to get through the prelim.

At that time I already knew I was a pacifist and I knew that I had a low draft number. I had gone before the draft board for a hearing when the draft started. As I sat in the waiting room, I heard an American Legionnaire talking to one of the draft-board members, saying "we'll never have any COs in this draft board." But when I went before the draft board, they were very fair to me. They quizzed me pretty hard, but when they learned that I had refused ROTC at Penn State in 1932, my sincerity impressed them. I said I was determined to work to try to prevent wars as long as I was alive. I think they were impressed because they gave me my CO classification. Then what they did, I'm sure, is bury me in the files so

I wouldn't be called from that board, because I was not called for over two years. When I was called, I had been changed in classification to 1-A. By then I was at Harvard and had to appeal.

After I took that prelim at Chicago, I realized that I wasn't going to buckle-down and write a thesis with a war going on, so I decided I'd better get a job and earn my own way. So I went to Washington D.C. to look for a non-war job. I didn't want a draft-proof job; I wanted one where I was still subject to the draft. So I went to the Bureau of Labor Statistics (BLS). I knew a couple of guys who had gone down there so I went for an interview. At the interview, the guy brought out a book that had just been published by Harvard, a study of the inter-relationships between industries and the economy and asked whether I would like to work on something like that. I said this is exactly what I'd like to work on, so I was hired on the spot. He asked whether I wanted to work in Washington or at Harvard. I said I'd like to do a little of each, so that's the way it worked out. After a short time I was sent to Harvard and I became one of the first people hired in what became a whole staff doing a new study for Harvard on the post-war economy, which would be the basis for post-war economic policy. They wanted to have that document for the purpose of deciding what policies to use right after the war. That research turned out to be the background for my final thesis later on.

I was almost never asked by anyone about the position I had taken as a CO, but during the war most of the male manpower was being drafted, so all of a sudden they didn't have enough people to teach the Principles of Economics course at Harvard. I got the BLS job in January, and by late summer, with September looming, one of the women on the BLS staff recommended me to the chairman of the department. Can you believe that I had the gall to say that if they could make it a full-time salary I'd do it, otherwise I was not sure that I could? The chairman said, "They don't normally do that, but I'll think about it." The next day he offered me a full-time job, so I taught full-time at Harvard for a year. Talk about the world working for me! This was phenomenal. I told him then that I could be drafted at any time. He said, "People have been drafted; we'll take a chance on you." The fact that I was through with my prelims satisfied him that I was ready to do it. The following summer I said, "Now I'm sure I'm going to be drafted" and he said "we'll take a chance again." By the time I finished that summer term I was called. And then, of course, I had to go through the appeal procedure.

When I got my notice I wrote to change my draft board to Cambridge. I told them about having been granted CO status by the Chicago draft board but an exchange with Frank Knight, my main professor in Chicago was in my file at the draft board. When the guy said "one of your professors" I knew it had been Frank Knight because I knew Frank Knight very well. One day on the elevator he asked me, "Do you believe in God?" I said "Professor Knight, I think you know better than to ask that question," because one of the things he stressed in class was that if somebody says he believes in God you don't know what that means because you don't know what he believes in. So that was the answer I gave him at that time. I didn't go any further. He knew the answer wouldn't mean anything.

I appealed, went before a nice judge, and he said "some of you guys are a tremendous problem. I know what to do with Jehovah's Witnesses but not what to do with you people!" But in the end he said we've got evidence from one of your professors that you don't believe in God. I said "how would he know?"

My CO status was reinstated. Then I went to a physical. At the physical were a bunch of young psychiatrists not much older than I was. I can remember the questions they asked me, "have you ever had sex with a woman?" And I said "no." They said "well, didn't you want to?" I said I didn't believe I should have sex until I was married. The result was that I was transferred to another military figure, who looked for all the world like a southern gentleman who had never faced battle, a nice, kindly old gentleman. He said, "Mr. Smith, I see that you're classified 4-F, the classification for those physically or mentally unfit for military service. How would you get a classification like that?" I said I didn't know I had that classification and asked where that came from. He said "the psychiatrists gave it to you." And I didn't put two and two together until later when I realized that they thought I was gay and didn't want any gay people in the military. The gentle old guy said, "I can't understand why you would have that classification. It won't help you in life, it will hurt you. Didn't you have a CO classification before?" I said "yes, I did." He said "didn't you expect to go to a CO camp?" I said I sure did; I'd been expecting it. So he reinstated my CO classification.

I was sent to a Big Flats, New York, Quaker camp and was there just short of three years. I had no choice. I was managing a forest in the winter and in the summer raising evergreen seedlings to plant for soil conservation purposes. The work was managed by the federal Soil Conservation Service, and for the entire time we were under that command of a military figure, assigned to work, penalized, and so forth, by military figures.

The head of the department at Harvard knew I was a CO and knew I was subject to the draft, so it didn't bother him. However, when I finished CPS[14] I went back and said I'd be available to teach in the fall. He said, "Harlan, you know I'd love to have you back. We appreciated the teaching you did; it was very good. But all we have right now are returning veterans, and I'm afraid to put you in front of servicemen all the time." I understood that; I didn't blame him one bit.

I knew that I was rusty economically and needed a review before I did anything else. I could have gone back to Chicago, but I had gotten to know some of the faculty at Harvard so I decided the brilliant thing for me to do was to get the benefit of some review at Harvard. So I enrolled as a student and took a limited number of courses. I got to know the faculty much better; it was an invaluable experience.

After a year studying at Harvard it became apparent that I needed to get a job teaching. Harvard was prepared to recommend me, so I ended up at Brown. That Harvard recommendation made things too easy for me! Brown never asked anything about my background; they took the Harvard recommendation. While I taught three years at Brown, I wrote my thesis for the University of Chicago. President Wriston decided Brown needed to staff its departments with faculty with national reputations instead of getting by with cheap Harvard labor, young Ph.D.s, so he warned us all to get out. I had known several people at Brown who had gone to Minnesota and I had helped them with some early work, so I interviewed at the University of Minnesota, was offered the job, and here I am. Since my retirement from full-time teaching 22 years ago, I have been teaching one course each semester.

At Brown I was in FOR[25] and went to a meeting one day where A. J. Muste[43] was supposed to speak. Of course I went to hear A. J. because I had gotten to know him in camp but he didn't show up for some reason. We went around the table and introduced ourselves. One of the girls at the table introduced herself as Margaret Guthrie, and Ted Morgan, one of the guys that had come from Harvard with me, had told me, "you're single; you should be looking out for someone here," and he recommended that I get to know Margaret Guthrie. When I heard that name and recognized it as someone who had been recommended that I should know, I walked her back to the dorm. She was a dorm mother at Pembroke. I was very slow and didn't ask her for a date for over a month, and then only after I had seen her in the audience where I had been on a panel debating something on foreign policy. One of the Vice Presidents at Brown said that my position was unpatriotic, and he lit into me for what I had said about world government. The political science professor had defended me and said the Vice President's attack was unwarranted. Afterwards I called Margaret Guthrie and asked her what she thought of that debate.

That Fall she was going to be in New York at Union Seminary finishing one of her degrees, so I said, "well, if that's where you're going to be, I can do what I want to do in New York too." So we took independent rooms in the same building in New York. I was doing a bibliography for the chairman of my thesis committee so I worked in Columbia library, and she worked on her paper. I invited her to visit Minnesota, where I would be in the Fall and then we'd know for sure whether we wanted to marry. So that's the way it worked. She came out, we had a beautiful Indian summer, and we were married that Christmas.

I have always felt that the CO position didn't warrant me taking a personal stand unless I was trying to prevent wars. I was not going to turn my life over to the military, because that might prevent me from working for the elimination of war. War causes suffering for untold numbers of people. It is the most wasteful enterprise of any. In teaching economics we fiddle around with inefficient operations like monopolies, for instance, whereas war is the most inefficient thing you can possibly do. Instead of improving anybody's economic status, it's making people suffer. It's the biggest economic problem there is, so it even enters into my economics teaching.

Quite apart from that, a friend from CPS[14] days, Bill Huntington, who became an architect, kept trying to get me to join the World Federalists. I said "that's exactly the right idea, we'll have to do that eventually to eliminate war, but people aren't ready for it." But the day the atomic bomb dropped on Hiroshima, I went to Bill and said "sign me up. We don't have five hundred years now." So, I've been an active World Federalist[73] ever since. Recently they've changed their name to Citizens for Global Solutions[12] to show that we're dealing with more than the war problem; we're dealing with any international problem that can't be solved by nations. I'm still active in that. I've been chair of the Minneapolis chapter and the St. Paul chapter when they were separate, and the state chapter, I've been on the Board every now and then. It's been my life work.

To this day I'm still doing war research, trying to find new ways to get people interested in the fact that there's a system that generates wars. We call it a deterrent system but even Kenneth Boulding,[6] who was a Quaker and a pacifist, says in one of his books that deterrence does lead to wars because you can't keep your threats credible in a mutual threat system unless you sometimes carry them out. So, this is the sort of approach I've been taking ever since 1932, and I'm still working on it.

I haven't achieved anything that I can be proud of except I'm lucky enough to be alive, still teaching, and keep my head working! My head's working as well as it ever has, and I can't believe it. I'm teaching better too because I'm always revising my material to keep it up to date and find new arguments to convince people of what I'm talking about. But I don't try to make converts. I've never tried to make people believe in God and I've never tried to make people believe in pacifism. I think they should make up their own mind. I tell them how I think and

challenge them to make up their own mind and not believe anything I say because I said it. I had some of the best economic teaching in my day, and as an undergraduate I could see where they were wrong. So I tell my students I expect you to give me a good hearing and show me on the exams you understood what I said, but you've got to make up your own mind and take your own stand on everything of importance.

I have no regrets whatsoever. I've had it too easy, much too easy. I have done nothing to regret and have achieved nothing to be especially proud of.

I did have hope that things would change, not just because of my CO decision but because of pacifist work, but nothing has changed. In fact, things are worse than they've ever been in my lifetime. The amount of terrorism, genocide, and ethnic cleansing now, the world is in far worse shape than it was in 1914. To be sure, it's not in as dangerous shape as it was during the height of the Cold War, because if nuclear war had really taken place and the Soviet Union and the U.S. had used all their nukes at each other, scientists were debating whether there would be any human life left, or even life left except turtles. We could have committed suicide. This is still possible, because the nukes are still there for the most part, and they could be retargeted in moments. Scientists are telling us ways to eliminate the possibility of retargeting quickly, but people are not interested. They're only interested in whether terrorists might get hold of an atomic bomb.

I would like all pacifist groups, including particularly FOR, of which I am still a member, to learn that they're not going to prevent wars by people becoming pacifists. Even Einstein thought that might happen, but it's never going to happen as long as we have the set-up that we have, with nations feeling they have to protect themselves by military means in order to be secure. It is a high ideal for people to be willing to go to war and to lose their life for their country. With the present international set-up, we are never going to have enough people take the pacifist stand to prevent war. We are only going to prevent war by convincing people that it is necessary to change the institutional structure and finally doing it. That's a lesson I think COs themselves must learn, and they haven't learned it yet.

Reed M. Smith *(1920)*

Harlan Smith's younger brother, Reed Smith, was unable to send a chronological interview. He did offer us this valuable picture of the rehabilitation work which was done in Europe by so many of our contributors. —*Editor*

After I was discharged from CPS,[14] I wanted to help the victims of war. I had been released from CPS camp in December and signed up for the service in Europe in February, 1946. I did not want to just be "put away" into a camp or work in a hospital. In January I received a post-card from a friend in Philadelphia reading: "The AFSC is sponsoring a transport program in Europe. Are you interested?" I wrote in reply: "Sure, I'd be glad to help." My mother and father asked me: "Do you really want to go to Europe?" I replied, "Of course I want to go." I served with the American Friends Service Committee (AFSC)[4] for about a year and four months in Europe. I worked with AFSC projects in France and in Poland near the Polish border with Russia.

It took some time to organize this new AFSC European Transport Unit. The Polish assignment was organized by Bill Edgerton, Russian professor at Penn State, who has since retired in Bloomington, Indiana. The delay pro-vided us with a longer training period — February, March and April, 1946 — at Pendle Hill near Philadelphia. We interviewed Quakers who had done relief work after World War I, some who had been in occupied France during World War II. In 1946 the war had just ended and we went there to help "pick up the pieces."

In France we worked in the city of San Nazaire, a city that had been completely bombed out, 90% destroyed, because it had also been a German submarine base. So we lived up the west coast in a little fishing village while we did "demenagement," which means moving remnants of households and their families. I was a "moving man" helping to move refugees. My title was auto mechanic and driver, but much of my "mechanics" was done with a sledge hammer! We purchased 6 x 6 trucks from the American army and had to drive them on war-damaged roads. When I had to change a tire, I always began the work with a sledge

hammer. I was a "sledge hammer man." Yet in that postwar period the job was exciting. I learned a little bit of French and later I landed a job teaching French. I was with a different family each day and it was very interesting to learn their stories.

When the Polish project finally opened up, several of us volunteered for that. We were not allowed to drive to Poland through the Soviet occupied zone, so we drove through the American zone. We weren't supposed to stop on the way, but we did. We visited Quakers in Frankfurt and gave them some grain and other things. We broke the rules. Then we had to drive down through Czechoslovakia, in order to avoid the Soviet zone. A few Americans sold cigarettes in order to get enough money to see Prague. In Poland we were stationed in Pulawy, a little city right on a river, the Vistula, which is Poland's central river, as is our Mississippi. Pulawy had been completely destroyed. A few of the Poles were living in holes in the ground and in shacks—wherever they could. Every house in Pulawy had been destroyed. We lived in our trucks and slept out in the field or in a few tents. Finally they built a barrack for us to live in. The winter of 1946–47 was a terrible winter. Many persons in Berlin froze to death because they lacked enough coal for heating.

Our barrack was full of holes and it was damn cold. I recall the ink in pens freezing. We had no water. We had to go into town where we could pump up some water. Our jerry-can of water would freeze and we'd have to light a fire during the morning in order to thaw it out. That was a pretty rough winter. The gasoline froze in the trucks because of condensation. We had to light fires under the gas tank! That was very exciting. I also had to learn Polish. I already knew some German, so I used my German to help me in learning Polish. Poland had just been occupied for four years by the Germans, so the Poles had learned much German, although they often didn't want to admit it.

That was a very exciting period in Poland. We helped reconstruct the village, which required us to haul in the materials. Most of the Polish men had been killed, or they had gone abroad or to prison camps, so it was mostly women and children and some old men who remained. Building materials were scarce. But Pulawy was on the river. Its banks had cliffs, which could be cut and broken by workers with hammers and chisels to provide stones for building houses. These workers would roll the stones down to us by the river, and we would haul them away to the construction sites with six trucks.

The roads were terrible. We had many flat tires that we had to repair. They had vodka. One time my truck hit a hole that broke both the tire and an axle, so we had to get parts from the USA, which took time. My team-mates accused me of having drunk too much vodka!

Driving those trucks was a difficult job. I also had to haul wood, which was scarce. As in France, we worked with a different family each day. We also had to haul quicklime because they needed cement. The Poles would shovel lime into a hole and pour water on it, so it would bubble and we could use that "quicklime" for cement. We didn't know enough to use masks so we got lime in our lungs and coughed our heads off. We didn't know enough to dump it out of the truck. It was pretty hard work but they built about 45 small houses that year. We didn't do the building, we just did the hauling. The women and the children had to do all that. When I got a chance, 25 years later, my family went over.

In February, 1947, it got so cold we couldn't drive the trucks, so I knew somebody, actually a girl I met there who was a student in Lublin where Poland had a provisional government. It was right on the Russian border, and in Lublin was Catholic University, the only private school in Eastern Europe. It had been destroyed by the Germans. They tore out the plumbing, the lights—everything. It was a difficult place to have a school. Poles managed it. I gave English lessons there.

I came back and finished up my work in political science at Oberlin in 1947. It was almost a letdown for me with all these languages and challenges abroad. In Europe we were not paid maintenance by the AFSC[4] all this time. I met David Richie, a famous Quaker who was running the Philadelphia work camps. He had been in the Polish unit with me. Somehow he had heard that I was looking for a job and he told me, "Well we have an opening in Westtown, you know, the big school near Philadelphia. So I applied.

Neil H. Hartman *(1920)*

"If I had signed up against my conscience, I am sure that in the long run, I would have regretted it."

I was brought up in the Methodist Church and in the Methodist church we were members of the Epworth League.[20] The Epworth league had conferences over the summer where we met other young Methodists and talked about various things. Of course we talked about war because war was looming. What really determined my course of action was my sister going to a Quaker work camp in 1939 in Philadelphia. When she came home, she talked excitedly about it and persuaded me to apply the next year—1940. That summer I went to a American Friends Service Committee (AFSC)[4] sponsored work camp in Michigan. The next summer they asked a bunch of us "veterans" (boys only) to go to an emergency work camp in Mexico to help with an earthquake relief program. Again, we knew that war was imminent so we spent every night talking about what a Christian should do in time of war. I became 21 that summer so I knew that after I returned to the United States I would have just five days before I would have to either register for the draft or refuse to register at all. I was very much under the weight of what I should do. Because of our discussions and the friends I made in the Mexican work camp, I decided that I should sign up as a CO.[17]

My family was a very strong Methodist family but they were not pacifists. Of the four children, I was the only one who became a pacifist. A brother and a sister became ministers in the Methodist church but not pacifists.

I was the only one in my family who was an athlete. I engaged in many sports, basketball and tennis being the two main ones. Other activities included milking two cows every night even after I entered college, since I

Interviewed by F. Evert Bartholomew

just had to go across the street to my college, Cedarville College in Cedarville, Ohio. When he got married, my father, moved to Cedarville mainly because it had a college where his children could get a good education very cheaply. The college was just across the street so we really had no choice as to where we went. It was an Old Side Covenanter College until the local church changed to the Presbyterian U.S.A. But the new church dropped the college since they already had Wooster College in Ohio and they did not want two schools so close to each other. So by the time I entered the college, it was an independent school although every member of the board was a Presbyterian except for one person, my father who was a Methodist.

The Epworth League was my mentor, I guess. Our minister was very active with young people. He was not a pacifist, but he was next door to one. It is very interesting that his son, a brilliant chemist, along with Dr. Harold Urey at Columbia University, helped develop heavy water, which was then used in developing the atomic bomb. However, one of the pastor's daughters became a pacifist. It was an interesting family and they influenced me a lot.

In school my favorite subject was mathematics. I became a high school math teacher. I also enjoyed plays and was very active in dramatics all through school and even when I was a teacher. The philosophies of the schools I attended were diametrically opposed to the decision I took as a pacifist. I lived in the Bible Belt of Ohio, a very conservative place. They strongly supported the war. In fact that was why I resigned from the Methodist church. The Methodist church had a very strong pacifist section on the national level but my local church did not go along with that position. They posted a list of the boys who had been drafted and they did not include my name when I was drafted as a CO. I resigned from the church in protest.

I have an A.B from Cedarville College and a M.Ed. from Temple University. My majors were mathematics and science. I took the science courses just because I enjoyed them; I certainly did not expect to teach science when I got a job.

Before I went to Mexico with the Quaker work camp in 1941, I had been hired to teach mathematics in junior high school. However when I came back from Mexico, I discovered that due to the lack of men because of the draft, my job had been changed. I was now to teach biology, physics, and chemistry in high school. So I spent my first year of teaching as a science teacher instead of mathematics, which I much preferred.

When Pearl Harbor happened, I had already signed up as a CO.[17] I give my family a lot of credit for my decision, although they were not pacifists. I was brought up in the church in a Christian family. They very definitely backed my decision even though they did not really understand it. They felt I was doing what I considered the Christian position and they supported me, which was important to me. The minister was also a supporter. Although I don't think he was a pacifist, he was a strong person and he very definitely supported me.

The major detractors were the leaders of the college. They did not support me at all. Neither did the people of Marysville, Ohio, where I taught in the 1941-42 school year. However, I was surprised by one married teaching couple when they said, "Neil, we suppose that you signed up as a CO." This one couple, although they were not pacifists, appreciated the pacifist position. I had not talked about my opinions since Marysville was also in the Bible Belt, but I guess my opinions came through by osmosis. I was not close to my colleagues since I thought many of them immoral.

My ambivalence ended in the work camp in Mexico. When I came back to the U.S., I didn't hesitate to sign up as a CO. I was not drafted until 1943. I resigned my school teaching job after one year during the summer of 1942 because I knew I was going to be drafted in a few months and I felt it was unfair to start teaching that fall and then have to leave during the school year. In the fall of 1942, I volunteered for social work in Monroe, Michigan, in a settlement house where one of my Quaker work camp friends was employed. I actually got drafted from there in April of 1943.

I was assigned to Merom, Indiana, but it was scheduled to close in two weeks. I was the last person assigned there. I hardly unpacked because I knew we were going to be moved. In two weeks we were moved to Trenton, North Dakota, to an old CCC[13] camp. I spent the summer doing land leveling work for an irrigation project in the Dust Bowl of the 1930s. I drove a D6 Caterpillar tractor that pulled a 14-cubic-foot Carryall to level the land. We ran the machines sixteen hours a day with two shifts.

In September we had a snowstorm in North Dakota and that helped influence me to volunteer for some other place. I volunteered for Byberry Mental Hospital in Philadelphia. After they accepted my application, they wrote me a letter to ask if I would be willing to volunteer as a "human guinea pig" for the study of hepatitis for two days a week. I came to Philadelphia in November of 1943 and worked as an attendant at Byberry Hospital four days a week and two days a week I traveled to the University of Pennsylvania to be a guinea pig for hepatitis. I was there until the fall of 1945.

During the war, I had to ride the public bus from Byberry Hospital to downtown Philadelphia two days a week for the hepatitis experiment. Since I was a young male coming from Byberry, everyone knew I was a CO so I frequently heard passengers talking about a "yellow streak down my back." After I got off the bus, they would sometimes step on my heels as we walked along the sidewalk. I also received some hate letters, not only during the war, but as long as forty-five years later after I made a speech in public.

During the war, Congress passed a law that said COs could not leave the country. After the war ended in 1945 that law was changed overnight. So after I was released from the draft in May of 1946, I volunteered for the Heifer Project,[33] which was sponsored by the Church of the Brethren[7] in cooperation with United Nations Relief and Rehabilitation Administration (UNRRA).[65] I made three trips to Europe as a seagoing cowboy taking cows and horses to devastated countries. I enjoyed the Heifer Project so much that I signed up with UNRRA as a supervisor of the seagoing cowboys. I made four more trips as a supervisor until the program ended in May of 1947 with my final trip to Shanghai, China.

I was unhappy with my colleagues when I taught in a public school so before I left the profession I applied to teach at a Quaker school. I knew my experience as a CO would be an asset not a liability, and I found that to be true. Before my China trip I was hired to teach that fall in George School, a Quaker boarding school in Bucks County outside Philadelphia. I started teaching there in the fall of 1947. I taught math there for two years during which time I met a school secretary and got married.

I met her my first year at George School, married that summer, and then taught another year at George School. We were both employed at George School just two years. She was an Episcopalian and she had never really heard much about pacifism so I had to educate her! We volunteered to go under the auspices of the American Friends

Service Committee[4] for relief work in Japan. We were there for three years. We called it a honeymoon!

We did not want to have children while we were in Japan. Our first child was born in the summer of 1952 while we were directing a work camp in Missouri, just after we had returned from Japan, but he died after four days. After medical treatment for the Rh Factor, we had three girls in 1955, 1957, and 1961. We had only girls, so we did not have to worry about a draft. My wife and I joined Friends in 1954 while I was teaching at Moorestown Friends School. We listed all three of our daughters as associate members of our Quaker Meeting. That meant that before they turned 21 they had to declare whether or not they want to be members of the Quaker Meeting. All three became members.

I've been very active in Quaker activities since I joined in 1954. I've served on both Monthly Meeting committees and Yearly Meeting committees, especially the peace committees. I've spent many hours standing in peace vigils even now. I have also sponsored peace vigils. I have recruited young people for Quaker work camps abroad.

I am very proud that both my daughters are Quakers and have taken an active interest. I say both because we lost one daughter in 1978. My first wife died in 1978 and in 1978 I married a girl I met in Quaker work camp in 1940. She was a pacifist but not a Quaker when I married her, but she has since joined the Society.

I do not have any regrets in taking the CO position. I am proud of it. I hope that I had some influence. I'm sure I had some but I don't know how much. Being a teacher for 36 years, I have had contact with hundreds of students and I am sure I had some good influence on some but maybe bad influence on others. I hope the good outweighs the bad.

I would say to future generations, "Don't be afraid to take a stand for what you believe. It may be inconvenient at the time but in the long run, you will be glad that you did what you thought was right. It is much better to do what you believe is right rather than compromise, even if you have to take some flak." If I had signed up against my conscience, I am sure that in the long run, I would have regretted it.

Kenneth D. Roose (1919)

*"Until we narrow the gap between the "have not" nations
and those with abundant resources, a peaceful world will
be very difficult to attain."*

I would describe my family background as religious but not pacifist. My father's grandfather was a Presbyterian minister and dad was a Deacon in our Presbyterian church in Topeka, Kansas. When we moved to California, he became a Trustee of the Community Methodist Church in North Hollywood. My parents gave equal support to their two sons, one of whom was a Lieutenant in the Navy and the other a CO.[17] I first became a church member at the age of seven when we still were in Topeka. My rejection of war and violence was shaped in my early years by religious training and belief. I particularly remember the Veteran's Day parade of November 11, 1936, when our Epworth League[20] group entered a float on which our streamer said, "In Christ there is no East or West"!

North Hollywood High School had some diversity because of the Japanese Americans and a small group of Hispanics. It was also in this period that I became addicted to the game of tennis, playing three winning years on the high school varsity and my freshman year at USC. This has remained a passion for me and my family to this day.

Fred Trotter, our minister from 1930 to 1935, never preached a sermon that did not contain reference to the need for pacifism as a way of life. Trotter, an Irishman, had immigrated to the U.S. with his brother a few years before we entered into World War I. In addition to Trotter's influence, the Methodist Youth Movement in the thirties had a strong strain of pacifism. This was especially true of the Summer Institutes that were held in the

Interviewed by his son, Kirk B. Roose

High Sierras. Almost all of the participating ministers were pacifists. I attended the summers of 1936 through 1938. It was during this period that I became committed to my pacifist beliefs.

The mentor who had the most influence in shaping my pacifist views was Dr. Robert B. Pettengill, one of my professors at the University of Southern California. I became an economist largely through his influence. Almost one fourth of my undergraduate work was in his classes. In the summer of 1940, after my graduation from USC, he was one of the leaders at a Methodist District Student Training Conference held at the San Anselmo Presbyterian Seminary, north of San Francisco, where I met my future wife, Gretchen Burns, who supported me whole heartily in all the strenuous years of the CPS[14] Camp, in the Loyalty Oath[9] controversy that will be discussed later, and in the raising of our children.

I was a very dedicated student and prepared lengthy papers on such widely divergent topics as "Public Education in America," "The Rise of Mussolini," and "The History of Prohibition." I read adventure stories, biographies and books on contemporary political developments. When it became time to consider college, I received a scholarship for the University of Southern California (USC). My parents, who were public school teachers, had taken their graduate work at USC. It would have been described as conservative but with an international outlook. Because of the numbers of Japanese Americans seeking higher education it had a somewhat diverse student body. I chose my major of economics in my junior year in college. We were still in the throes of the Great Depression, so I wanted to learn about measures that might be taken that could provide more jobs and more adequate incomes.

To summarize my academic degrees, I graduated as number two in my high school class in June 1936. Then I graduated from USC in June 1940 summa cum laude, Phi Beta Kappa and winner of the Lottie Lane medal for highest grade average in the College of Letters, Arts and Sciences. All of my graduate degrees were in Economics from Yale University. The M.A. was in 1943 while the Ph.D. was awarded February 1948. During the years 1940–1942 when I was at Yale, I served as the secretary-treasurer of the Yale All University Peace Committee. Senator Gerald Nye, Wendell Willkie and Charles Lindberg all spoke at the New Haven downtown square in 1940–41.

During the 1940-1941 period, I was a regular attendant at the Yale University Chapel. Contributing to the strengthening of my pacifist beliefs were the sermons of John Haynes Holmes, Henry Hitt Crane and E. Sherwood Eddy. On the other side, I also heard from Reinhold Niebuhr, who was particularly challenging, Henry Pittman van Dusen, and Henry Sloane Coffin, Sr.[15]

When registration for the draft was first scheduled for October 16, 1940, I was not yet 21 so it was not until September 1941 that I had a hearing before the draft board to register my request for classification as a CO. Two people appeared with me to testify to the sincerity of my beliefs. The first was Dr. Glenn Randall Phillips who had been my minister when we first came to North Hollywood in 1928. In 1941 he was the minister of the

Hollywood Methodist Church and some years later he was appointed the Bishop of the Rocky Mountain States. Dr. Robert B. Pettengill was the second person to appear with me before the draft board. I eventually was given the classification of lB but I had established my claim for classification as a CO.

At the time of Pearl Harbor, I was 22 years of age. With the graduate program at Yale closing down, I took a position as a Junior Staff Economist at the Post War Planning Unit of the Department of Commerce. It was while there that I received three separate draft designations beginning with 1A, then 1AO, and finally 4E. The latter two resulted from appeals.

On the 16th of February 1943, I reported to Camp 76 at San Dimas, run under the auspices of the American Friends Service Committee.[4] My service extended over 3 years, 1 month and 17 days. The final five days were after Camp 76 became a government camp run by Selective Service. One interesting incident from my CPS[14] experience is that my local church was faced with a dilemma. Since the church had posted a list of men from the church who were serving in the military, what recognition would be accorded to COs? With only two such in the congregation, both sons of Trustees, it was decided to post their names in a separate column.

In my camp experience, my commitment to pacifism was put to the test at times. For three years I served as the foreman for the statistical crew that was stationed in the town of Glendora. Since most of the campers were strongly opposed to the force embodied in the conscription process, our relationships in the Quaker camp were always in a state of tension with the Selective Service System and the Forest Service leadership. Under such circumstances, to serve as an intermediary between the assignees and the forest service was a most delicate assignment.

As the war drew to a close, I was somewhat concerned about my future prospects having taking this extremely unpopular position of being a CO. To my great surprise and relief, I experienced no antagonism. My good fortune, initially, was that the Chairman of Graduate Economics at Yale was E. Wight Bakke, a Quaker. We kept in touch during my CPS days. It was he who told me that since I had taken my required examinations for the doctorate, the remaining course work would be waived. I could simply return to Yale and write my dissertation. Another illustration of the support given me by faculty at Yale was that almost two years before my release from camp, I received a letter from Kent Healy, the new chairman of the economics department in which he expressed his good wishes and said he was looking forward to the time when I could resume my work at Yale.

It was also reassuring to receive several letters from S. Morris Livingston, my boss at the Department of Commerce in Washington, D.C., where I was working when I was assigned to CPS camp. He was urging me to return to my job in his unit.

From these recollections you can see that my service as a CO did not open me up to discrimination after the war. In fact, one other incident suggested that my position was seen in a positive light. In January of 1951, I received a job offer from Max Millikan, son of Robert Millikan, the Nobel Prize winner in Physics. Max had been my professor and later colleague at Yale. He had just been appointed the Assistant Director of the newly established Central Intelligence Agency. He wanted me to be his Assistant. I replied by indicating I was not ready to make another move at this time. Also I suggested that he may have forgotten that I had been a CO which might well disqualify me for this position. In his next letter he said, to the contrary, my being a pacifist would be all to the good: "We are trying to prevent any future wars!"

I was also aware that some ex-COs had a different experience. In particular, John Buttrick, who had been in graduate school with me, applied for a job when I was in the Department of Economics at the University of California at Los Angeles. In my initial communications with him, I indicated his application was being well received and that I thought shortly he would be offered a position. Sadly, a week or so later, I had to advise him that no offer would be forthcoming because by the grapevine, I heard one department member had said that one CO in the department was enough.

After finishing my work at Yale, I took a position as an Assistant Professor of Economics at the University of California at Los Angeles. Things there went along smoothly until the summer of 1949 when, with the growing tensions that became the Cold War, the Regents of the University of California decided to require all employees to take a Loyalty Oath.[9] Drawing upon my stand as a CO to World War II, I could not in good conscience sign such a Loyalty Oath. Just as I believed in freedom of conscience, so, too, I believed in freedom of speech and freedom of association. Had I not had my CPS[14] Camp experience perhaps I might have compromised my principles. But for the next eight months or so I continued in my opposition to the Loyalty Oath, even though it became clear that unless I signed, I would be fired from my position.

As this outcome became clearer and clearer, I cast some lifelines to institutions where I had hopes another job might be offered. Oberlin College, to its credit, eventually offered me a position without even an interview. I knew only one person at Oberlin, a graduate student from my Yale days. Oberlin College had such a prominent role in the Abolitionist Movement and to this day has cherished freedom of speech on its campus.

My years of social activism in Oberlin were largely directed to questions of civil liberties.[3] I served on the

Board of Directors of the Cleveland Civil Liberties Chapter Number and was one of the founders of the Oberlin Civil Liberties Chapter. I also served as Treasurer of the Ohio Civil Liberties Chapter. Although we were unsuccessful, I was among those who opposed the invitation for the establishment of a Naval ROTC on the Oberlin College campus in response to the Korean War.

In 1956 and 1957, I was a Senior Staff economist on the President's Council of Economic Advisers in Washington, D.C. Arthur Burns was then the Chairman and I was able to get a little taste of political life in the nation's capital.

In the mid 1960s I was Dean of the College of Liberal Arts at Pennsylvania State University when student unrest beset campuses. My pacifistic leanings were revealed when I convened a group of angry students to meet with a civil liberties lawyer and me to air their grievances.

One measure of one's accomplishments is in the contributions of one's progeny. My older daughter spent 38 years in various aspects of library work, my older son was a CO in the Vietnam War and has a law practice solely devoted to Social Security Disability Law. My younger daughter is developing a Master of Teacher Education Program at Oberlin College. And, finally, my younger son is the Chief Mediator for Public Employees in the state of California.

Our interests in peace have never faltered over the years. On the material side, we have been supporters of the AFSC,[4] the FCNL[27] and FOR.[25] In 2006 we returned to our roots in Oberlin by taking a cottage at Kendal, a Quaker retirement community at Oberlin.

I am not overly optimistic about the prospects for a peaceful world in the long-run future. At the end of World War II, because of the explosion of the nuclear bomb, I doubted that there would be a world in the 21st

Century. We have made it, but the problems of achieving a peaceful world appear almost insurmountable. At the very least, we should take the counsel of President Jimmy Carter and open up a dialog when we have disagreements. Until we narrow the gap between the "have not" nations and those with abundant resources, a peaceful world will be very difficult to attain.

What am I most proud of? I can think of three things, all of which I think required some degree of courage and I still take pride in them. First, it was to be a CO, second to be a non-signer of the Loyalty Oath[9] and third to be, with my wife, parents of four such fine children.

Samuel P. Hays (1921)

"..be independent, think your own mind, do what you want to do."

L et me say first of all that becoming a CO[17] was no big deal for me, no big decision, no controversy, nothing at all. I grew up in a series of events that led to this very naturally. I was very much influenced by my mother. I grew up in a small town in southern Indiana, Corydon, which was the first state capital of Indiana, an historic town. My ancestors had come there from the early 19th century. I have more pioneer ancestors in my genealogy than almost anyone. So they were two families who had long been there. My father and mother married in 1916, and I was born in 1921. I was one of three children. I grew up in town but my folks had three farms that were all inherited from years ago. My father was a small town lawyer who developed a Guernsey dairy herd and I spent a fair amount of time with it. Over the years I got interested in farming as social action.

It was a mixed religious setting; my father was an ardent Methodist, typical, we historians might say, of a Methodist-Prohibitionist-Republican, all in combination. He was the leader of the Sunday school and Treasurer of the church. My father left all the problems of raising children to my mother, although he did read to us. Clearly most of my ideas about this and other positions are due to the fact that I was very close to my mother.

My mother's family was associated with the Disciples of Christ, known then as the Christian Church. Mother was never very much active in the church. Her mother, the mother of ten children, went to the Christian Church, and one of those children, a maiden aunt, took me to Sunday school regularly, so I grew up in the Disciples of Christ Church.

Interviewed and transcribed by Wendy Underhill

I wasn't par-
ticularly interested
in social issues at
all except that the
minister happened
to be acquainted
with an officer
of a church in
Indianapolis that
had a peace section.
In 1937, it was very
popular around
the country to sign
what was known as
the "peace pledge,"
where young peo-
ple would sign a
pledge saying they

would not go to war. Their minister brought this to our
congregation and my mother, who rarely went to church,
took me to hear the presentation he gave. Both of us were
of very much the same mind, and I signed the peace
pledge. That was not something that was a decision of
any kind. I was very close to mother, and she was always
interested in social issues. She read a lot of magazines
such as the *Progressive and Survey Graphic* which was for
social workers and I sort of absorbed that. Throughout
my college correspondence we were constantly discussing books we read. We had discussions of the ideas, so I
sort of grew up along with her attitude, and from then on
it seemed a very natural thing to do.

Mother got a degree from Wellesley in Latin, Greek,
French and German, and taught all of them, so she was
very much oriented toward education. She was also a
pianist of some accomplishment. So, in that atmosphere
I made a decision about college. My brother and sister
went to Grinnell. I got a scholarship to Grinnell and I got

a working scholarship to Swarthmore, and so she put it to me to make the choice. The other thing she said to me was that "if you go to Grinnell, you'll be a big fish in a little pond. But if you go to Swarthmore, you'll be a little fish in a big pond." Well, I was always challenged by something that seemed to be a little bit difficult to do, so I went to Swarthmore. All I knew at that time was that I shouldn't go to a big school. Indiana University was off limits to us. It was a party school, had a football team, and was nothing but a business school, no liberal arts.

We became more involved with Quakers as time went on. The first thing was a work camp. I'm not sure how she knew about Quakers. My older sister went to a summer work camp in Chester, Pennsylvania, when I was a sophomore in high school. I went to a Quaker summer work camp in eastern Tennessee in 1941. We built a barn for a demonstration farm in the Tennessee Valley Authority area, and I learned a lot about the problems of the South. The next year I went to a work camp in southeastern Missouri that was right in the midst of black-white tenant farmer problems. I became more involved with the American Friends Service Committee[4] that sponsored the work camps. From then on it was logical. In fact I can see from my correspondence that I was deciding to register as a CO even in 1941 or 1942, before I did register. So, all that was very natural.

At college I learned to write papers which I enjoyed very much. I liked to read widely and write my own thoughts about what I read and that's what Swarthmore provided me an opportunity to do. I had never written a college-type paper in my life in high school, and I had no idea what some of the subjects were. I remember my roommate came back and said he was taking Political Science, and I said, "What's that?" I'd never heard of that before. Sociology I'd never heard of before. I had fun with Philosophy. We had graduate seminars in which we had small groups where we had a lot of discussion. I decided after a while that Philosophy was too esoteric for me. I wanted something a little more concrete, based more on human things, so I ended up majoring in Psychology, only because that was the easiest thing to do. When I went back after the war, it was with the idea that I would go into History. History interested me because it was so comprehensive, and I could run my way around and do my own kinds of things. I like to read widely and write about it, and that was something you could do as an historian.

I had never joined a church, so the draft board took my application and they told me, "None of us are ministers so we can't tell if you're sincere or not, we don't have the ability to do that, so we'll just give you a 1A, which is the regular draft number, and you can appeal." So I did. The appeal went very nicely for several reasons. In the first place I'd been in work camps for two years and I had sponsors from AFSC[4] on my behalf. But the most interesting thing was that I was majoring in Philosophy. The best-known philosopher at Swarthmore at that time was named Brand Blanchard and he was a Quaker, and kind of an icon at Swarthmore, but anti-pacificist. I wrote papers for him on pacifism and we'd had quite a number of arguments, very nice, very principled, strong arguments. Brand Blanchard went to the Director in my appeal, and that impressed the Hearing Officer. Two or three other people came and testified on my behalf. The Hearing Officer said, "Oh, there's no problem here. The only problem was that the draft board passed you over because you're not a member of any church," but he added "Your case is pretty clear." So I never had a problem.

I was in the CPS[14] starting in June of 1943 and served for almost three years. For the first two and a half years I worked for a federal forest agency in western Oregon, the western Cascades. The last six months I worked in a in Laurel, Maryland, in a school for what we called "low grade kids," low intelligence kids from the District of Columbia. There were over 50, most of whom had to be taken care of. It was a custodial job. We kept them fed, cleaned, and clothed, but there wasn't much beyond that. There were two or three with IQs over 50 who could learn how to sweep the floor and make the beds, and they were the "high grades." I had three years of college before CPS,[14] then after three years with CPS, I went back to college.

The honors program at Swarthmore is a program in which you don't take classes your last two years. Instead you take two seminars a term and the seminars meet once a week. At the end of the second year you have examinations in all eight of your seminars in the space of one week, given by people you've never seen before. The psychologist who came in and examined me in social psychology was Jerry Bruner from Harvard and he offered me a fellowship right on the spot. I never made a decision to do graduate work or become an academic. That wasn't something I sat down and did, it just came along. I had already made up my mind in favor of History because I like to sit and think and that's what History did for me.

I went to CPS from a rural area, so I knew about farming, but I had never gotten acquainted with forestry. I did forestry work in western Oregon with CPS. This means I fought fires, planted trees, worked in a blacksmith's shop and so on, so when I went to Harvard I was interested in what you would call Natural Resources Management. I did a thesis on the conservation movement during the Theodore Roosevelt era, which had never been done before. That started me off in the field of conservation. The thesis turned out to be a book published in 1958, which is still in print.[32]

At first I tried to get a job teaching the history of conservation, and every agricultural college in the country responded positively. That's a case where my experience in CPS[14] really carried over into the subject I chose. I went to my thesis adviser early in 1952 and asked him about getting a job and he said, "don't worry, don't worry, don't worry." About two weeks later I got a letter from the Department Chair at the University of Illinois offering me a job sight unseen. This is the old-boy network working.

From there I went to the University of Iowa for seven years. In 1960 I was offered a job as Chair of the History Department at the University of Pittsburgh (Pitt). This was a very interesting case because Pitt was unknown, what we called a "street car school." It had no real dormitories and it had a pretty poor record except in football. There was hardly a Ph.D. on the faculty. Most of them were M.A.s, and they had got their M.A.s from Pitt. They got a new chancellor to try to make a modern university out of it, and they hired a lot of good people. I saw this as an interesting opportunity. It wasn't really a sensible decision in terms of getting to a place that was well recognized, but I thought it was a good challenge, and I was there as chair for 13 years. I retired from being chair in 1973.

At that point the environmental movement had started, and it was very vigorous. I had really not paid much attention to it in the 1960s, but I decided that I would then go into the field of Environmental History. The time I was chair I wasn't able to do a lot of research and writing. I found that the job of building the department had been so successful I could just about write my own ticket, which I did. I began to teach what I wanted to, and had a lot of fun doing that. I didn't retire until 1990 from teaching.

I met Barbara in 1947, and we married in June of 1948. Barbara was also a student at Swarthmore when I was. At any rate I asked her for a date once. She was attending the checkout desk at the library. I just went up to her and asked her for a date. It was a movie, Henry VIII or something like that. She accepted right away, and then she turned to the student next to her and said, "Who was that?" We found very quickly that we were simpatico in many ways. In a general way we were both interested in the same sorts of things, both into social questions and issues like that. She went to Radcliffe. She was interested in Ecology and Biology. The problem was that she was going into Biology and I was going into History and she applied to Chicago and received a fellowship at Chicago. I ended up going to Harvard and she got an M.A. and taught at Simmons College for a while and was the breadwinner there for us for a while.

When we were married in June, 1948, I remember her father was a little bit anxious because we had no jobs, no money, and no income. Looking at all my letters I can see that we were getting a little bit here and a little bit there. And we finally figured out that we had enough to go.

We were living in big house in Pittsburgh by ourselves after our kids had left, which took a lot of time and energy. We wanted to get rid of all that and live a different life, so we came to this retirement community in Boulder Colorado in the year 2000. We have two daughters and three grandchildren here, so it was the logical thing for us to come here.

Looking back, I am proud of what I did at the University of Pittsburgh. When you're chair of a department, the big thing is the department you make. We had an excellent department there for quite a while. I went there with the idea to develop a program in modern history with the city of Pittsburgh as a focal point. We needed to build up an archive based upon the historical records, which took a long time to get going. First I had a half-time graduate student in a small room. We collected records and developed an archive that grew and grew.

Then in the library we had a section and we got a new librarian who was very interested, and they've started now a major archival location away from the university a couple of miles in several old warehouse buildings. When we were back there two years ago, I was just absolutely amazed at what this archive had become. Most of my books and manuscripts are there now and all of my professional papers. That is a permanent achievement.

Another thing that is less spectacular has to do with my hometown. I inherited two farms from my parents and in 1970 I gave one of them to the county park commission to start a new park. It was a good thing for that community. Through the imagination of one particular leader in town they started a County Park Board. They had six or eight different park areas and I gave them 320 acres, a half section of farm, which is now the largest one and a major part of the park commission. I have started an endowment to help manage the part that is a natural area. That's going to be there forever, another permanent achievement.

I began to learn what it means to be a man of peace when I did a few things as a student. At Swarthmore, I was Secretary of the Race Relations Committee, and we were interested in the possibility of letting blacks enroll. We knew that the President had the same thing in mind. He had approached the Board of Managers at Swarthmore, but they were very negative about it. So we tried a new trick. We went in pairs to each one individually, asking them about it. The replies were uniformly, "well, I'm not opposed to this but I think my fellow managers would be." We presented it to the board one night and it ended up that the next year they did have one black admitted. He was the son of Wilbur White who was the head of the NAACP and he was so light-skinned that you wouldn't be able to identify him unless you knew it. That was before the war. We came back after the war and lo and behold Betty Hunter, who was obviously black, had been admitted. That was the beginning and Swarthmore has had a very cosmopolitan racial and ethnic composition ever since.

When I was chair at Pittsburgh I established one of the first courses in black history in the country. We were not able to hire somebody to teach this particular course so six of us took pieces of it and integrated them into a course on Black History. It was only a beginning, but it was a beginning. Then we hired a black historian who did the work from then on. So that is a contribution. Even though I've never been really active in civil rights, we did some interesting things that are useful.

What I would tell others is, "be independent, think your own mind, do what you want to do." I've always been able to do that, although I'm sure a lot of people can't. But if you can, do as you want to do and don't feel as if you have to do something because your employer wants you to do it.

Be independent, be an independent thinker and really explore the world. This is one of the reasons I like the Internet so much. You can sit down and find out about all kinds of things if you have an exploratory mind. I'm surprised at how many older people just sit and watch television. You can't explore with television, you have to accept what it gives you, whereas with the Internet you can explore.

I hope that things have changed because of my decision in the sense that I'm interested in environmental subjects. People can get very negative about what's been achieved but I think that it's a slow steady increment in the right direction, even though this book I've just written tells you how terrible the Bush policies have been!

D. Thurston Griggs (1916)

"You have to meet people where they are and then figure out how to move in any direction tactically in terms that are acceptable with them. That's what pacifism really is but it's hard to put into practice."

I was a pacifist when I was a child, but I didn't know what to call it. It was a matter of temperament. I was told that I was the most agreeable of the six children. My parents were Presbyterian missionaries; my father was a doctor. He had been in China from 1902 to 1907. They were not pacifists.

When I was a child, I liked sports and music. I liked a sport if I thought I was good enough at it. If it was a sport that I was not good at, I wouldn't touch it. I was good at backyard football, skating, riding a bike, and riding horses. I could run faster than most kids. I went through a spell where I was playing tennis very well. I swam almost daily all the way through graduate school. I liked diving, but I didn't care for distance swimming. I stayed away from baseball, volleyball, basketball, and some of the track things like throwing things and jumping high or broad.

In the family I was the youngest and there was always something going on. We had a large library at home and my parents were intellectuals, so that I read a lot of the classics as I was growing up. I remember reading Dickens, Mark Twain, and Robert Louis Stevenson, some books many times. I've been playing the cello since I was eleven, which is eighty years. I always liked Geography and languages. I never got into Math, but everything else I liked.

After kindergarten I went to public schools in Tacoma, Washington. They were excellent schools. Then I went to

Interviewed and transcribed by Beth Edelstein

University of Washington for three of my four years. The second year was spent in China as an exchange student in a Chinese university where they used English because they didn't have suitable textbooks in Chinese. I had a Chinese roommate there. I went into Chinese Language and chose schools that taught the Chinese Language, of which there were only five American universities at that time. I had five years of graduate study at University of California at Berkeley, University of Chicago, and Harvard and went on to get my Ph.D. in Chinese History from Harvard. The philosophy of the schools I attended was liberal. The best was the University of Chicago. That was at the time of the *Great Books*.

I spent my junior year of high school in Nazi Germany where I made a lot of friends because I could speak German. I joined the Fellowship of Reconciliation[25] in 1935 and stayed with the Harvard Pacifist Society. I was classified 4F - 4E. Through my associations in college in my studies, the year in China and the months I spent in Germany, Austria and Denmark, I had an international outlook and I couldn't see making war.

I was twenty-five at the time of Pearl Harbor. My family supported me as a person when I decided to become 4E. My father had died at that point. He would probably have been the most adamant in the other direction. I had two brothers who were also pacifists by their own conviction. The women didn't want me to go to war, but they didn't feel that taking a stand was practical. They didn't try to stop us, but decided to tell the truth. In those days women weren't subject to being involved in the conflict.

I was in two Friends CPS[14] camps. For a while it looked as though I was going to get to go to China in a Friends ambulance unit. That took me to Philadelphia, New York and Yale University for preparation for the assignment, but the Selective Service nixed it. I had three months of specialized training in linguistics to get ready to go to China, but they wouldn't let the Friends do it, so I worked in the Philadelphia State Hospital for two years. It was a total of four years.

After I got out of CPS, I first I went to work for United Nations Relief and Rehabilitation Association (UNRRA).[65] I worked there for a little while trying to prepare people who were going to go abroad for what they would encounter. In that connection I was approached by the State Department and asked if I would set up a training program in China for Foreign Service Officers who were there for two years to do nothing but study Chinese and Chinese culture. Because of my graduate training in the language and family background—I had a sister who had lived in China for twenty years—I probably was a logical candidate for that work. In 1946 I went to Beijing and worked there for a year setting up a program for those Foreign Service Officers. At that point Senator Joe McCarthy tried to persecute anybody who had been connected with China on the theory that they were responsible for the communists taking over China. Things closed down and those guys that I trained hid it as much as they could so as not to be picked on. Fortunately, they managed to survive. Only one of them left the service.

The McCarthy hearings also had ramifications in the educational field and made it difficult for me to get a job teaching. When I got my doctorate at Harvard, I taught at the Fletcher School of Law and Diplomacy, Drew University for two years, and the University of Maryland. At that time the Chinese bamboo curtain of no contact put a crimp in anything Chinese except laundries and restaurants. I changed into administrative work in the academic field, but I did teach Chinese History in the evenings. I was at the University of Maryland in College Park for 20 years as Physics Administrator. I had a high school course in Physics but I didn't have to know Physics. All I had to do was to know how to push people and papers. We had about 150 graduate students and many of them were foreign, coming over to this country after World War II. I handled their problems of housing and immigration, and so forth. I also managed the teaching assignments for the professors. We had 75 professors of physics.

At the time I was in CPS, I was attracted to one of the nurses with whom I worked in the psychiatric hospital. After I went to Cambridge, Massachusetts, I missed her and asked her to come up there. That's how that marriage occurred. We lived together as a family for four years. But it turned out, unfortunately, that she had schizophrenia. We had two sons and she took them with her to Maryland. When she went I didn't realize that I wouldn't be able to get those children from her. I tried very hard, worked through the courts and so forth trying to get the children. She had two breakdowns where she was hospitalized. While she was hospitalized, the children came into my care for a few months at a time. I also commuted from New Jersey every other weekend to see the boys. At that time the courts did not ever favor giving the children to the male if they could help it.

Then the second marriage occurred when I was teaching at the University of Maryland. I married a teacher whose brother knew my family out in California. I didn't know it at the time but she had been hospitalized and had many shock treatments. Suddenly the sickness burst out. I got a phone call telling me that she had loaded a moving van with all the furniture. I called the county police who came and she was hospitalized. Her brother came from California and got her released in his custody. Then he drove her back here and they stole our child, my third child. I went to California, hired an attorney, and got a *writ* of *habeas corpus* to get my boy back. I brought him home.

One of them has been a teacher for about 20 years now in Pennsylvania and he's an excellent teacher of

German, Latin, and computers. He likes to teach elementary level.

The second boy lives upstairs with me. Randy has
had health problems and is now under disability. He was
rejected by his mother. He was badly treated by her. He
was militarily inclined, spent 11 years in the National
Guard and was a correctional officer. Then he got into
drugs and alcohol. He was in prison for three years but
he's all right now, straightened out. The third boy was
learning to play the oboe and going to Johns Hopkins.
He said, "Oh, I'm going to take Chinese." I thought, "He's
going to find out how tough it is." He always tries things
and drops them. After the first year of Chinese, he moved
so fast that he could read some things better than I could.
He stayed with it and went to China for two years on
a scholarship. He had a scholarship to Johns Hopkins.
After he came back from China, he found that the faculty
had changed at the University of Chicago and they were
specializing in Japanese. So he went to Japan for two
years and he and his wife are both trilingual. The children are now speaking both Chinese and English. The
children have been to visit China and they're going again
this summer. Their Chinese grandparents are living with
them right now.

Before I was drafted I worked for the Quakers. I was
called to the Japanese evacuation from the west coast. We
had the first hostel in Los Angeles where we kept the families of imprisoned Japanese men. I had to eat Japanese
food for six months there—seaweed—I hated the food.
It was an important service. I visited some of these people with the Quakers in the Internment camps, one in
Arizona and one was Marianna, California. I spent some
time with Chinese seamen who were rescued when their
ships had sunk, but they couldn't come into the United
States because of the anti-oriental legislation. So they
were held at Ellis Island. Another CPS guy and I went in

there to try to teach them English to give them something to do. I regarded that as a pacifist action.

I started learning to fly an airplane when I was still in CPS[14] service. I couldn't contact people I knew in Europe and in Asia during the war. The mail service was interrupted completely. I felt isolated from my interests. It meant that there was a new world I had to adjust to. I wasn't sure at first what role pacifism might play in that because my role as a pacifist had been pretty isolationist from being in CPS camp to being in a situation where I wasn't supposed to be seen or heard. However, being in academia made a difference because there were people in academia who were not closed-minded or narrow-minded.

For the last ten years, I've been going down to Washington D.C. for lobbying with the Peace and Justice Committee for the Presbyterian Church. We are first briefed from the Presbyterian office on what was current legislation and then go to the congressional offices. I talk to their Staff representing our pacifist point of view, speaking for the Presbyterian Church. For the last twenty years I have written pacifist editorials for the newsletter of my church.

I've been surprised that I've been able to do that because there are some die-hards. Now we are beginning to be pressed to stay quiet and shut up in pacifism. Before they thought we were under control and they didn't have to worry about us. We could talk, but we weren't going to change things. Now, they're worried, so they're putting the screws on us. The Peace and Justice Committee was cut from nine people to five. A new Chair has been chosen by the Presbytery, and we have been given hints that we had better shape up. This is going on right now. It means we have to become real pacifists now. Our response to them has to be in amicable terms.

I'm most proud of the Chinese language computer program that I developed for instantaneously translating speech into printout. I regret that I had an invention that I got five patents on, but couldn't get funding to put it on the market. I needed $500,000 to complete the research necessary. I sold my house to get the money to carry on that research work. For over 18 years I worked on it, but I had to drop it because there was no funding. They came to me last summer and asked for all the materials that I had. They have it now but they've done it a different way and it has a lot of flaws.

I've been lucky that I've been able to do a lot of things. I've been versatile enough that if I was blocked in something I'd move to something else. I published three books and six plays so I had a chance to get the pacifist message across.

I regret my marriages. I don't regret the offspring but I regret the anguish they were caused. I blamed myself for not being sensitive to women. It helped to have two brothers who were pacifists.

It was a great surprise to me when things started changing. I think World War II surprised me. I had expected the Germans to win partly because I had spent so much time in Germany and partly because they were winning up until 1944 when they suffered defeat in Europe. Then there was the rest of the war fought with Japan. The valedictorian from my high school class was a Japanese girl. I visited her in Japan both before and after the war. It was pathetic the situation she was in Tokyo.

My grandson he told me, "I'm going to be ..." and then described a pacifist. I'm giving him my cello. He already plays his own small one. So I believe in genes. It was there, in the genes, and unfortunately his father is not. My grandson has learned how to deal with his father who pushes him to achieve. I think he's seen how I do it. I felt that he is going be hard; the boy takes it out on his sisters. I'm not so sure that pacifism is a complete virtue.

I take a lot of comfort in my ability to get along with people. It's the pacifist thing. I've come to realize that you don't get something for nothing. This is a proverb also in Chinese culture. You want everybody to be good to you but you can't expect it unless you're good to them. You have to meet people where they are and then you have to figure out how to move in any direction tactically in terms that are acceptable with them. That's what pacifism really is and it's hard to put into practice.

I've come to understand a little better who I think God is and what I think God is and it's kind of closely related to the pacifism we're talking about. I think God is like time, immeasurable, immense and supreme, and we have been given the power of choice. We have to make decisions that are the best we are able to make. Our existence here on earth is a gift of grace, and it has both a dimension of beauty and a dimension of joy.

It's been a lot harder reconciling myself religiously. I had the illusion that I wasn't very good in the material world. I had to try one thing after another. Because I had enough of Jesus in my heritage it supported the pacifist tradition for me and I'm satisfied with what it's been. Human beings have a lot of problems with sex. But I've really been blessed by a long life of propriety and, although I did feel some persecution by various folks, I managed to survive without recourse to violence.

Roger D. Way (1918)

"The only way that we are going to create a better world is for the mass of people to do the right thing."

I was conscripted into the Patapsco CPS[14] camp on May 15, 1942. That was so long ago that I have forgotten the details of my becoming a pacifist. Because I was born Quaker, I became aware that I was a pacifist, beginning soon after I entered primary school.

My family were members of the Religious Society of Friends,[52] Centre Monthly Meeting of Baltimore Yearly Meeting (Park Avenue). The Meeting was located in Halfmoon Valley, Port Matilda, Pennsylvania. My family were regular attenders of the meeting and were always pacifists.

When I was six years old, I was given the job of driving a team of horses to harrow a field. I never had any hobbies. In primary school and in high school, I never volunteered to play in any competitive sports. My brothers and I played some baseball at home. At a young age, there was never any non-family member who was a mentor with whom I consulted on any subject.

In primary school, my favorite subject was Geography. In high school, Physics and other sciences were my favorite subjects. I had no reading preferences, reading only that which was assigned to read in primary and high school. To the best of my knowledge, my primary and high schools had no philosophy under which they operated. Both schools' total aims were to get the kid educated and out of there.

After high school, I chose to enroll as a freshman at Pennsylvania State University (Penn State). It is a world-class university and I lived nearby. My father was a farmer who was growing apples and peaches on a commercial scale and I wanted to follow in his footsteps. I majored in Horticulture, electing courses which emphasized fruit-growing sciences and graduated with a Bachelor of Science Degree in Horticulture in June, 1940.

In 1941 I returned to Penn State and earned a Master of Science degree in horticulture in May, 1942, completing my studies just before I was conscripted into CPS.[14] I was 23 years of age at the time of Pearl Harbor. For me, it is logical to believe that war is totally immoral. I was part of discussions with some members of the State College Friends Meeting. Other major supporters were my family, especially my mother, and John Ferguson who later became director of a CPS camp.

I had an insignificant amount of direct confrontational detraction. The farmer next door once expressed his disapproval to my father about my being a CO. The only other detraction that I remember was when I was having my physical exam, along with a couple dozen other potential army recruits. This took place in a public primary school building in State College, Pennsylvania. During the process of dressing and undressing, a rumor began circulating among the recruits that there was a CO among them. I did not reveal my identity and the incident passed without serious consequences. I never had any ambivalence! I was of a mind set to go to prison if necessary.

I first went to Patapsco, Maryland, but was there only a couple of months. Then I applied for a transfer to CPS Camp 34, Beltsville, Maryland. Beltsville was the only camp which was administered by a combination of all three service committees: Friends, Brethren, and Mennonite. The government "work of national importance" assignment for me was to serve as a Research Assistant at a research station of the U.S. Forest Service. Because of my technical training in plant sciences, it was appropriate for me to serve as an Assistant to a Forest Research Scientist. For me, it was a good experience. Then, after CPS, I was able to cooperate with the scientist in publishing the results of our research in a technical publication. This served me well in future job applications.

While I was in CPS camp, I volunteered with the American Friends Service Committee[4] to serve with the Friends Ambulance Unit in China. After two and a half years in China, I came back hoping to find a job in my field. I went to my former professors at Penn State and asked about openings. They knew of a new Research Associate position in the Department of Pomology at New York State Agricultural Experiment Station, Cornell University, Geneva, NY. I enrolled at Cornell University and earned the Ph.D. degree in Pomology (fruit science), graduating in 1953. I worked there for 51 years, during which time I was promoted to Assistant Professor, Associate Professor, Professor and finally, Head of Department. My job was to create new varieties of apples. Among others, I introduced the Jonagold and Empire varieties of apples which are now widely grown on a commercial scale the world over.

Being a CO has never had any negative consequences in my professional work. All of my colleagues knew that I was a CO but they rarely challenged me about it nor exhibited any obvious hatred toward me. The only roadblock that I remember occurred was when I was first hired at Cornell University. I was required to sign an oath of allegiance to the State of New York. I hesitated. But then I consulted with another CO acquaintance who was already on the Cornell faculty. He assured me that it was OK.

I married Mary Elizabeth Otis in June, 1953. She is also a birthright Quaker and pacifist. We totally agree on our pacifism. We watch Amy Goodman on Democracy Now every day. We have three sons and a daughter, now in their 40s and 50s. Our daughter crossed the line at the School of the Americas in Columbus Georgia and spent three months in federal prison. She is currently with Christian Peacemaker Teams in Colombia, South America. If put to the test I do not know whether or not our sons would be COs.

Since my life has been very full with a professional career, other than CPS[14] and China, my lifetime CO activities have been minimal. I have been on a couple of peace marches and have attended peace conferences. Sometimes, I have written my congressmen about peace matters. I subscribe to and faithfully read several peace magazines. But I cannot claim to be a strong world-improving CO activist.

I consider my time in CPS as one of my greatest achievements in life. Volunteering in China also rates high as one of my proudest achievements. Earning the B.S., M.S. and Ph.D. university degrees ranks high. I invented new apple varieties which are now being eaten by thousands of people every day, all over the world. This, I think, is a worthy achievement. Like every person, every day, I wish something had gone a little better. But I cannot think of any major, lifetime regrets.

I had hoped that the world would be in a better state than it now is. Although I never expected my COism to reform the world, I am confident that my COism did, in fact, help to make the world a slightly better place. But

I never had any delusions or even expectations that my being a CO would make the world right. The only way that we are going to create a better world is for the mass of people to do the right thing. One right thing everyone could do is to become a CO and refuse to go to war. This would be a good beginning toward making this a better world.

Chapter Five
Hard Timers

Chapter Five
Hard Timers

Chris Ahrens

Delbert D. Blickenstaff

Harold Blickenstaff

Thomas C. Hall

Phillip Kelsey

Douglas R. Johnson

A ll independent thinkers do not think alike! Some who trust their intuition float through life on a straight, well-lit path to their ideal goal. Others find themselves constantly and unexpectedly challenged by life circumstances while they persevere.

Our first contributor led a life of dedication to ideals few of us could begin to emulate. To him it was not a hard life. But for others, ambitions were thwarted and jobs lost. Some chose to go to federal penitentiaries rather than cooperate with the draft. But even in prison they also acted on their convictions. Drawn to injustice and people in pain, they chose solitary confinement rather than eat in a racially segregated mess hall. They modeled more than preached their pacifism. Only one of them feels that there is no hope left for the human race.

Chris Ahrens *(1916 - 2007)*

"We had agreed from the beginning that we wouldn't be held down by possessions we might accumulate, but would always be free to move as guided."

I first became aware of my objections to war through activities of the youth group in my Presbyterian Church in Queens, New York. The Spanish Civil War was in the news daily, and many Americans were going to Spain to fight against the "fascists." We went to lectures by representatives from the Fellowship of Reconciliation,[25] War Resisters League[68] and others, and agreed on our own conscientious objection to war status. We spoke to groups at churches in our local region, sharing our reasons for a CO[17] stand and against the slaughter in Spain. As it seemed that the U.S. would have a draft, members of our church group discussed what they would do, go to Canada or South America? When the draft did come, I was the only one who actually took the CO position.

Although my parents were regular church-goers, they were not pacifists and found it difficult to understand my position. But they and our local minister were very supportive of my stand. It was my mother's scrapbook of newspaper notices, showing my youthful activity in speaking against war that probably helped the local draft board understand that I had been of this mind for a long time and acted honestly in it, before the issue of a draft arose.

I attended Brooklyn Technical High School instead of a more usual public high school, as I knew that I wanted to do something technical. Work with my hands on concrete projects was more important than book-reading to me. I learned more from this experience than from ten subsequent years of college. Brooklyn Technical High

Interviewed and transcribed by Kathryn Parke

School had a new building, with rooms large enough to build a full-size house and in another area, a full-size airplane. So we got hands-on experience in choosing and using materials and real tools.

Even in hobby work, I've been engaged all my life in model-building, including model airplanes. I was active in most sports during these years, including sailing, field sports, and skiing, as well as minor-league team sports like basketball and football. The small boats attached to a large ship which was beached and wrecked near our town, were turned over to some of us young people to rehabilitate with metal patches, etc. We fitted one up with a sail and a motor and used it on Long Island Sound.

I began my college education with night courses at New York University, and, after the war, received my degree in Civil Engineering. Later, through a non-resident program at Goddard College in Vermont, I earned my Master's degree specializing in City Planning, working with mentors at Goddard College and at VMI (now Virginia Technical) in Blacksburg, Virginia.

I had major supporters of my CO stand. When war broke out during my college education, the church groups I had been connected with stood by me. The major detractors were usually just casual contacts, like young men standing on the street corner with me, as I awaited a pickup to go home to see my family. Those exempt from the draft for medical and other reasons were less sympathetic than the men in uniform, who were much more open than those in civilian clothes.

I had a variety of experiences in the CPS[14] camps I was sent to, all under supervision of the American Friends Service Committee.[4] The first was a forestry project in Cooperstown, New York. This ended when a number of the men were sent west to fight forest fires. My next assignment was in Beltsville, Maryland, where I built storehouses for a research project, using whatever materials I could find. My third assignment was to Orlando, Florida as Director of a unit on hookworm control, mainly building privies that would not pollute the water, to prevent the spread of the disease. My final work was in the mountains near Zalduando Yuquiu in Puerto Rico, as a medical social worker, again cleaning up privies.

After the war, in 1947, I found a partner, Olga, who joined me as we felt led, in accordance with Quaker values. We married and as a honeymoon that summer, directed a work camp of young college women in Tetelcingo, Mexico. We had agreed from the beginning that we wouldn't be held down by possessions we might accumulate, but would always be free to move as guided. After returning to the U.S. and finding housing, we established our family, two sons, and I accepted a job offered by the Congregational Board of Home Missions, in Huancayo, Puerto Rico. Here I was assistant business manager at their hospital, but much of my time was spent overseeing the building of the first residential nurses' training school. We recommended and then supervised a work camp there, building a recreation field for the local children. Through the years, we started and/or supervised other work camps for the American Friends Service Committee[4] in Charleston, West Virginia, blacksburg, Virginia, and Elmira, New York. Then, employed by the Office of Economic Opportunity, I served eight- to eighteen-month stints in at least eight different locations. I also worked for the Peace Corps for a time and for the Federation for Cooperative Housing.

After a few years as Engineering Manager at Mohonk Mountain Resort in New Paltz, New York, then owned and operated by the Quaker Smiley family, we joined the nearby Society of Brothers (Bruderhof)[8] community, which was intentional living in poverty in upstate New York, and were members of that for three and a half years.

Subsequent leadings took us to a three-year stay in Colombia, South America, as technical staff for CARE/ Peace Corps projects. We also worked for the Federation of Cooperative Housing in Washington D.C., in Central America, and in Charleston, West Virginia. I was invited to join a special technical assistance group of the new Office of Economic Opportunity (OEO) poverty program, as a specialist on low income housing. This took us to Kentucky, to several sites in Virginia, to the Virgin Islands, to Elmira, New York and to New York City. In all of these my work was to get projects started by finding financial resources, making plans for housing and small industries, then to move on, leaving these projects in the hands of newly trained local people.

With the demise of OEO looming, I accepted an invitation to join Volunteers in Technical Assistance (VITA) as a contracted employee at the World Bank, reviewing housing contracts and recommending use of local materials and appropriate technology where feasible. I've always been most interested in sustainable and simple living. After retirement, Ollie and I spent one year as volunteers for the Fellowship of Reconciliation,[25] then helped start the first international service programs for students at Warren Wilson College, and later taught Appropriate Technology at the College.

It's hard to choose one thing I've been especially proud to be connected with. I have no regrets about any of it, although I'm sorry to say I don't see the world getting better in spite of my life's work and witness. If anything, it is getting worse.

If I have a message for today's young people, I guess it would be: "What will be, will be. Don't expect things to work out exactly as you would hope. One of the most important outcomes of taking a stand on an issue is that you learn a lot from taking that stand, even though it may be contrary to the general opinion. It may mean a great deal in terms of the future, both general and personal." For me, it turned out that I used my engineering in simple procedures, worked strongly on appropriate technologies in developing countries, traveled a great deal with my wife and sometimes with our two boys, and kept free to move as required, responding to our leadings, recommending use of local materials and appropriate technology where feasible.

Delbert D. Blickenstaff *(1924)*

"..there was a real need for physicians who were consci-
entious about their work and wanted to ease people's suf-
fering. Once that concept got settled in my brain I never
questioned my decision about wanting to take part in
that type of profession."

I think my first recollection of having any feelings about
the effect of war on me and other people was when I
was younger than draft age and was at Camp Alexander
Mack in Northern Indiana. Looking through their rather
meager library I ran across a book that had a whole bunch
of pictures of soldiers with their legs and arms ampu-
tated. They were sitting on the edge of a rather large seagoing vessel. I don't know whether it was a military vessel or not. But anyway, they were sitting on the edge and
they had their arms and legs exposed so it was perfectly
obvious that most of them had some kind of an ampu-
tation. That picture remained in my memory for a long
time and I realized that I didn't want to be part of any
activity that caused that kind of damage to humans no
matter if they were Americans or foreigners.

My family were members of the Church of the
Brethren[7] and were pacifists.

My main hobbies were sports, music and art. My
favorite subject was Art because I thought I wanted to
be a commercial artist. I don't think I read very much
besides the subjects I was supposed to learn in college.
Although I did do some reading while I was in CPS[14] and
I remember, vaguely, reading about Mahatma Gandhi.

Besides my parents, I think some of my early mentors were the teachers that I had. One person that I do
remember was Arlo Gump, one of the camp leaders at
Camp Mack.

Interviewed by Bill Kidwell and transcribed by Peggy Kidwell.

Most of my college work was taken at Manchester College in Indiana. Being a church-related college the professors there were well acquainted with the Christian religion and I think applied their understanding of Christianity in their teaching. I can remember taking a course about the New Testament from R. H. Miller at Manchester. He and I got into some rather lengthy discussions about religion and whether the world was getting better or worse. He enjoyed arguing and discussing these items with me and other students. Most of my college studies were concerned with science, Chemistry, Physics and Biology.

My twin brother Harold and I chose Manchester College mainly because both of our parents had attended and graduated from Manchester. We didn't even consider any other schools. We spent our freshman year together at Manchester and then I decided to go to Chicago to study Art and work part-time. My brother stayed at Manchester and finished his degree in Chemistry. I took a few classes at University of Dayton and also at Northwestern University in Chicago. That was during my CPS[14] experience and I chose those schools because they were available where I was stationed.

I would like to describe how I came about changing my vocation. My decision to go into medicine came rather suddenly. I had never even thought about going into medicine when I first started college. Nobody in my family suggested that as a possibility and I really don't know where the idea came from. But one evening as I was walking down the road towards the Dayton State Hospital Farm where I was assigned, the idea of becoming a physician suddenly entered my conscious thinking. Once it got there I was unable to ignore it. So I changed my mind completely and, although I was still interested in art, I decided not to pursue a vocation in art. So that was when I started taking pre-med classes. I was able to continue some class work at Northwestern University in Chicago. And then after I completed CPS, I went back to Manchester and finished my degree with a major in Chemistry and a minor in Art. And I think I'm the only Manchester graduate with that combination.

I was twenty years old at the time of Pearl Harbor. As you might expect, there was a lot of discussion among the students at Manchester about what was going on and their reaction to it. Many of my friends were drafted and went into the military, and some of the rest of us decided not to go into the military and were drafted into some type of alternative service.

I think the major influence that I experienced was my own father who had been a CO during WW I. Since the church did not have an alternative service program, Dad and other COs were sent to prison. And my dad spent a certain amount of time at Leavenworth Prison in Kansas. Although he didn't spend a lot of time talking to us boys about that, we were aware of what he went through and had a great respect for his ability to withstand an enormous amount of public pressure in his life and take the stand of a CO. When I had to make the decision, it was fairly easy for me because there were a lot of other fellows in the same boat at Manchester. Through our joint discussions we tended to support each other. Also we had an understanding draft board and I know that was not common. In fact some draft boards didn't want to be saddled with any COs and made it extremely difficult for a few fellows. But the board at Manchester was used to facing that problem and so they didn't give me any trouble. Also, I don't think I had any detractors. My major supporters were my family and close friends who were also going into alternative service.

The only ambivalence was that when I first realized I was probably going to be faced with the draft and was still interested in art I thought about the possibility of going into the armed forces and doing art work because I knew there were a lot of non-combatant types of service that some of the fellows did. I thought I could probably get into some type of work like that. It would not pose a major danger to me. I did talk that over with my parents a little bit and they convinced me that I really didn't want to be a part of any military machine.

I was drafted into CPS[14] in August of 1943 and spent about three months at Camp Wellston in Michigan which was a forestry camp. Then I sought transfer to Dayton, Ohio, to work at Dayton State Hospital, which was a mental institution at that time. The main reason I wanted to be in the Dayton area was because that was where my fiancée lived and worked. Later on we got married. I spent a year and a half at Dayton State Hospital. Most of that time was on the farm outside of the city limits on the east side of Dayton. Then I sought transfer to Chicago when I learned about a nutrition experiment that required the cooperation of individuals who were called "human guinea pigs." And I was transferred up there. That was after Louise and I were married in 1944. I spent the last year of my three years of service at Northwestern University Medical School Passavant Hospital Complex being the subject of a nutrition experiment about pellagra, which is a vitamin B complex deficiency disease.

I chose going into medicine on a rather sudden impulse. I've often asked myself how that came about. The only way I can explain it is previously I had not considered medicine probably because I thought there were enough doctors and everything was being taken care of adequately. However, while I was at Dayton State Hospital I saw several things going on that indicated to me that there was a real need for physicians who were conscientious about their work and wanted to ease people's suffering. Once that concept got settled in my brain I never questioned my decision about wanting to take part in that type of a profession.

1945-46 Pellagra Experiment CPS Unit at Northwestern University Medical School Chicago, *(back row from left)* Gary Heisler, Ed Crill, Harvey Dibrell, *(front row)* John Smith, Roy Miller, Lee Smith, Delbert Blickenstaff.

I had one disappointment, but I don't know if that was related to my CO position. After I graduated from Manchester and was ready to pursue my education in medicine, I went back to Chicago and worked in Dr. Andrew Ivy's Department of Clinical Science at the University of Illinois in Chicago. I was working and doing graduate work in Physiology and trying to figure out how to get into medical school. This was right after World War II. There were thousands and thousands of people in the same position that I was whose education had been interrupted and they were anxious to get back into many professions, including medicine. Those who did get into medical school had to have either straight A's or some kind of political pull or both and I didn't have either one of those. So I found it difficult to get into medicine at that time. However, there was a program in Illinois similar to the National Health Service Corps whereby

students could agree to work in a medically underprivi-
leged area after they got out of school and those communities would help finance their education. I applied for
that type of a program and was sent to Danville, Illinois,
to be interviewed by some people there. They seemed to
be favorably impressed. However the final decision had
to be agreed upon by a committee representing the university and a local committee from Danville. Each one of
those two groups informed me that I would be approved
by them if the other decision makers approved me. But
neither group wanted to stick their neck out and say,
"okay, we'll take this guy." So as a result I didn't get in
that program. I have no idea whether my position as a
CO had anything to do with that. They didn't tell me that.
So I didn't get into the University of Illinois. But eventually I got into the University of Oregon and went to
school there.

Louise and I met at Manchester on a student volunteer trip to Bridgewater College and Washington, D.C.
We became acquainted on that trip and started dating
immediately after we got back and we've been dating
ever since. We got married in May of 1944 while I was
still in CPS at Dayton State Hospital. Then we moved to
Chicago when I was transferred up there. At that time we
had our first baby by the name of Theron.

Louise had graduated from Manchester with a
Bachelor's degree and a teaching certificate so she taught
school one year while I was in CPS. That was very difficult for her. She didn't like her teaching job and she had
to carry the baby to a baby-sitter. We didn't have a car
so she had to use public transportation. She said that's
the only year she's lost weight because she worked pretty
hard.

At the end of that year I was released from CPS and
we spent the rest of the summer on Louise's father's farm.

I helped him with the farm work and that's the first time he ever took a vacation. He and some of his relatives went back to Virginia where he grew up. While he was gone I did the farm work. Following that summer I went back to Manchester and finished my degree.

We have four children, three boys and a girl. They're all completely different. Two of them are physicians and two of them are school teachers. Louise and I never really argued or differed much about how we would take care of the children. For some reason or another we seemed to have the same general attitude.

I have continued to be an active pacifist only to the point of writing letters to the Editor and talking to my close friends about books and articles I've read and either agree with or disagree with. I have not been involved with any public demonstrations.

I am probably proudest of my work as a physician. As I mentioned before, I was not a straight A student. I was generally a B student and I had to work extremely hard at learning what I needed to learn to become a physician. I saw other students around me that seemed to just breeze through without much effort, but it didn't come easy for me. I was proud of finally being able to accomplish that goal. I have a vivid memory of how I felt after having done my first appendectomy. I was supervised by a surgeon, of course, but I did the operation from beginning to end, and it was a great accomplishment for me. I really enjoyed doing surgery.

I can't think of any regrets.

I have always had hope that things would change but not necessarily because of becoming a CO. My hope is that eventually people in general will see the folly and the utter stupidity of engaging in war and find better ways of dealing with international problems. But I don't know when that is going to happen, if ever.

The only lesson that I think I've learned is that it is extremely difficult to change people's minds about anything, at least in a short period of time. The result of that realization is that my motivation for saying the things that I believe in and trying to live a style of life that I believe in is to present an example which some people will understand. Other people won't, regardless of what I say. So I've become rather skeptical about whether I can change very much. My motivation for doing the things I do is personal rather than attempting to change other people. I'm very skeptical as to whether that will ever happen. But maybe as people see the way I live they will eventually have some understanding and respect and try to emulate what I am trying to do.

Harold Blickenstaff *(1921)*

"*I don't see society in general giving up on the use of force and violence as a way of trying to solve social problems. I don't believe in punishment or force or violence as way of trying to prevent crime or bring about social change.*"

M y first exposure to the idea of conscientious objection or being a pacifist was when I attended a camp of the Church of the Brethren,[7] Camp Alexander Mack, which is named after the founder of the Church of the Brethren. After having gone to this summer camp I went back home and talked to my father about it. And that was the first time I learned that he had been a CO[17] in World War I. During World War I there was no provision for COs, so he had been court-martialed and received a twenty-five-year sentence and served two years in Leavenworth Prison. But he didn't really publicize this fact because he was a school teacher, and the school principal in a small town in Northern Indiana. Although the general attitude in Indiana at that time was that America's entry into World War I was a mistake and we should do everything we could do to keep out of getting into another war, the fact that he had not supported the war and had refused to support the war, was considered unpatriotic.

I was about twelve years old at that time. And I regret that he never talked to me more about his experiences in prison. When he was principal, the local people found out about his war record, and he was fired from his position for having been a CO in World War I. After hearing about his experiences, I have likewise been careful in terms of publicizing my own experiences. Though I taught in public schools for a number of years, never did I ever, in a class in a public school, talk about my experiences as a

Transcribed by Mary R. Hopkins, from an interview by a radio station in Reno, Nevada by Alan Stahler, KVMR, Nevada City, CA.

CO based on the experiences of my father.

I subsequently learned that my family background goes back about nine generations in that my great-great-great-great-great-grandfather was called Anabaptist Blickensterfer. The family name was originally Blickensterfer named for a village near Zurich in Switzerland. But my ancestors became Protestants and/or

involved in the Anabaptist religious movement and moved to Southern Germany because, Zurich is in a Catholic canton. Then around 1720 he and his four sons came to the United States to escape German militarism. The Anabaptist religious movement fathered the Church of the Brethren[7] and Mennonites,[42] both of which are the historic peace churches. The three historic peace churches are, of course, the Quakers,[52] the Mennonites and the Brethren. All have basically the same values in terms of pacifism and opposition to violence and war.

My family was very, very religious. My father was an ordained minister in the Church of the Brethren. My maternal grandfather and my maternal great-grandfather were also ministers, so religion was a very important part of my family's life. We went to church meticulously every Sunday and I went to Sunday school classes and every meal was always preceded by saying grace. Religion was very important in my family and upbringing. It's impossible for me to see how anybody could read the New Testament carefully, the things that Jesus said, and support war.

I was in Indiana at that time and the general attitude was that WWI was a mistake. The reason that we had got involved in World War I was because people were trying to profiteer from it so we had the embargo acts passed to say that the United States cannot trade with any belligerent country. In general during the 1930s in Indiana there was general acceptance of the idea that war is wrong or stupid.

I went to Manchester College, North Manchester, Indiana, which is the largest college of the Church of the Brethren[7]. There was never much of any question that I would go anywhere else because both my parents were graduates of Manchester College and my older brothers and I, all three of us, went to Manchester College. At that time I didn't know what I wanted to do occupationally. I remember taking an aptitude test when I was a senior in high school. I scored high in being a school teacher and being a carpenter. At that time I said, "I don't want to do either one of these." Amusingly both of these things are things that I have subsequently done. But at that time I thought maybe I would be a lawyer or something else. I didn't really know what I wanted to do.

Likewise, it took me a while to formulate what I really believed. I never could really accept Jesus Christ as my personal savior and some of the rituals of the Church of the Brethren I found somewhat meaningless. One of the rituals is that they re-enact the Last Supper, in that they get together and they have a foot-washing ceremony. I was baptized when I was eleven years old. But I noticed that I didn't really feel any different after being baptized than I did before, and they didn't really tell me what I should believe. I didn't find the foot washing the Church of the Brethren meaningful to me. Though some of the

theology I haven't accepted, I accepted the basic values
of the Church of the Brethren, which are basically iden-
tical to those of the Quakers—simplicity, honesty, and
abhorring violence. Though I have had difficulty accepting some of the theology, I have never had any question
about accepting the basic values.

One of the persons that I became acquainted with
that has influenced my thinking in various ways is Dan
West. Dan West was a college classmate of my father's at
Manchester College and I became acquainted with him
in about 1940 when he and my father worked to establish
a project in Northern Michigan that later became CPS[14]
camp number one. When they began to write the draft
act in 1940, the historic peace churches got together with
General Hershey[34] and Hershey said, "We don't want
these guys in the army, they're more bother than they are
worth." So they wrote into the draft act that, "If because
of religious training and conviction a person is a conscientious objector, they should do work of national importance under civilian direction." But the government did
nothing to set up the alternative service programs and
it was up to the historic peace churches to do that. Dan
West[69] and my father were responsible for setting up this
first project.

Subsequently the thing that Dan West is most known
for is starting the Heifer Project[33] which is still going on
today. I was a bit surprised the first time I heard him
say, "Relief is always wrong." What he meant by this is,
just giving something to somebody, if that's all you do,
you make them subservient. This is the basic idea in the
Heifer Project. Instead of just giving them a cow you give
them a way of becoming self sufficient. When you really
help somebody, you help them to help themselves, rather
than giving them just a donation.

I remember him pointing out whenever you state an
opinion or write something, you should put a date on it,

saying this is what I thought or believed at this time, but tomorrow I reserve the right to change my mind. So I am very careful to include a date whenever I write an opinion and I get after other people for not putting a date on something that states an opinion. I agree with Dan that one should reserve the right to change one's mind if one becomes more enlightened.

I was able to get two years in at Manchester College before I was drafted as a CO and then I served three years in CPS.[14] Then following the war, Manchester College said that though COs weren't covered in the G.I. Bill, but that they would give free tuition to anybody who had been a CO. So I went back to Manchester College for two years and by that time had decided that I did want to become a school teacher. I got an Indiana teaching credential with a major in Social Studies and a minor in Physical Education. I was interested in athletics and I had observed that in high schools coaches had more influence over many of the young men than other teachers. So being a good Hoosier, I enjoyed playing basketball and was always very much involved in sports and athletics. I got married then also. My first wife, Dottie, had attended Manchester College. I got acquainted with her by the fact that she had lived with a cousin of mine at Manchester. Her father was a Methodist minister.

We decided then that we wanted to do two years of service in some way or another and so we wrote to the Methodists, to the Brethren and the Quakers offering two years service. The AFSC[4] responded first, so we went to Poland in 1949 where the AFSC had this transport team with a small fleet of trucks that was hauling building materials and supplies for people who were interested in rebuilding their homes in some of the devastated areas.

We were sent to a town about fifty miles north of Warsaw where the Russian-German front had stood for about six months and was very heavily devastated. We worked under the Ministry of Reconstruction. We spent a year in Poland until the Iron Curtain began to drop down more vigorously and it became apparent that people who became too friendly to us, as Americans, would often be questioned. So it was decided to end the work in Poland because we were endangering some of the people we were trying to assist.

We left Poland and then spent another year in Europe in International Voluntary Work Camps. I directed one for the AFSC in Germany in the summer of 1949 and then we participated in others in France, England and Greece. There had just been a civil war in Greece and some of the areas had been devastated. The idea of International Voluntary Work Camps was an idea started by Pierre Ceresole (1879-1945) after WWI. The idea was that if you could get young people of various countries living and working together they would evolve various kinds of friendships and understandings that would make war less likely to happen.

When Pearl Harbor happened in 1941, I was a freshman at Manchester College. I remember it was a Sunday and I had gone for a walk on the Sunday afternoon, came back, and found out about it and I can remember then listening to the radio in the boys dorm at Manchester College, to Roosevelt give his speech, "yesterday is a day that will live in infamy" because of the dastardly attack.

I regretted that the attack had happened. I think one of the things that many people don't know is all the things that we had done that provoked it. We had said to Japan that we will not continue to trade with you unless you pull out of China. Japan had been invading Manchuria. It had been their whole policy of expansion. Actually, we had become quite involved in the war even before Pearl Harbor in that our Navy had been convoying ships across the Atlantic with orders to fire on German submarines. So actually Pearl Harbor really wasn't the beginning of America's entry into World War II, we were already involved. I think that President Roosevelt knew that something like Pearl Harbor would have to happen to get the American people agitated and behind the war effort because, at least in Indiana at that time, until Pearl Harbor took place, there was not the general sentiment that we should get involved in the war.

Because the draft had started before Pearl Harbor, I was aware of my CO[17] position. The draft act had been passed in 1940. In CPS[14] Camp One, which my father directed in Northern Michigan, I had become aware of COs and alternative service even before Pearl Harbor took place. I never had anybody trying to convince me otherwise. I felt supported by my family. Likewise, all the time that I was a CO during the war, if I was questioned by anybody who was in the armed forces, I never got any criticism. The most common reaction was, "If I'd known I could do something like that, I'd have done it too." The only time that I ever felt any resentment was during the times I would occasionally hitchhike. When I was picked up by somebody and they would say, "Why is a strong young man like you not in the armed forces?" I would look at them and decide how much I wanted to tell them. If I didn't want to give them my complete status I would say, "Well, I am in Civilian Public Service." Most people didn't want to expose their ignorance, so they would just accept that. The only time that I can recall ever having any adverse kind of reaction was if I told some mother who had a son in the armed forces that I was a CO, then she might feel that I wasn't doing my duty to God and country. But I never got any kind of an adverse reaction from anybody in the armed forces for having been a CO.

I was sent first to a camp in Virginia which was working for the National Park Service helping to build the Blue Ridge Parkway. I worked there for about four months. Then the opportunity came to volunteer to work in a mental hospital, so some of us volunteered. I was sent to Lyons in New Jersey which was a Veterans Hospital. I worked there for a year. Most of the men who were in the mental hospital at that time were Veterans of World War I. We were only beginning to get men from World War II who were suffering mental problems as a result of being involved in the war. I worked the longest in that mental hospital on the admission ward, which was very interesting. Men who were there from World War I were mainly suffering from what was called "general pare-sis," which was the latter stages of the effect of syphilis. This was before the days of wonder drugs. Many of them had contracted syphilis during World War I. In the later stages, syphilis attacks the nervous system but it didn't destroy their bodies, so their body was still functioning but their mind was gone. That was the most common kind of patient in the hospital.

We were beginning to get young men who had bro-ken down in combat. They were being discharged from the Army, but with the provision that they had to be checked out through a mental hospital. I had a course in abnormal psychology and it was interesting to me to see these various stages of kinds of mental illness. Many COs worked in mental hospitals during the war. One of my older brothers worked in one in Dayton, Ohio (*see p. 226*). Most worked in state hospitals rather than in veterans hospitals. COs made a significant contribution towards the more humane treatment of the mentally ill.

A notice came out to all the CPS camps that they were contemplating a starvation experiment[64] and they asked for volunteers. I decided to volunteer and I understand that they had about four hundred people volunteer for thirty-six positions. I'm not sure what criteria they used for selecting, but I volunteered and I was chosen. During World War II a religious fundamentalist was a CO who was not necessarily a pacifist, did not have a pacifist philosophy, but said that "The Bible says 'Thou shalt not kill' and it's my job to obey the Bible and unless I obey the Bible I won't go to heaven." In the base camps of the CPS these were the majority of men and they didn't necessarily have a social conscience. Another type of CO was the Jehovah's Witnesses, who are not necessarily pacifist either. They said this just wasn't God's war. If it had been God's war they'd have been pitching in there.

But among the men who were selected for this starvation experiment, none of these Religious fundamentalists or Jehovah's Witnesses were selected. Everybody who was chosen seemed to have a social conscience. They varied in age from twenty to thirty and I, as twenty years old, was next to the youngest one in the whole experiment. Everybody who was in it had at least two years of college and this was a very unusual and talented group of young men.

This was conducted at the University of Minnesota. We lived in the football stadium at the University of Minnesota. They set-up classes for us because we were told that the experiment itself would only take half of our time and that we would have the other half to prepare ourselves to do relief and reconstruction work once the war was over. Most of us were interested in doing this and many of us, as I said, did do that once the war was over. We were involved in drama and music. I sang the "B Minor Mass" and also sang in the church choir. One of the fellows had been a ping-pong champion in Long Island and taught me how to play ping-pong much better than I ever had before.

I think it turned out to be much more rigorous than most had anticipated. They told us the objectives were first to find out what happens to people mentally, physically, and psychologically as a result of starvation and then, most important, to find out the most efficient way of rebuilding people who have starved as to caloric level, percentage of protein in the diet, and whether or not supplementary vitamins would have a significant therapeutic effect. The experiment was designed to last for a year, divided into three segments. The first was a three-month standardization period in which they were going to find out how we were normally. We were given very extensive physical, psychological, and mental tests plus many of the tests we had to do often enough that we had reached our peak performance on them. One of the simple tests was reaction time test in which, while you were walking on a treadmill, you had a paddle on your each hand and you had three lights up in front and if the red one went on you hit the left paddle, if the green one went on you hit the right paddle and if the white one in the middle went on you hit both paddles. It recorded the length of time between the time the light goes on and the time you hit the paddle. And so naturally the second time you do this you'll do better than you did the first time, so we had to do such a test often enough until we had reached our peak performance. During the standardization period it was a very jovial, fun-loving group of young men.

But when we starved this changed. The goal was that we should lose a fourth of our normal weight in order to achieve the objectives of the experiment. In my case I weighed 165 when I went there. During the standardization period I lost 15 pounds, so I weighed 150. They took a fourth of 150 which is 37.5 pounds so my goal was 112.5. I had actually dropped to 110 at one point. But one of the things they found was on the average there was an 80% loss of big muscle strength, which mean that I was really quite feeble. It was as I imagine perhaps being 90 years old might be, although I haven't quite reached that yet. I think that it turned out to be more rigorous than the laboratory had anticipated it would be. One of the things that they found out was at that stage of malnutrition, weight is no longer a reliable indication because your body picks up extra cellular fluid and most of us were carrying maybe ten to fifteen pounds of extra water around.

Although there was no deterioration of our mental power, there were many psychological changes as a result of the starvation. But many men went through periods of elation and depression and one even got to place were he was contemplating suicide. They kept pretty close track of us, so they counseled him. I know I can't remember anything that I ever looked forward to as much as I looked forward to the end of the semi-starvation period. Not so much because of the physical discomfort though when one looses that amount of weight just sitting on a chair isn't all that comfortable because your bones stick out. Most of us carried cushions around so that we could sit a little more comfortably.

The physical aspects of it were not as troublesome as the fact that the food became the most important thing in one's life. The things that I ordinarily enjoyed doing I couldn't do or couldn't enjoy. I couldn't be a jock, I couldn't sing, I was no longer really interested in girls and if I went to a movie I wasn't particularly interested in the love scenes but I noticed every time they ate and what they ate. So the things that made life meaningful weren't really enjoyable.

They wanted to find out the optimum level to feed people and what they found out for us was that for a group of young men about the optimum level was around three thousand calories a day. But if you'd been starved three thousand calories a day isn't going to satisfy your hunger yet they found that three thousand calories was about the maximum that your body could take and utilize constructively. Anything in addition to that would just be put into terms of fat which doesn't assist in terms of rehabilitation. When I hear someone say, "Oh, I'm simply starved," depending on the situation, I may say, you don't really know what you're talking about.

They found the most important factor in terms of rehabilitation was the caloric level and the percentage of protein in the diet didn't have any significant effect. This meant that they could just send grain rather than having to try to send meat or something into starved areas because the body will take the carbohydrates and convert them to protein. And at that time the supplementary vitamins didn't have a significant effect but the most important thing was the caloric level.

During the starvation period we didn't argue and debate because that took too much energy. But when we began to get more to eat, then some of these dissatisfactions and arguments began to come up. A group got together and said here we've been here all this time, they've been telling us what to do, and we haven't had any voice in what's going on, so we got organized and there was some movement for self government among the men in the starvation experiment. If you want to keep people subservient, keep them hungry. If you give them more to eat, then they are apt to rebel and to assert their independence.

Coming back from Europe in 1950 I was asked to direct the high school work camp for the American Friends Service Committee[4] in Missouri. Then I looked around in Missouri to see if I could get a teaching position. Whenever the question came up as to what I did during the war, if I told any prospective employer, I didn't get the job. After trying for awhile to get a job in Missouri and Indiana I decided I wasn't going to get a teaching position. I went to Portland where one of my older brothers was living and got a job for awhile in a reform school in Oregon.

Then I was offered a position by the American Friends Service Committee[4] in the Bay Area to come to San Francisco to develop a program for high school students. I did that for two years with limited success. Then the financing for this project ran out. I looked around and my Indiana teaching credential qualified me to teach junior high, so I was able to get a position in Downieville, California, teaching six, seventh and eighth grades in one room. I found that it wasn't advisable whenever applying for a teaching position to tell a perspective employer about my wartime experience. Likewise, as a school teacher in the public schools even though I taught US history and it would have been quite illuminating to a U.S. history class to know about my experiences, I never felt free to talk about my experiences as a CO.

I got involved with the College Park Friends Educational Association, which was interested in establishing a high school program in Northern California. I taught in summer school and then directed a summer school before they bought the property for the John Woolman School.

After 1969 I went back to University of California Davis and got a Masters Degree in Political Science. When I had difficulty getting a teaching position, I became a general contractor which I have now been for thirty years. I have built many houses including the one we now occupy. I no longer have a license or employees, but I still build ramps for handicapped seniors who use walkers or wheel chairs to get in and out of their houses.

Two things in my life that I am proud of, one as being a CO and the other is being Principal of John Woolman School. I don't see society in general giving up on the use of force and violence as a way of trying to solve social problems. I don't believe in punishment or force or violence as way of trying to prevent crime or bring about social change.

My youngest son, Jacob, is a professor at the Western Washington University in Bellingham, Washington, and is involved in teacher education, how to teach science. I was invited to talk to students about how my pacifist convictions have affected my teaching position. One of the persons raised the challenge; how has pacifism ever been effective? I cited two examples at that time, one being Gandhi in India and the other being Martin Luther King in the United States. Subsequently I added Women's Liberation. Women have become liberated in the United States, not by force or violence, so force or violence doesn't bring about positive social change. But I don't see this being universally accepted.

Thomas C. Hall (1921)

"All progress is through the law of mutually supportive shared union. This is the point at which religion and science come together to share the one law of survival — love."

I became aware that I really am a pacifist during my freshman year at Harvard College, in the Fall of 1940. There was a big move by the government to get popular support for joining World War II. I had decided several years before that Christianity meant carefully and fully following the precepts and actions of Jesus. But when it became apparent that the U.S. entering the war was inevitable, and the draft required a decision, active personal commitment became necessary. I realized that to join the military machine as a non-combatant was still to accept a machine for killing and maiming for an objective, and that I must reject the machine and not cooperate in any way. So I wrote a letter saying that I would refuse to register.

My family of origin consisted of a devoutly Roman Catholic mother who died when I was four, and an agnostic father who sent me to Catholic Parochial school to honor my mother's wishes. My father's second wife was a non-observant Lutheran who sent my younger brother and me to Lutheran Sunday schools, but who, like my father, never went to church. My parents were not pacifists. My father was a World War I veteran who did not permit us to play with guns, indicating some hesitancy to accept guns as problem solving. My step-mother was a Neo-Nazi who admired Hitler and objected to the U.S. going into that war. My hobby as a child was reading, my sports in school were gymnastics and I had an athletic letter in the low horse. At school I played softball, but especially hand ball. Competitive team sports were

Briefly interviewed by Lorina Hall and written himself.

not big in poor communities in the inner cities during the Great Depression.

My neighbor playmate, Spencer Gillespie, came from an observant, Methodist family. They followed Jesus' precepts regarding pacifism, community and simplicity. They used no utilities that required anyone else to work on the Lord's Day. So, they walked to and from church, used no public transport, and any utilities such as light, or buses. They cooked for Sunday on Saturday and kept meals warm with hot bricks. This consistency between faith and behavior impressed me greatly. It was reinforced in my sophomore Psychology course, in which the Professor Alport asked us to consider "The Behavioral Equivalent of Consciousness,," or the science behind "Do as you say."

My favorite subjects in high school were History and Physics. I read everything and anything, particularly modern and older plays. During the Great Depression,

Mr. Roosevelt instituted a program to rehire teachers, so that my high school got a number of extra teachers who enriched the curriculum. There was also a program to bind unsold books and use them to enrich teaching. I remember especially a small green-backed book of Browning's poems some of which I remember to this day.

All of the family had to work. I began after school at age 13 in a dry

cleaning store. So, regular college was out of the question. I got a full time job in the fall of 1937 and began City College of New York City at night, intending to get engineering training and a job. However, most of the courses I took were in Spanish, English Literature, Musicology and Sociology. When I got a scholarship to Harvard, I continued to take History and Sociology, but added Biology, Psychology and Anthropology. My intent then was to become a pastor. My younger brother chose medicine and said we'd be "sawdoc and sky pilot."

I had just turned 20 when Pearl Harbor came. My decision had already been made, so I got a leave from college and went back to New York City. My draft board sent me a notice to register. I returned it, explaining that, as I had written them earlier, I would not register. They sent me a court appearance date, sentenced me and I was placed in the West Street New York Federal Detention Center. My stepmother thought I should reconsider, but my dad was supportive of my making my own decisions, and the Gillespies and others in the Methodist Church were supportive. My tutor at college Clyde Kluckhohn, was a Major General in the military, but supportive of me. During my first college year I had attended the local Methodist Church. During the second, and since, I attended Friends Meetings. I had yet to get to know others in the Meeting, but no others, to my knowledge went the non-registrant route. This was also true at Harvard.

I was sentenced to two years in Federal prison, and spent the first month or so at West Street. There I met a goodly number of COs, some non-registrants, some who were refused CO status, and refused to enter the military. We formed a group who put on skits for the other inmates and protested the racial segregation at meal times. I was transferred to the Federal Penitentiary at Chillicothe, Ohio, where I again protested the segregation at meal times, and spent the rest of the time in solitary confinement as punishment. Thence to the Federal Prison Camp at Mill Point in West Virginia where there was a small group of COs and non-registrants. There I was a cook, dynamite monkey, ran a jack hammer, and "napped" big rocks into little rocks on a road gang. I also taught arithmetic at nights to the large population of "hill-billy" illegal pot-still operators.

My final stay was in the Federal Penitentiary in Ashland, Kentucky, where I had the opportunity of working in the medical dispensary along with several other COs some of whom were pre-medical students. There I began to think of medicine as a life work. Once again I spent time in solitary confinement for refusing to line up for segregated meals.

I was paroled in the care of Father Kenneth Viall, Abbot of the Anglo-Catholic Society of Saint John the Divine Monastery in Cambridge, Massachusetts, to work at MacLean Hospital in Belmont, the psychiatric division of Massachusetts General Hospital. I worked the 7 p.m. to 7 a.m. shift and returned to college in the day time. There my main emphasis was to complete pre-medical requirements. My parole officer permitted me to change to employment as a night-orderly at the Peter Bent Brigham Hospital, directly across the alley from Harvard Medical School (HMS) in Boston. When I was admitted to HMS I was able to continue working at the Brigham as a late-in-the-day relief switchboard operator, receiving room and board. My freshman advisor at college, John Lydenberg, lent me the $400 initial year's tuition.

My intention to follow my Anthropology tutor, Clyde Kluckhohn, to the Navajo Nation as a physician was altered when I saw the opportunity to try a war gas, nitrogen mustard, to inhibit lymphocytes functioning to cause an experimental form of allergic nephritis in rats. The war was over, and I took a year off to complete and publish this experiment, which started me on work in chemotherapeutic intervention which has been my career ever since.

The State of Massachusetts had to be convinced in a public hearing to grant me a medical license, even though President Truman pardoned non-registrants after the war.

I convinced a young Wellesley sophomore against the wishes of her family to marry me and live in a cold-water flat whilst commuting by bus from Boston to Wellesley. After fathering 6 fine children, I left the marriage and hoped that by paying their expenses and providing a second weekend home for all of the children, my selfishness would have minimal impact on them. Although my wife remarried happily in time, all of the children were hurt, and have trouble forgiving me, as I do myself. My second marriage did not work out, and after 18 years, and an amicable divorce, I met and married my present wife, with whom I share a daughter and a son. I believe I have learned how to be a better partner and parent during the past 28 years, but still am learning and am grateful for her support.

I am listed as a Draft Counselor at our local Peace and Justice Center, Clerk the Peace and Social Concerns Committee of our local Friends Meeting, and am active in anti-war protests and highway bannering. I write letters and sign petitions daily on the Internet for pro-peace, anti-violence campaigns. I contribute financially to Quaker groups, FOR,[25] and Alternative to Violence[2] projects in Rwanda.

Medically, I'm proud of successes in new drug trials, in the establishment of Cancer Centers at Harvard, the Universities of Rochester, Southern California, British Columbia and Hawaii. My regrets concern my selfish behaviors which have hurt my wives and children.

I knew that my not registering with the war machine was critical. During the Korean War, one registered as a

CO, not with the military, but in hopes the military would excuse you. Hence I registered as a physician and was assigned to do cancer research at a public hospital. So, we non-registrants seemed to have helped create recognition as a non-military entity. However, Mr. Carter and subsequent executives have gone back partway by taking the category CO off the registration form.

The process of evolution is by mutual aid between entitites. The ultimate best destiny of a human individual is to join with others to create new entities capable of further evolution. The law $E=mC^2$ states that matter is created when the energy created by the First Mover becomes quark-matter. All our universe results from quarks, that join together, then attract electrons to make atoms by mutual aid. Molecules are made from atoms by mutual supportive attraction, thence life through the supportive aggregation of molecules, species through mutual support and evolution and, finally, humankind. Then we, the ultimate social species, form families from *eros*, children from *storge**, brothers and sisters through *filia* and interact altruistically with others in our species family through empathy and *agape*. All progress is through the law of mutually supportive shared union. This is the point at which religion and science come together to share the one law of survival—love.

The military is based upon the illogical, demonstrably unsustainable, repeatedly failed concept that the unsharable greed for power of a sick few acting against love, by the violent diminishing of the personhood of others, in the human family, can somehow be "good."

---

storge is one of the Greek forms of human love. It means the love between parent and child. This form of love has on one side a completely dependent entity and on the other, its parent creator. The exchange between them and their joining is asymmetrical and unearned, and hence may be the primary source for our self-esteem. It grows and changes as the years go by and in an incomparable flowering of diverse richness that forms much of our joy in ourselves. It precedes our personhood, and we are loved unquestioningly. It occurs in mostly living higher animal species, and so is probably wired into our social brains.

Phillip Kelsey (1915)

*"We formed a peace group in Andover that I partici-
pated in. We used to march in front of the post office on
Saturdays and write letters to the editor. Consequently
the church got rid of me."*

I can't remember when I was not a pacifist. I had dreams
of stopping war as early as I can remember. My father
was the head of the mission in Ramallah, Palestine and he
was a preacher. He came from a family of preachers. His
mother was a Quaker preacher and her four sons were
all Quaker preachers. I suppose they all were pacifist but
it wasn't discussed much because we were Quakers. My
sister was a nurse in a CPS[14] work camp. She married one
of the campers and he was a teacher at Westtown School.
I can't remember that there was any special conviction in
any of the other members of my family.

I was in Ramallah most of the time until I was 12
years old. I went to school in Beirut because they had
an American boarding school. I learned Arabic because
all of my friends were Arabs. I had two languages until
I was 12. In Beirut was a Presbyterian congregational
group and they were very religious people, not fundamentalists, but liberal religious people. They had a medical school, liberal arts college, and nurses training school.
The whole staff and a young people's group met once a
week for devotions and singing. I left Ramallah when I
was twelve, but I've always had a soft spot for Palestine.
I've been back there twice as an adult. I took Roz, my
wife, over there in 1968–69. Then I went alone on an
Fellowship of Reconciliation[25] trip when I retired. I still
have some Palestinian Ramallah friends who live in this
country.

I left to go to high school at Moses Brown School in
Providence, Rhode Island. I can't remember if they were

a particularly Quaker body at that time. I think we had one teacher who was a Quaker and taught chemistry, but I wasn't particularly interested in chemistry. There was an English teacher who fascinated me, but I don't think he was a Quaker. He was a good English teacher and I got a lot of basics from him. When I was young I was not much of a reader, that is, reading for recreation was a very small part of my life. But I did major in English in college and in my later life I got to reading much, much more and I still read.

I can't remember any particular religious influence at Moses Brown. The Principal was a Quaker, but he celebrated Memorial Day by reading a list of students who had served in the armed service without batting an eye. At that time, I didn't think too much about it. It was the thing to do on Memorial Day. But when I went to college, it was a different thing. Guilford was deeply committed to the Quaker philosophy. I never lost my loyalty to my college. We used to go to reunions, our 50th and 55th.

At Guilford it was the Dean of Students, Adam Vital, who influenced me most. He was not a Quaker, but he was a strong pacifist. He used to take his classes to prisons. The last time I visited him in 1964, he was President of a black college in Mississippi. The first time I went to Guilford College was on the train. When I got to Washington, they announced that all the black people had to go into a different car and I was shocked! I lived in Rhode Island where there weren't many black people. It never occurred to me that I would be in this kind of situation. I developed a very strong feeling against racial segregation. I'm not sure if that was because I had grown up playing with Arab boys. To me separating people because of race, background, or any other artificial thing was an anathema.

I went to Moses Brown because I was sent there, but I chose Guilford because colleges in the South were much cheaper than colleges in the North. I had a consideration that I wanted to be as little a burden on the family income as possible. I'm sure that was the reason that the Guidance Counselor showed me different schools and Guilford appeared to be a Quaker school that didn't cost an awful lot. Being introduced to Quakerism at an early age led me to go there. I have a Bachelor's degree in English and I was always interested in becoming a Minister, but it wasn't a very promising career for a Quaker. There were Congregationalists in New England and they were a very liberal denomination and that's what I joined when I started studying to be a pastor at Boston University, which was a Methodist seminary. I followed this path for the next few decades, but never lost touch with my Quaker roots. Later in my life I rejoined the local Friends meeting in the Atlantic City area. When I finished my studies at Boston University, I got my Bachelors of Divinity degree. Later on I went to Hartford Divinity School and got a Master's degree in Religious Education.

I was 26 at the time of Pearl Harbor. All during a work camp, a year before, we had known that the draft law was going to be passed. It was passed in the fall of 1940 and we all became draftees. Everyone was expecting the United States to give in to the war and we did. During high school the Public Affairs Committee on Organization in Providence, Rhode Island, used to send tickets to the college for their events. I accepted a ticket once and went to their dinner. A Japanese man was the featured speaker and I can remember his raising a tea cup and he put his fist down to emphasize a point that the United States was cutting them off from their markets all over the world. And they needed markets because they were an island nation. I never forgot that.

When I got my draft notice, I had to decide whether I was going to register. I didn't think registration was a step I needed to fight, but I did register with some trepidation. I had to go to several hearings and be denied. I guess they just got tired of me. I wasn't a very good convincer. But finally I was given CO[17] status and was drafted a year and a half later.

First I was assigned to West Campton, New Hampshire, up in the White Mountains. This was the fall, and winter was coming on. We had to chop wood because we lived in old CCC[13] camps and had to keep warm during winter. That was about all that we did and we were already discussing whether or not to stay in CPS[14]. We had heard rumors that some war resistors were walking out.

We were belly-aching about the system of slavery and what really shocked me was getting a check from the American Friends Service Committee.[4] They realized we had no money for travel, to buy clothes with, for incidentals, or to ask a girl out for a date, even if you knew a girl. When I got that check, I thought, "What in the world are they sending me a check for?" Well, I guess it turned out that they sent a check to every CO who was a member of a Friends meeting. Most of them were not Quakers. That shocked me and further pushed me out.

Three of us decided that we were going to join the walking out movement. We didn't know how long the war was going to last. It hadn't been underway a year yet for us. England had been in the war for two years, but we had war on two fronts in the Pacific and Europe. Was it going to take us until we were 35 or 40, or when? If we were sentenced, we would be sentenced and know the release date. So, it wasn't a great idealism, but a sense of reality. This is slavery. Are we going to become slaves? I remember the Director of the camp saying he was sorry I had gotten under the influence of two non-Quaker rebels. They didn't have very much trouble convincing me. I was my own man. I didn't have to go. To me it was the right thing to do, but the Quakers were very critical of these deserters. They had worked hard to make this arrangement that was friendly to the Government. The Government didn't have to support us, they didn't have to police us, and they didn't have to pay us. So I got more hostility from the Quaker community than from anywhere else.

I would guess I was there about two or three months before Thanksgiving when I joined with two other COs and walked out. As soon as we got settled and had an address, we sent our address to the Selective Service Board because we didn't want to be fugitives.

After walking out, I was in Brooklyn, New York for two or three months. I worked to earn my living and then two FBI men came and took me to court. The first time was a hearing when the judge set my bail. The War Resistor's League put up bail for me. I had two or three more months before I appeared in court to be sentenced. The second time we tried to testify, but we had no lawyers and it was pretty much what the judge decided. We were absent without leave (AWOL). The only question was how long would the sentence be. Some got short sentences, some got longer sentences. It depended on the judge. My sentence was four years, which was medium long. After you served one-third of it, you were eligible for parole.

First we sat in a county jail in Manchester, New Hampshire, until they had transportation to take us to a federal prison and the United States just paid our board while we were there. Then they sent us to Lewisburg, Pennsylvania. I was there until I was paroled.

At first we were not particularly conspicuous, but we became conspicuous because we didn't cooperate with the racial segregation pattern which they had in prison. We would take our food trays and sit at a colored table, so they threw us in the "hole," solitary confinement. Hearing of our plight, other COs in the prison, did the same thing but they didn't have enough cells in the hole to accommodate all of us. So they put us all in a big room with cots and three meals a day. I don't think the other prisoners cared very much what we did. Most of the blacks were not educated and they didn't mind. If a white person wanted to sit at their table, they were welcome.

We were segregated for two or three months, and then we had to decide, are we going to stay here the rest of our time or should we just compromise and go and accept the pattern of segregation that all prisons have? We had quite a little educational experience while we were there. They gave us Bibles and we took turns reading out loud and then have discussion periods. They took us out for a walk every few days. It was a very close-knit bunch. Eventually we went back into the population.

I don't think being in a Federal prison was any handicap later in my life. I went to the seminary at Boston University and said I wanted to study to be a Minister. I remember the Dean saying, "You know, this is in the middle of war and you can't dodge the war. You can't choose after the war starts." And I said, "I just came out of prison." I had been on the path to seminary school when I was first sent to the CPS[14] camp, but I never even thought of dodging the war that way.

To be paroled from prison, you had to have a job to go to. That was a universal requirement if you wanted to be paroled, and I certainly wanted to be paroled. I went to Massachusetts General Hospital where they had a unit of COs, so I blended in with the unit when I went there. The difference between the unit and me was that I got buck private's pay and they didn't get anything. I got my meals and I could have had a bed with the others, but I wanted to have my own living quarters. I took what money I had and got a coldwater apartment just a half a block away from the hospital, so I got my meals and I had a place. If I wanted to get married, I had a place I could bring a bride to, and I wanted to get married.

There was a meeting of FOR in Boston and the camp gave us a station wagon for all of those who wanted to go. I knew the names of FOR people because they were public names, but I didn't know any faces. Then I spotted Roz. She had been in work camp with me a whole summer. I gravitated toward her and asked what she had been doing. She had graduated from college and, because her brother and sister were in the service and her father had had a very severe stroke, she went home where she was needed. She had worked in a woodworking shop where they made small furniture, until they got war contracts. Then she quit. She wasn't going to work on war contracts. She was substitute teaching in the local school. I said, "You know where I am, but I'm not going to be there very long." I said, "We decided that jail was a better choice." So we left. I didn't hear from her, but I had a cousin who was keeping me up on the news of the work campers and she had mentioned that Roz was a social worker in Boston. I was heading for Boston if got my parole so when I went to Boston I looked her up. Apparently I was one of her heroes because I went to jail! So, we have been going together ever since.

Being on parole, I wasn't supposed to cross the state line, but Roz and I were going to get married in New

Hampshire. I didn't tell them when I went across the state line; I just did. I did tell them I was going to get married. The war was over three days after we got married, and after that the Parole Board didn't care anything about what I did.

After going to seminary, I got a Congregational church in Andover, Massachusetts and had a career that lasted until the war in Vietnam. At that time I started being an activist again when they had the march on Washington for jobs and housing. We went to Washington but we didn't hear the "I Have a Dream" speech because we were too far away to hear. But the people at home heard it over the TV. The next summer was Mississippi Freedom Summer and they asked ministers to volunteer to go down to Mississippi so they would have some older people to balance the college students and I went on that.

We formed a peace group in Andover that I participated in. We used to march in front of the post office on Saturdays and write letters to the Editor. Consequently the church got rid of me. That's how I reconnected with Quakers. At first I got a job in public schools, where I taught for one year. My daughter had gone to Sandy Spring Friends School. She got me connected with the Principal down there, so I got a job teaching English. Then I got back into public school until I was 60, after which I got a pastorate in Philadelphia and had a few more years as a minister. I already owned this house at that time and had an apartment in Philadelphia.

If I had married somebody who didn't believe as I did, I might have had trouble convincing her to let me go to Mississippi and to get involved in peace activities. When I got fired in 1965–66, there were hard times in my marriage because I was so hurt. I didn't regret doing anything, but it hurt when you get rejected like that. But my family seemed to survive. When one of my daughters was in the third grade in Keene, New Hampshire, there was a militaristic program that they were giving. It was a very patriotic holiday and she refused to take part in it. Another daughter teaches in Somers Point and she is very strong in her support for liberal causes. My oldest grandson Rory went to George School and I think if they drafted him, he'd refuse. I have two granddaughters in North Jersey and they are both very strong liberals.

I can't say I have any regrets. I have had hard times but I wouldn't change that. When I was fired from my church, I had friends who would have nothing to do with me. I was surprised, but then there was a fundamentalist Baptist preacher who drew me into any ecumenical activity that was going on. I had nothing in common with

him theologically, but he drew me in. And there was an Episcopal rector who invited me to preach in his pulpit. You have the nice experiences to balance.

Recently I've thought of how things change. During the Vietnam War they used to call the Vietnamese "gooks"—what a dirty thing to do, calling them "gooks." The phenomenon of war resistance grew and GREW during the Vietnam War and that was a sign of hope. During this war, I have heard no derogatory things said about the Iraqi people. There is almost a sense of apology, like "I hate to do this," and that's a sign of hope. I feel that the time will come when the whole world will recognize people simply as people, and that's a sign of hope. I don't think I ever became a tired liberal.

Douglas R. Johnson *(1917-2009)*

"When I look at the people who are religious today (not the Quakers), most of them are concerned with saving their own souls, personal salvation, that kind of thing. They are not concerned with the way they act toward others. They have missed the important Christian message, 'Do unto others as you would have them do unto you.' They have faith. People that have faith are dangerous, because they don't ask questions, they know all the answers."

From the time I was five or six until I was twelve or thirteen or fourteen, I was a member of a religious family. I came from a small town in Minnesota. Everybody was quite religious, or belonged to a church. We were Lutherans. There were several Lutheran churches, but ours happened to be the English Lutheran Church. I went to church; I went to Sunday school and still have medals to show that I had perfect attendance for a couple of years. When I was twelve or thirteen, I went to confirmation classes and became confirmed. There was a ceremony and I was admitted to the Lutheran Church.

I stopped going to church when I left home. Prior to that my family had stopped going to church. We didn't belong to a church after I started high school. When I look at the people who are religious today (not the Quakers), most of them are concerned with saving their own souls, with personal salvation. They are not concerned with the way they act toward others. They have missed the important Christian message, "Do unto others as you would have them do unto you." They have faith. People that have faith are dangerous, because they don't ask questions, they know all the answers. I read the other day that Philosophy is the study of questions that have no

---

Interviewed and transcribed by Ruth C. Schwaegerle, assisted by Shirley Johnson

answers; Religion is the study of answers that have no questions. We were not of any particular faith.

I chose Antioch College because my best friend was going there. His family members were church goers and his minister told him about Antioch College. This was a college where you could go and work half time and go to school half time. We thought that would pay for our college, but it was not so. It did help, and Antioch College is a great place. Antioch College required courses in Art and Aesthetics, English Literature, Social Sciences, Philosophy, Geology etc. It was a very broad liberal arts program and the professors were all very good. But the most important thing about Antioch College was the work program. I worked in Waterbury, Connecticut, making nonferrous tubing and I worked in the Neenah/Menasha, Wisconsin (factory) making Kleenex. I was introduced into the everyday world by having those experiences. I got a Bachelor of Science in Civil Engineering. Shirley and I were married the day we were supposed to graduate. We didn't stay to graduate, we left and got married instead.

I became aware that I am a pacifist during the last couple of years I was at Antioch College. We had a strong pacifist group that was pretty much all faiths and non-faith. We had meetings and talked about the evils of war. We studied the philosophy of Christ and Gandhi. Martin Luther King wasn't in it yet, but these are the people that I revered or honored in college. Personally it was just what was moral for us. The church had nothing to do with it. It was the study of history.

Some of the people we associated with were "fellow travelers," communists or communist sympathizers. Then Hitler went through Poland and attacked Russia, and within a very few days those of our group who were fellow travelers turned on the pacifists. The head of the Communist Party addressed our group and said that all the pacifists should be lined up and shot because they were traitors to the country.

We didn't think of pacifism in terms of being a CO because that came a little later. The Selective Service decided they were going to have a special program for COs. When we graduated we stayed in Yellow Springs and worked there and continued associating with the people that were of this pacifist conviction.

I was twenty-four at the time of Pearl Harbor. I didn't do much thinking about it until I came to the point where I had to make a decision. When the draft act was passed in 1940, they had all the young males older than 18 sign up. That was my first contact with officials of the Selective Service. I knew the draft had provisions for conscientious objectors, so when I signed that card, I wrote on it, "I am a conscientious objector."

I was classified 1-A, that is, they did not accept my declaration of conscientious objection. It was very rare for anybody to be given a 4-E classification in Greene County, unless they definitely were Quaker,[52] Brethren[7] or Mennonite.[42] The draft board in Yellow Springs included a Catholic priest who thought that married men ought to be exempted to stay home and have children. I had to fill out a special form to let them know where my beliefs came from, what they were, and their basis. I took a couple of character witnesses to my hearing, a teacher and the Vice President of the college. I was the first person in the county that we knew of that was given a 4-E classification without a church affiliation.

My wife Shirley and I debated for some time about whether I should accept the CO registration. Some of our best friends were in jail, or on the way to jail. But since I was the first non-religiously-connected CO to be granted that status, we felt it would be a mistake to turn it down. It might never be granted to anybody else like me.

I was sent first to Coshocton, a Brethren camp in Michigan. Many of the camps were CCC[13] camps, built for 150 to 250 men. There were as many as 125 in this camp. I was 15 months at Coshocton. That camp was closed at the end of the war and in March of 1946 I was transferred to a government camp in Gatlinburg, Tennessee. I was there until the middle of July when I was discharged. There was no difference between who ran the camps, government or churches, but the churches supported their camps.

I never had any problem with any people bothering me about my pacifist position, but in many of the areas in which these camps were located they were not particularly friendly toward the inmates. We weren't paid, but the American Friends Service Committee[4] gave us an allowance of $2.50 dollars a month. My wife worked, but she didn't make a big salary either. Compared to World War I, it was a very enlightened treatment, and the government got good value out of it. We did things that had to be done.

When we graduated it was the Depression and jobs were tough to get. I managed to get a job with a building contractor in Yellow Springs, Ohio. We built houses and a bank building, and I became fairly skilled in the building trades. We knew I was going to be drafted and we didn't know when that was going to happen. After I got out of camp, there were plenty of jobs, but they were in war work and I was not going into war work. I went back to Yellow Springs and worked for an architect who was building a dormitory for Antioch College. I was clerk of the works on that construction.

Before the war Quakers had a self-help housing project in Pennsylvania near Pittsburgh. In the 1930s there were a lot of unemployed coal miners. The Quakers organized a group of these coal miners so they could build their own houses. They were nice houses and it was written up in *Reader's Digest*. After the war, Steel Union members in Lorain, Ohio, read that article in the *Reader's Digest* and said "Why don't we do that?" They contacted the Quakers and the Quakers solicited me and Max Ratner, a fellow Antiochian who had been in prison during the war, to manage the project.

We came here knowing we were going to do that project, but it was a year before it could get organized and financed, so we built our own living quarters in Oberlin. Max and I built a duplex and did all the work ourselves. We had to get plumbing and electrician licenses to do our own work. When the project started, most of those we were directing were veterans and they knew we were COs. We were on that project for two and a half years and then we built some houses in Oberlin for faculty members. I had been studying architecture and Max had studied architecture when he was in prison. He passed the state board and became a registered architect. Then I studied and passed the state board, so we had an architectural practice. He went into Cleveland and worked on various projects and I went to Cleveland and worked part time for a year or so with him. Then I went to work for a firm of architects in Berea, Ohio. While I was there for 10 years, we designed schools in all the suburbs on this side of Cleveland and did some hospital work.

We have two adopted children. They knew I had been a CO, but thought that was in the past. In his youth our son Eric was very strongly opposed to the Vietnam War. I think if he had to face it, he would have been a CO. Our daughter would agree with that, too.

I've had a good life and I've done a lot in local government. I've been on a lot of committees and on the Council. I'm sorry about it, but I think the human race is not long for this world and it's our own fault. And there's not much the individual can do about it, it's too late. We do not have much more than 10 years before disaster and it's not just global warming. We are living on oil and there's not much left. If you stop to think about it, our whole economic system is based on communicating and getting in your car and burning up oil. You and I will not experience this because we won't be here that much longer, but it's not very far down the road. Not only are we running out of oil, but in burning it up we are adding to the carbon dioxide in the atmosphere that's going to warm things up. We are polluting the oceans, ruining the soil, and cutting down the trees. The carbon dioxide in the atmosphere is making the ocean, not acidic, but less basic, and destroying the coral reefs and all the life that is living on the coral reefs and in the ocean.

I admire the Quakers and the Fellowship of Reconciliation and do make contributions to them, but I'm afraid it's hopeless. It's too bad but...

Chapter Six
Movers and Shakers

Chapter Six
Movers and Shakers

John H. Michener

Ross Sanderson

George M. Houser

Three preacher's kids, confident, verbal to verbose, intelligent to brilliant, forge new paradigms of pacifism. Their paths to conscientious objection were clear and well lit by their fathers.

One says he follows wherever continuing revelation leads. Another will struggle for justice if the struggle is non-violent. Finally, seeing things in black or white when he sees wrong, he takes the most immediate pragmatic action. Hard-headed, practical and aggressive do-gooders who brook no obstacle to their visions of perfect societies, they courageously rack up enormous accomplishments.

John H. Michener *(1925)*

"I ended up refusing, some four or five times, to do things I needed to do to keep my job, or doing things I knew would cost my job. These decisions weren't directly based on conscientious objection but were derived from the same source as my conscientious objection, refusing to do something I thought was wrong or doing something right my supervisors would not accept."

My family of origin was a religious one, Quaker on both sides. The first Michener in America came over in the household of William Penn. We've been a Quaker[52] family since then. Both my folks were very heavily involved in University Friends Church, now University Friends Meeting, in Wichita, Kansas. Both were very active working for the social good.

Dad expected to go to prison in World War I as a Quaker non-registrant. But my mother was an ardent believer that war was the "war to end all wars" and talked him into going into the army. So he became what we call now 1AO. He was in the medical corps as a front-line medic. Although Mom started believing it was the war to end all wars, she ended up an ardent pacifist and led the Kansas Yearly Meeting Peace Committee for years. This brought her into a very bitter conflict with the Yearly Meeting during World War II. The Yearly Meeting felt its young men should go into the armed services as noncombatants rather than going into alternative service. So Mom and the Yearly Meeting came to loggerheads. After the war she was hired by Friends University to teach English. The Yearly Meeting told the University that if they hired her the Yearly Meeting would cut off its funding. The University cancelled her contract. The conflict was the subject of an article in the *Kansas Historical*

Interviewed and transcribed by Beth Edelstein

Journal. Both of my parents had been on both sides of the issue, but both ended as pacifists.

As a child, I always liked Math and still do. I remember my dad telling me about π (pi) when I was in grade school. I didn't get much into competitive sports, although I was on my high school swim squad. I dropped that because I needed a job and it conflicted. I was active in Boy Scouts and liked being outdoors. My grandfather had several acres with a house ("cabin") on the Little Arkansas River north of Wichita. Our family spent the summers out there and I was outdoors a lot. I also had jobs.

My mentors were my family. My grandfather, H. D. Baker, was campaign manager for U.S. Senator George McGill, who was elected in 1932, the first Democratic senator from Kansas for a generation or more. FDR appointed Grandpa as District Collector for Internal Revenue (now IRS) for a five-state region. Grandpa was a straight shooter and got in trouble for it when he started a property foreclosure to collect on delinquent taxes. He was told "this guy's a good Democrat," to which my grandfather replied "good Democrats pay their taxes" and went ahead and seized the property. I admired his full adherence to his standards.

My other grandfather, Homer Michener, was a doctor back in the 1900s, the turn of the century. He helped found the Wichita Medical Society and was its president a number of times. He experimented with x-rays and lost one hand through x-ray burns. When I knew him he had a couple of fingers with a thumb on the other hand. He also experimented with electrical current. The medical society threw him out because he was not adhering to accepted practice. He was also an ardent Quaker pacifist.

My father was President of the student body at Friends University. He made a presentation to the university's Trustees in which he stated that he and Dr. Stanley, the university President, had made an agreement. The agreement had become controversial and Dr. Stanley denied making the agreement. Dad turned to Dr. Stanley and said that he was a liar. The Chair of the Board told dad he could not call Dr. Stanley a liar. Dad said "Very well, Dr. Stanley is a prevaricator." The next year my father went to the University of Kansas. He wasn't expelled but he got a clear message to get out.

Dad was elected to the school board after he retired from teaching. My brother-in-law, Bill Busch, was also elected to the board at the same time. That was the time Wichita came under the first desegregation order from the U.S. Office of Education following Brown vs. Board of Education. Dad was leader of the group that believed Wichita should have desegregated years earlier. Bill's stance was that the Board didn't take orders from the federal government and should fight the order. So we had that conflict in our own family. Both Dad and Bill got death threats.

Mom was on the American Friends Service Committee's (AFSC)[4] Des Moines Regional Executive Committee. She led the drive to desegregate the YWCA, which became the first place a Black could eat in downtown Wichita. During the depression she helped found what was called Southwest Wichita Community Center. Mom ended up in the Wichita Women's Hall of Fame. When she died the City Council had a moment of silence in recognition of her work. The School Board named a new elementary school the John and Anna Jane Michener Elementary School.

In school, my favorite subjects were Math, English, Linguistics, Science, and Social Studies. I always went to public schools. Unlike the Quaker schools, they didn't have an articulated philosophy.

I went to the University of Kansas (KU) because I won a statewide competitive Summerfield scholarship. Mr. Summerfield, the founder of Gotham Hosiery, was a KU graduate and gave a large sum of money to these scholarships. At KU I joined an independent student housing co-op, which was integrated and very democratic. My initial major was Political Science but I did Math in my spare time, so I switched to Math. Then I realized a career along that line would probably be restricted to teaching math or work as an insurance company actuary and I didn't want to do either. Since I was also very active in trying to make a difference in the world, I went back into Political Science and got my Bachelors and Masters in that field at KU. I got an offer of a small graduate scholarship at Harvard, a small co-op scholarship at the University of Minnesota and an offer of a teaching assistantship at Berkeley. I went to Berkeley.

I was drafted in my freshman year. Ann and I got married while I was home on leave from CPS.[14] We were both freshmen and after the war we completed college trying to take one course together every semester. Our marriage was fully collaborative. In 1948, after we had returned to KU, we participated in a Congress on Racial Equality (CORE)[16] sit-in at an off-campus student hangout. The Kansas football team was called in and I was pitched out on the street with the other male participants. The women were allowed to walk out.

At the time of Pearl Harbor I was sixteen. Because of my background as a Quaker, it wasn't hard to decide to become a CO.[17] I had some ambivalence but I realized that I could always opt to go into the armed services. My ambivalence was short lived and didn't return until a number of years after the end of WWII. My family and University Friends Church were very supportive of my decision. A family friend who was also a member of University Friends was denied a CO classification by the local draft board. He ultimately won on a Presidential Appeal. We had a pretty liberal draft board after that.

I worked some at my aunt's flower shop. She lived a couple of blocks away and was at our house several times a week. She had major reservations about COs and thought the COs could choose the luxury of sitting back in safety only because of the sacrifices of "the brave boys in the armed services." I didn't feel that way because we were eager to do dangerous work, but Congress had prohibited our service overseas. She was a major detractor because she made pretty sharp comments.

I was assigned to Trenton, North Dakota, and worked some on the land reclamation project there, but I was primarily in the kitchen. When they closed Trenton I went to the Gatlinburg camp in the Smoky Mountains National Park. I started off on the trail crew maintaining park trails, but then they stuck me in the kitchen again. I had 28 months in CPS.[14]

I started out wanting to be a Constitutional Law professor in Political Science and got my Doctorate in that field. In the beginning I thought it would be helpful to also have a law degree. Then Ann and I refused to sign the just enacted California Loyalty Oath.[9] Ann was fired but I wasn't. They just cut off my pay. I voluntarily continued teaching the rest of the semester without pay to make the point for the record that my work was satisfactory. There were two reasons for our refusal. One was as a protest against the rampant McCarthyism. The other was that the oath stated we would accept without reservations any civil defense assignments we might be given in the future. Such unqualified acceptance of undefined future obligations was impossible for us. We had criticized the Germans for not opposing Hitler. But how could we criticize the Germans for not taking actions that would have put their lives at risk and then knuckle under to McCarthyism ourselves?

As Ann was expecting, I needed immediate employment, so I applied for an opening at Standard Stations, a subsidiary of Standard Oil of California. That diverted me from a teaching career and I never got back to it. I quickly got a promotion at Standard Stations and was told I had a promising career there, but neither the company nor the career appealed to me. I took the U.S. Civil Service entrance exam and was offered a job with Social Security in Sacramento. That started me toward an administrative career I never left.

My CO position resulted in a number of roadblocks in my career. I ended up refusing, some four or five times, to do things I needed to do to keep my job, or doing things I knew would cost my job. These decisions weren't directly based on conscientious objection but were derived from the same source as my conscientious objection, refusing to do something I thought was wrong or doing something right my supervisors would not accept.

The Social Security District Office Manager who hired me, Mr. Hewitt, was a bigot. He had no use for anyone with a university education, for minorities, Jews, Hispanics, Catholics, or, especially, COs. Believe it or not, we became good friends. I asked him why he'd hired me when I represented everything he detested. He said

"I knew since Standard Oil had promoted you that you couldn't be all bad."

Later I was offered a job without an interview at Social Security's headquarters in Baltimore to help set up the disability program. I asked my supervisor why I was picked without an interview and was told my record showed I hadn't signed the loyalty oath. They wanted someone who had convictions and demonstrated integrity. I might say this positive result from my CO stand happened repeatedly.

Several years afterwards I was offered a job in the National Library of Medicine working on its project to computerize the Index Medicus. The position required a security clearance and that was turned down. The security people told me two things kept me from getting a security clearance, the loyalty oath and that I was a pacifist, so I didn't get that job. But my friend Charles Miller was Assistant to the Assistant Secretary for Administration of what was then the Department of Health, Education and Welfare (HEW). Charles went to the Assistant Secretary and said that the refusal of my security clearance was a great disservice both to me and to HEW. The Assistant Secretary reversed the security denial and gave me the clearance. The original position I had been offered had been filled almost a year before I finally received my clearance, so I ended up with another job in the Office of the Surgeon General. Later I moved on to some other work in the Public Health Service. When Medicare was approved I was asked to come to Social Security and help set up Medicare since I had extensive Social Security plus Public Health Service experience.

After Medicare had been in operation for a while they set up a study commission to evaluate how it was progressing and to pinpoint any problems. I was assigned as staff to Jack Young, Assistant Secretary/Comptroller of HEW. Jack gave me a stack of material and an outline and told me to see him in two weeks with a first draft. Two weeks later a red-faced Jack pounded the table and yelled, "Goddammit Michener, you didn't follow my outline!" I had looked at the materials and the outline and it just didn't work. I thought, do I tell him it doesn't work or do I just go ahead and write it the way I think it ought to be written? He looked at me and, after a long pause, said "Good!" Once again I did what I thought was right rather than blindly following directions.

Two or three years later I was working for Social Security in Baltimore. I had a call from my boss saying Jack had called about some work he wanted me to do. When I got to Washington, I learned that I was one of two staff persons to study the possible reorganization of HEW into two new departments. The other staff person was a business executive in a White House/business exchange program. I called my boss at home and told him I didn't know when I'd be back. We prepared the options that were used in setting up the Department of Health and Human Services and the Department of Education. It was over half a year before I returned to Baltimore.

Shortly thereafter the Commissioner of Social Security let it be known that Social Security itself must do much better in ensuring equal employment opportunities for minorities. I asked if we were in this for show or for real, because if we were in it for real, then an admonition alone wouldn't be adequate. I said we would have to set goals, enlarge recruitment pools, measure progress, and ensure that standards have not been lowered. The upshot was that Social Security changed its program. I was asked how I had the courage to do this. My reply was that if you make a practice of saying what you think, it does not require unusual courage to take a stand.

I was good friends with the Associate Commissioner, Lou Zawatsky. Al Henderson, who had worked with me, filed a complaint charging Lou with discrimination. Al complained that Lou was not pushing equal opportunities to the extent required by law. Lou felt that proceeding that fast would cause a backlash which would ultimately slow progress. Lou gave Al a performance evaluation stating he exceeded expectations in almost all areas but the overall evaluation was "not satisfactory" on the grounds that Al was not a team player. Al felt his unsatisfactory rating represented discrimination against him as a black man for continually demanding that the law be followed to its fullest extent. Al asked me to represent him in his complaint of discrimination. Representing Al against Lou was something I did not want to do, so I told Al I would think about it.

Lou called me into his office for a friendly conversation. He noted that he was a strong supporter of civil rights and equal employment opportunities. He also noted I had a high reputation and that many opportunities lay before me in Social Security. However, he'd heard I might represent Al Henderson. He would not hold it against me but others would. I would not get promoted again. I just wouldn't hear about the opportunities.

I realized Lou's remarks could be seen as blackmail, but I thought they were intended as friendly advice and were an accurate prediction. But Al needed representation and I would not desert him in the face of this kind of pressure. I told Al I would take his case. As both of us expected, we lost. That left me knowing I could expect to be sitting at my job, for an extended time. It was a price I was willing to pay.

Before the year was out the National Federation of Integrated Neighborhoods (NN)[44] began looking for a new executive director. NN had a multi-year grant from the Ford Foundation, but Ford decided to switch its funding from integration activities to neighborhood empowerment and notified NN that the grant would be ended after two years. NN's director immediately resigned. I had been on NN's board for years and had served as its president. Ann and I felt it was important for NN to continue its work, so I took that job.

It was financial suicide. I left a good federal job with full benefits for a job that paid less than half of what I had been earning and provided no benefits, not even Social Security coverage. In addition I had to commute to Washington every day and pay my own parking. Ann and I put in sixty hour weeks over there, with Ann's time being unpaid. We solicited everyone we knew, told them what we were doing, and that we would appreciate contributions. In a short while we raised a few thousand dollars that bought time for NN to build a better financial base. Then we got disgusted with the NN Board. We had both given up a secure future, had taken a drastic cut in income, and were working day and night. All the Board did was to say "you're doing a great job." They wouldn't do anything! We felt the whole Board had to help.

Then I got an offer from Buzzy Hettleman, the newly appointed Secretary of what is now the Maryland Department of Human Resources (DHR) to be his Special Assistant. Ann and I believed in what we were doing at NN but weren't willing to continue without Board support, so I said, "I'll come." Once again a setback led to a new opening. Buzzy's offer came because of the National Neighbors, and that came because I represented Al Henderson in his unsuccessful complaint against Zawatsky.

Several months into my job as Buzzy's assistant he became aware of problems in a program called Judicare that paid for legal services for people with low incomes who needed an attorney but could not afford one. At that time the program was spending about $2,500,000 yearly, approximately three times its budget, so the state legislature was moving to end the program. Buzzy thought I was the person who could save Judicare. While I was working at Social Security in Baltimore I also went to law school at night, so I had a law degree and had been admitted to the bar. Reforming Judicare was a major struggle that called on both my administrative background and my legal training, but I got the program whipped into shape and the legislature allowed it to continue.

Then the Maryland State Bar Association set up a pro-bono program, the Maryland Volunteer Lawyer's Service (MVLS) and we ended up with an interlocking coordination of the State's compensated Judicare program, the Maryland bar's pro-bono MVLS program, and county bar and other pro bono programs. For example, the Judicare program couldn't pay court and other incidental costs but MVLS could. So I set it up so MVLS could pay court and other costs incurred under the Judicare program and if an attorney took a pro-bono program case under MVLS or one of the other pro bono programs and put in twenty-five hours, Judicare would reimburse him for further work at the Judicare rate of $30 per hour. This encouraged attorneys to take pro bono cases because it alleviated the risk of an unpaid case unexpectedly becoming so time consuming as to prevent them from taking sufficient new fee-generating cases necessary to sustain their practice.

One outcome of my simultaneous work for the State Judicare program and the private nonprofit MVLS program was that I got investigated by the Maryland State Ethics Commission for a conflict of interest. For the first and only time in the Ethics Commission's history, it approved simultaneous related work in the public and private sectors by a State employee.

Our marriage was fully collaborative. I supported Ann when she wanted to do things. One day I was in a conference and Ann called, saying to the Secretary, "I'm going on the Freedom March to Montgomery tomorrow. I just decided. John needs to know." The secretary marched right into the conference and told me to go home. We arranged for the kids to stay at a friend's home, and she was off the next morning to Montgomery for the march.

We agreed on how we would raise the children. We consulted privately on disciplinary matters and never contradicted each other in front of the kids. I was on the board of Friends School, but we thought public schools were important and needed a student body from families with a wide range of educational and income levels. So we sent our children to public schools rather than Friends School. Our daughter was the only white kid in her class the year Martin Luther King was shot.

How did we make sure our children had good educations? The schools our kids attended were not the best in the world, but they weren't bad. That was not crucial since we thought the quality of the schools, above a certain minimal level, was not relevant. The important factor was that kids need to be challenged. It could be by the teacher, it could be by other students, or it could be by something else.

To ensure that challenge we supplemented their education. If they showed an interest in an area, we got a magazine in that area at their level. Sometimes those magazines came from abroad. We never said we were ordering a magazine. They just appeared on the coffee table. The kids would fight over who got to which ones first. Sometimes they complained they weren't learning enough at school and we'd say "Well? It's your job to learn. The school's job is to help you. What are you going do about it?"

Our daughter wanted to go to Pimlico Junior High, a very good school at the time. The Principal of her elementary school told us the elementary school was not good enough for Pimlico to accept any of its graduates. I told the Principal that our daughter ought to be judged on her own qualifications, not the elementary school's reputation, and that I would appeal all the way up to the Board of Education if it took that. She was admitted.

I traveled a lot for the Public Health Service and Social Security. When I was sent on a protracted trip we notified the teachers that the children would be away for the period involved. I took the family along for the trip by car, camping out along the way. I paid for everything not covered by the travel money and the extra time required to go by car was charged to my vacation. We thought the travel was broadening for our kids and that they would learn far more from seeing the country than by remaining in class.

They learned on our trips how to handle disasters. A spring on our camping trailer might break or something else might go wrong. But we always worked our way out, so they learned not to be afraid of strange or unpredictable circumstances.

We told the kids we wanted them to go to college, but that a lot of very good people didn't attend. They had to be serious enough about college to be willing to try to raise the money they needed for the first semester each year. They could have scholarships, get jobs, or obtain student loans, but they had to try to raise their share. Then we'd pay for the second semester. However, if they'd made a real effort to raise the money they needed we'd make up whatever they hadn't. We wanted them to prize education and know that it came with a cost.

I was on the AFSC's national board for six years and one of its vice-chairs for a couple of years. During that time the AFSC[4] was asked to send an observer to the International Peace Conference in Tehran following the overthrow of the Shah. There was not time to call a board meeting so Steve Carey got the other Vice-Chair and me together to decide what the AFSC[4] should do. The Department of Justice advised the AFSC[4] that sending an observer would constitute a criminal offense that could send us to prison. Some folks in the State Department hoped we would send an observer who could give an objective report of what happened at the conference. The three of us decided to send the observer. Fortunately for us, we were never prosecuted.

Because of my work with affirmative action at Social Security, I was the first Chair of the AFSC's National Affirmative Action Task Force. I went to a number of AFSC[4] regions around the country that did not like the affirmative action plan. We were getting some real flack on that. And then a number of years later I was back for another term on what had become the National Affirmative Action Committee. Currently I am serving on another Board committee.

Ann and I went on a Christian Peacemaker Team (CPT) to Chiapas, Mexico, immediately after the massacre at Acteal, where 40 women and children were murdered as they were praying in the Catholic Church. A member of our Meeting, was co-leading the CPT team and asked Ann and me to go along with her. We said we would even though we had an active desire not to go. It was scary. We never felt safe and probably never were.

We lived in an integrated neighborhood in Washington. Along with some other neighborhood friends, we set up a corporation to purchase houses going on the market before speculators could get to them. We'd rehab and sell them on an integrated basis. We moved several houses but we found that housing is not something you do in your spare time. It needs to be a full-time job.

Because of my work with NN, I was on the Boards of several organizations related to fair, open housing. NN had been set up by a group called Sponsors of Open Housing Investment (SOHI), initiated by Morris Milgram, the first housing developer to build and sell only on an integrated basis, and James Farmer[23] of CORE[16] and later Assistant Under-Secretary of Housing and Urban Development (HUD).

New Hope Housing managed three apartment complexes in Washington. Morris Milgram was asked by the State Department to provide decent living quarters for diplomats of dark color who could not get such housing in Washington. SOHI created a new organization called the Fund for an OPEN Society (OPEN). OPEN ran a national pro-integration mortgage program providing mortgages at below market rates for moves that were pro-integration—blacks moving into neighborhoods that were predominantly white, whites moving into neighborhoods that were predominantly black.

Baltimore Neighborhoods, Inc. (BNI) was the Baltimore metropolitan (now the Maryland state) fair housing agency. HUD asked for proposals for affirmative action plans, so the Greater Baltimore Board and BNI submitted a collaborative proposal, the Baltimore Plan, which was approved by HUD. I served on the Baltimore Plan board for a while. Residual distrust between the Board and BNI eventually undermined the Plan and led to its termination. This distrust stemmed from lawsuits BNI had filed earlier against various brokers because of discriminatory practices.

I chaired the Housing Committee of Baltimore's Citizens Planning and Housing Association (CPHA), which for three generations had been the training ground for Baltimore's leadership. Windsor Hills Neighbors was a neighborhood in Baltimore City that became integrated in the late 1960s and still is. I became president of Windsor Hills and applied what Ann and I had learned from NN. Instead of trying to conceal the fact of integration, we talked about its benefits. We told everyone to be proud of integration. It was my work with BNI, CPHA, and

Windsor Hills that led to my appointment to Baltimore's Board of Municipal and Zoning Appeals.

I have had a deep involvement with the Stony Run Meeting of Friends, including being a past Clerk. Ann and I supported the establishment of Broadmead only after there was agreement that once it was on a sound basis it would address the medical and other needs of older persons. I came on the Broadmead Board in 2000 and we moved in a year later. Currently I am the Chair, the first resident Chair of the Board.

I am also involved in Friends Care, another corporation under the control of Stony Run. Friends Care now carries the broad charge originally given to Broadmead of addressing the needs of older persons not choosing to move to a retirement community.

I am proud that Ann and I have been happily married over 61 years, and it just keeps getting more wonderful. We're proudest that we've stood up for what we think is right. I didn't end up doing what I originally wanted to do, teaching Constitutional Law, but we haven't paid the heavy penalties some have for living their beliefs.

Our oldest son, who has a doctorate in engineering, has worked for a number of computer companies handling various aspects of information technology, including security architecture. He repeatedly told the companies their products were defective, but they were put on the market anyway, so he wrote an article that users of defective and insecure software could successfully sue the companies for damages resulting from their use. Afterwards he was hired by Microsoft where his views are heeded.

Our second son is at Duke Medical School. He spent his non-teaching time treating people rather than doing research. He's done a lot to change the way medicine is practiced at Duke and now heads the leading family medicine program in the United States.

Our third son has a Ph.D. in botany and is Curator of the Botanical Gardens and Arboretum at the University of Michigan. He placed an ancient Islamic cenotaph in one of the University gardens. He says gardens are often designed around artwork, and that the cenotaph is a piece of art from a different culture that should be given an honored place. He was Clerk of the Quarterly Meeting for a number of years.

Our fourth child, our daughter, worked for Social Security, as I had. She was a Claims Technician in a Payment Center. There was congressional pressure to approve a certain difficult case that had been referred to her that she would not approve because the claimant did not qualify. The case was forwarded as though she had approved. She tracked the case and made sure the approval was revoked. She was dismayed when the case went through after she retired on disability.

All the kids have stood up for what they believed in. We told them if they ever found us not acting in accordance with our values they should challenge us on the spot. They did occasionally. They are now meeting that same challenge for themselves.

When the Prince Edward County Schools in Virginia were closed rather than comply with Brown vs. Board of Education, we volunteered to take one of the students into our home. Howard was part of our family for the school year. We took him on trips to visit our families in Wichita and siblings in Michigan. A close relative refused to let us come over to visit if we brought Howard along. We were unwilling to leave Howard behind, so we did not go.

We told Howard we would like to take him with us on a trip to California once the school year was over. But, since we were really hard up for money, he would need to try to earn enough money for his own food. We said that if he worked to raise the money we would cover whatever he didn't. He didn't make any effort. We learned later his uncle told him Whitey would take him anyway. We really wanted to take Howard with us since we thought it would be a good experience for him, but we had an advisor from Morgan State University, an historically Black university in Baltimore, who told us we had made the agreement with Howard and should stick to it. We told Howard we were going without him. It was hard to do.

On the 50th anniversary of Brown vs. Board of Education, MSN-TV ran a special on the impact the closure of the schools in Farmville had on the students and their lives. Howard was one of the persons featured in that special. We learned from the special that he had expected to be in a Black family, but it was a white family that took him in. It was a shock that forced him to re-examine how he felt about whites.

The special enabled us to get back in touch with Howard. We learned that his stay with us and our trips led him to realize there was a big world out there. Our decision not to take him to California also made him realize there were standards that had consequences if the standards were not met. The stay with us was the turning point in his life. For years he stayed away from Prince Edward County and Farmville. He finally went back because the place hadn't moved forward. He's doing what he can to bring about needed change.

Change comes in two ways. Often times it comes incrementally over a long period. At other times, there are blockages and things don't change until there's a crisis. Then radical change can come quickly and a lot that has been going on quietly before has a major influence on the resolution that comes out of the crisis. Although you may not see any results in your lifetime I'm quite convinced those results may surface long afterwards. You just have to work in the faith that when that crisis comes your work will help make a difference. So my advice is to work for what you believe in.

I went into World War II as a pacifist on a biblical basis. Back in college afterwards I did a lot of reading of Gandhi, nonviolence (including the nonviolent anarchists), and the British experience in India, particularly with the Sikhs. My pacifism shifted more to a moral basis and pacifism's ability to reach across the barriers of violence to persons on other sides of the conflict. These interactions permit creative outcomes that do not breed further violence. But with nuclear weapons and the

increasing mechanization of war the personal interactions that give pacifism its efficacy are becoming increasingly rare. What is the efficacy of nonviolent resistance to ballistic missiles with nuclear warheads?

Although I think violent solutions are almost always bankrupt, I also think that nonviolent resistance is not always the answer. While I'm overwhelmingly on the nonviolent side I cannot regard myself as an absolute pacifist. Not accepting the legitimacy of what is being done, but resisting openly and nonviolently can destroy the legitimacy of the violent solution and open the situation to other alternatives. I call myself a pragmatic pacifist—a pragmatic nonviolent resister.

Ross Sanderson (1917)

"Don't be too dogmatic in your views or in your feelings about what you think. There's always the possibility of new revelations."

I don't know how and when I became aware that I am a pacifist. When I was in high school in Baltimore a classmate said "You're not a pacifist, are you?" I gave him an uncertain response. I didn't know where the question was coming from, and I really didn't know the answer at that point. After WW II, I found out that his brother was a CO.[17] Becoming a pacifist was a very gradual process. A Quaker work camp the summer of 1938 had a lot to do with my coming to more certainty about it. There I met a lot of neat Quakers, including Rufus Jones,[38] Clarence Pickett,[51] and David Day, who had a tremendous influence on me.

My father was a Congregational minister. He was primarily in administrative work in the Council of Churches and the YMCA.[74] He wasn't a pastor of a church at any time in my younger life before World War II. I was influenced by various friends of my Dad's that would talk about World War I. They talked with an anti-war attitude, saying that war was so terrible, and we shouldn't be involved in those things. It was always hard to separate isolationism from pacifism. I remember one pastor saying that he would never participate in war again, but when World War II actually came, his son was in the army and he was obviously not opposed to the war. He was still quite friendly with me. Everyone I knew was very supportive when I made my decision to register as a CO.

In my earliest times in Wichita, we all played cowboy and Indians, and we had various games in the neighborhood, none of them of a particularly pacifist nature. When I was 10 years old, I went to a YMCA camp where,

ironically, I got a medal for marksmanship in rifle training. The first summer a very authoritarian gym teacher
from our high school was head of the camping program.
I was really unhappy about his leadership, particularly
because he bullied a counselor at the camp who was of
quite a different temperament.

I went to Oberlin College because I was a pretty
immature teenager. My father and other relatives had
gone to Oberlin and I didn't know what else to do. I
applied, was accepted and was very happy there. There
was a peace society at Oberlin and other organizations
that were peace minded. The President of Oberlin had
a Peace Institute after the close of the school year. One
year I was asked to stay to put out a special edition of the
school paper containing the speeches of guest speakers at
the Peace Institute. The President of Oberlin was an inter-
nationalist, but not a pacifist nor were my political science professors. Oberlin influenced me a great deal, but
it was the complex relationship of pacifism, communism,
Trotskyites, and Fascism. There was a national movement
among college students in 1938 to sign a peace pledge
that we wouldn't go to war, a standard pledge across the
whole United States. Many at Oberlin signed that peace
pledge, but I refused to sign it because I didn't know that
I wouldn't go to war under any circumstance. I was willing to be influenced by new revelations. Although I didn't
sign it, I was one of very few that kept that loyalty oath
that I'll never go to war. I often wonder how all my classmates that did sign felt when they changed their minds
and went to war against Hitler.

When I was a senior, it was very difficult for me to
figure out what I was going to do after I graduated. I got a
postal card advertisement for a graduate program at the
University of Pennsylvania in Public Administration that
looked interesting, since I was a political science major.
I was accepted on a scholarship to go there the second
year of the program's existence. We got an M.B.A. degree

that was really a Public Administration degree. The fortuitous part was that it brought me into Philadelphia Quaker meetings and built on the work camp experience.

I was on an AFSC[4] committee related to CPS[14] and Quakerism. Douglas Steere was on that committee. Sometimes we met at the Germantown home of the father of a future CPS man, Steve Carey. I became acquainted with a lot of Quakerism and heard discussions about the coming war. I got a job in Reading with the Housing Authority where, with fortuitous good circumstances again, David and Mary Ritchie had a work camp that summer. I was working, but in the evenings I joined the campers for discussions. I had a valuable relationship with the Friends Meeting in Reading. After Meeting, some of the younger people often stayed to talk. I remember a guy always asked me "What's more important if you're a Quaker, to follow your conscience or to be a CO?" I said, "To follow your conscience wherever it leads you," which was what he wanted to hear.

I had a certificate from my Congregational Church that I was a sincere CO. I just sent in the certificate and my statement about why I was a CO and I got my classification right back. I didn't have to prove it to a skeptical draft board. I feel a little guilty that I had that easy time to be classified, but practically everyone I met in CPS had to have hearings, which means they were spared CPS for at least six months. I was drafted in January of 1942.

At first I served briefly in a soil conservation camp in Ohio. Then we were asked to go fight the great conflagration of forest fires in California because the Japanese were supposed to set all the forests on fire. That never happened, but there was a normal forest fire season which we served. We were delighted to have fires because we had something to do. The rest of the time we were doing routine forest work or putting up telephone lines for the war service. As soon as opportunities to work in mental hospitals opened up, I went to a hospital in Washington State and was there about six months when an overseas training program started. I had just left Medical Lake, Washington, to come on the train to Earlham College when the whole program was cancelled.

I was very active in protesting AFSC's running of CPS. I was asking if AFSC[4] was going down the wrong road running CPS[14] the way they did, especially after Congress passed a law that made AFSC deal with the Selective Service. It was supposed to be under civilian leadership and the AFSC would train us to do overseas work so we could do ambulance or relief work. But it was still a question of serving in some way or following the people who went to jail because they refused to register, refused to serve in CPS, or weren't granted CO status.

I was at Earlham for six weeks. As soon as I could, I got a mental hospital job in New Hampshire State Hospital, where I stayed for the rest of the war. Mental hospital work was extremely educational, as educational as any course I had in college. In the meanwhile, Holly had obtained a Masters degree in Psychology so she was able to obtain a staff placement in the hospital. We had a lot of married people at the mental hospital in Concord. It was really very tough for a number of people. In my experiences, the antagonisms were minor, but I don't think that was true of everybody.

After I was released, with help from AFSC's search for jobs, I got a job with a citizen's organization that worked on mental health, public health, and prison work. A Quaker staff member, Leon Stern,s was head of the prison program. I was under the person working on mental health issues. When he retired, I was given his job. I was working around the state on mental health problems and legislation, visiting every institution for the mentally ill or retarded in Pennsylvania. This was a great experience; we tried to influence the mental health programs.

A new governor came in and asked a state senator, "I want to do something for mental health – what shall I do?" The state senator came to our organization and we said "We've been telling you for ten years we need this." He said, "Okay, we'll do it." The senator got all the credit because the governor said, "I asked Senator so and so what to do and he told me to do this." It was really the long years of work that had been done by our organization that had resulted in that one improvement.

It was difficult after the war to pick up my vocation. After I did the mental health work for several years, I was offered a job with the City of Baltimore. While waiting for the civil service job to materialize, I worked with AFSC[4] for a few weeks. Then I went into a career with the City of Baltimore. I took the job in Baltimore because it was the first inter-racial program of employment in City government. We were fighting a racial battle with the rest of the city agencies to get their cooperation. The prejudice among the city agencies and bureaus was terrible. We managed to have an integrated program for the first time ever with the whites or the blacks.

We had a promotion in the housing bureau. We promoted a white man to a supervisory role and one of the black men who was relatively new in the program vigorously protested. But it was the other black men and women that came to our defense and said no, they appointed the best person for that job. We had the inspector and the professionals all integrated but the clerical staff was not. We had a job to fill and we filled it with the most competent person on the list, a black woman. One of the top staff, who was white, strongly objected saying our program was too important to completely disrupt the clerical staff and have a completely unhappy group of people working here. She claimed one of the main clerical persons would quit if we appointed this black person. I, as the Assistant Director, and the Director said, "No, she deserves to get the appointment." We appointed her. Nobody quit. In fact, the person who allegedly would quit if we appointed was the most helpful in mentoring this black person. It all went very smoothly and we were able to integrate more people. I finally lost the job I had been doing in housing and found a job with the Health Department.

I was the first person to appoint a black person to a professional job in the Department of Public Works in Baltimore City. It soon became sort of passé, but that didn't help me much with some of my colleagues in the Department of Public Works that were very anti-integration. A black Deputy Health Commissioner told me, "You don't know what kind of flack I'm taking from some of my fellow blacks because I appointed a white person for that job. They think it's my duty to appoint black people to jobs."

I never considered my conscientious objection a hindrance. I always put down on all my applications and exams to get promoted that I had served four years in CPS. Most people didn't know what CPS was so they didn't pay attention to it. I didn't make any secret of the fact that I had been a CO and my immediate superiors always knew it. One of my supervisors asked, "How much were you aware of whether your having been a CO was hurting your career?" I was startled because I knew that some people weren't pleased that I'd been a CO, but they didn't really have much influence on my work. It may have had more influence on my career than I thought.

When I got a job in zoning which was one of my first advancements, another guy wanted the job and didn't get it. Then he came in with a permit application that I couldn't approve. He said "You will approve it."

I said, "No, I'm not going to approve that. It's not possible; it's not something that is legal for me to approve."

He said, "If you don't approve it, I'm going to pass the word around that you're anti-Semitic."

I didn't approve it and I don't know whether he did anything or not. My friends knew I wasn't anti-Semitic. We were a fairly large department, the department of housing and urban renewal. We had different attitudes in different divisions of the department. It was very racially mixed. My boss was a prominent black person in the community.

They had a printing office run by a black man. Whenever I went over to get anything, he said, "When do you need it?" I said, "When it's convenient. I'd like to have it as soon as possible, but whenever." I always got it right away. Some of my colleagues kept complaining that they couldn't get things promptly. Maybe my racial attitudes did help sometimes.

I undertook other peace activities, pacifist activities and anti-war activities especially in the sixties and in the Vietnam era. There were a lot of protests. It was the era of the civil rights in Washington. We went to a number of protests and demonstrations for peace. Sometimes it was the whole family and sometimes just me. The first one was the most impressive because that was early in the Vietnam War. It was a Quaker-developed demonstration, a silent protest completely around the Pentagon. Just a circle of silence, but some of us went occasionally to talk to someone who wanted to know why we were out there. When we told them what we were doing, they said "That's good. We really need your prayers." That was the best one that I ever attended because it was so Quakerly. There was no anger. Subsequent demonstrations became mixed up. I remember we had one demonstration where a young Quaker was very angry and shouted violently at somebody, perhaps some passing soldiers. I was upset about that.

A group went over to Washington to demonstrate. There were two things going on at the same time. A group of Friends went up on the Capitol steps to worship, testing the right of worshipful assembly. Then the poor people's campaign came along and they were doing something that was real civil disobedience, just a short distance up the steps from the Quaker demonstration. People from the Quaker worship group said, "We're not doing very much here. Let's go join them." So they did and got arrested for something entirely different from what they started out to test. I thought this was not a very smart thing to do. They had abandoned their project and gone to the other project. We never got the results of the Quaker project. They were thrilled by their experience in jail as a truly transforming experience. That illustrates the various different routes we go.

Some years ago the Pope visited Baltimore and our Meeting was asked by a dissident group to allow a demonstration on our property when the Pope was passing from downtown to our Cathedral neighbor. We had a difficult discussion about that in Stony Run Meeting for Business. Some people just thought that it was absolutely necessary for us to join that gay and lesbian effort and others of us thought that it was unneighborly and that it was more important for us to maintain a friendly relationship with our Catholic neighbors. The third group, the one that I was in, thought it was a lot of nonsense because the Pope probably wouldn't ever see the demonstration anyway. There was no northward parade but a quiet circuit route up I-83 and southward to the Cathedral. These issues keep coming up in various ways amongst Friends.

Gradually, our kids grew up and went off. I guess we were just getting too old and tired to do things. Holly and I were looking for a retirement community. We didn't like Quaker Broadmead because it was too plush, so we came here to Pickersgill, but I never realized quite how thoroughly they were committed to the flag and Mary Pickersgill who sewed the big flag for Fort McHenry. All this nationalism at Pickersgill surprised me. It doesn't change the treatment we get. They have several COs living here. But it gets a little uncomfortable and boring after a while.

I always did regret that those of us who really worked hard to get the AFSC[4] out of CPS[14] before the war was over didn't succeed. There is no post-war history because the COs were so diversified. Only a small proportion were Quakers, but the post-war history is written by Quakers who were sympathetic to what the AFSC did. I wasn't a Quaker until after the war. The AFSC CPS committee that met was composed of a bunch of Quakers primarily from the Philadelphia area plus the 10 or 12 representatives from CPS elected to represent the camps, mental hospitals and other assignments. The question was, the year before the end of the war, "Should AFSC continue their contract with the Selective Service?" All non-Quaker representatives were opposed to the Service Committee continuing its relationship with Selective Service. The two representatives who wanted to continue were Quakers, but the representatives were only a small part of that total committee. We really didn't know much about "sense of the meeting" and how to reach unity. There was no consensus about what should be done so the thing continued.

In a newsletter that went out to a large AFSC[4] supporting group, the representatives wrote that all but two of the representatives had "voted" against the decision, which was not very Quakerly terminology. At the next meeting Clarence Pickett, one of my heroes, everybody's hero among those close to him, was very upset about our having published this. He said, "How do you expect me to raise money to support all of you in the camp when you say that you don't want to be in this program?" He was very upset, the only time I ever saw him upset.

I was very proud of the individual services that we gave to the mental patients where we served. I think that was very important. Although that was something I'm proud of, I am also humbled by it because I learned as much from the patients as I helped them. Another thing I'm really proud of is getting an opportunity to work in the inter-racial program in the city of Baltimore where I had an influence in the way the program went.

I don't think I had any illusions about changing things. The theological perceptions that stood me in good stead during CPS are not the same theological perceptions that I have today, yet I still consider myself a pacifist. At that time I thought maybe life on earth was just a precursor to a different kind of evolution of that battle between good and evil. Being a pacifist means you seem to be accepting evil as something that you are not going to fight against because it will take care of itself in eternity.

I don't think in those same theological terms any more. *A Course in Miracles* has influenced me quite a bit during recent years, so now I really dislike the dualistic term evil. Some of my good pacifist friends are amazed that I say that because they can say with great elegance "War is evil, that's what we're against."

I would like to pass on to future generations, don't be too dogmatic in your views or in your feelings about what you think. There's always the possibility of new revelations. I feel that is important because so many of my fellow COs think that they have the answer. They know how they felt in 1941 and they still feel the same way today. While theologically I don't feel the same way.

George M. Houser *(1916)*

"*The campaigns against colonialism were just really getting started. It was an exciting ordeal*"

I guess became aware that I am a pacifist when I was in
high school. We lived at that time in Berkeley, California.
I was influenced by my activity in the Methodist youth
movement. My father was a Methodist minister and I
grew up as a preacher's kid. I participated in our church
youth group, which was called Theta Pi. We had summer
institutes and conferences, which included groups from
many different churches located in Northern California.
A major emphasis was put on peace and race relations
from a Christian perspective. I was introduced to the
word pacifism at that time. This was in the early 1930s. I
graduated from high school in 1934.

Two students came to speak from UCLA, Al Hamilton
and Al Reynolds. Both of these young men had refused
to take part in the ROTC[53] program at UCLA and were
expelled. They impressed me a great deal. At that time
there was the Green Shirt Movement. Those who wore
the green shirts, as Hamilton and Reynolds did, were
identifying themselves as pacifists who would not agree
to participate in wars. It was, I think, just after this, that
the Oxford Pledge Movement got started. The Oxford
Pledge was started in England at the Oxford University.
And those who took that pledge were saying that they
would not participate in any war. I was one of those.

It was during my high school period that I became
conscious of the rest of the world out there, after World
War I. We had seen awful pictures of the gruesome deaths
and the destruction of the war. And this was unthinkable!
My position was a Christian position that we as followers of Jesus would not participate in war. It was a violation of the gospel of love. It was at that time that I began

---

Interviewed and transcribed by Philip Greenspan

to think of myself as a pacifist. I became conscious of the War Resister's League.

I was born in Cleveland, Ohio, in 1916, just at the time that the U.S. entered World War I. We lived in Ohio and from there my folks went as missionaries to the

Philippines, so my earliest memories are of growing up in Manila. My father was a good preacher, very poetic preacher, and he made gestures. He was quite a popular speaker. I can still see him as he was gesturing, making his points preaching. I was greatly influenced by the fact that my family was based in the church and had a Christian outlook on life. My father's life was in the church. I developed my own social consciousness as a result of my activities in the youth movement of what was then the Methodist Episcopal Church.

We left the Philippines after five years and moved to western New York. We were in Buffalo, briefly, before moving to Troy, New York, where my father was the Minister of the Fifth Avenue State Street Methodist Church. From there, we moved all the way across the country in 1931 to Berkeley, California where I went through high school. After a year at the College of the Pacific, I spent a year in China as an exchange student at Lingnan University in what was then Canton. That had a great influence on me in terms of widening my view of the world. I had a Chinese roommate. This and my years in the Philippines must have had something to do with developing my idea of racial equality, that all people were basically the same, that any discrimination was to be resisted.

My grandfather on my mother's side was Frederick A. Mills. My middle name is Mills, George Mills Houser. He was a Methodist preacher also, so my mother grew up with a very religious background. My folks met at Allegheny College, which is a Methodist school in western Pennsylvania. That's where they met, fell in love and got married in 1910. I was the third child to be born of four.

We went on summer vacations for two weeks to a month. I can remember going to places like Maine, the Adirondacks, Vermont, or later to the Sierras of California. We sat in front of the fireplace and learned hymns. I can remember learning some of the old hymns that appear in the hymnbooks these days, John Wesley and Charles Wesley hymns. We were a singing family. Not just hymns, but good folk songs, old time songs. This was an important part of the family background. We had Bible readings. My father and mother always prayed at every meal. And at devotional times I remember in summer periods before the fireplace there was always some reading and some discussion of what a particular passage of the Bible might mean. This was basically my younger years.

My parents were pacifist in practice, but they were not part of a movement. When I refused to register for the draft in 1940 when the Selective Training and Service Act[57] came into effect, it was quite an experience for my folks. My father at that time declared himself completely in sympathy with me. At that time he was the Minister of the big downtown church in Denver, Colorado, Trinity Methodist Church. He preached a sermon that made the papers, the Denver Post and the Rocky Mountain News, supporting his son who was in Danbury Federal Correctional Institution for violating the draft. My picture was on the front page of both those papers because I had been a graduate of the University of Denver and my father was a prominent clergyman in the city.

My father and I did a lot of fishing together. It started in the Philippines where I remember fishing along Manila Bay along what they called the Luneta. I remember our hiking into the back country of the high Sierras when we lived in Berkeley. We would go for several days, hiking back carrying our sleeping bags and fishing tackle. We would spend two or three days catching trout in some of the lakes that were not available to most people. We did a lot of camping in our family. Jean and I still have that tradition.

We liked baseball. My first baseball game was in Manila with my father. That was before independence of the Philippines so it was still a colony of the United States. I played a lot of catch with my dad. I played on my grammar school baseball team. I played shortstop sometimes and I played center field. I did a lot of roller-skating. I skied in the winter. Marbles was a big thing. I was a pretty good shot. I must have had a thousand marbles that I had won by hitting somebody else's marble. Another game we played was with horse chestnuts. I haven't seen this done any place else. We put a hole in them on the end of a string and hit them in a contest to try breaking the other's horse chestnut. In high school I was on the swimming team. I could swim fairly fast. I remember if you won a particular race you'd get a double scoop of ice cream as a reward, at a YMCA camp in Troy, New York, Camp Vanskoonhoven.

When I was in grammar school I was particularly fond of music and I was always pretty good. I had a good ear for music. I always liked Geography class.

Maybe that's one reason why I did quite a bit of traveling and why I got interested in international things. Later in school, I was interested in Philosophy, Religion and Social Sciences.

When I was a kid I read the Tom Swift series of books and called *The Boy Allies* which had to do with two young men in World War I. I loved *Tom Sawyer* and *Huckleberry Finn*, Mark Twain's books. Serious reading came later. I was particularly interested in international relations, peace, race relations, and then Africa. They became the staple of my reading.

In college I majored in Social Sciences. I was in three different colleges. The College of the Pacific, now the University of the Pacific, in Stockton, California, was a Methodist school. I particularly liked the social sciences. I took a lot of survey courses—Economics, Philosophy, Astronomy, Physics, Chemistry—but I never was oriented towards Chemistry or Physics. I was interested in Astronomy, the mystery of it all.

Then I had a year in China as an exchange student at Lingnan University. There were twenty-five American students on the campus of this very lovely university at Canton. That was an important year for me. I had special courses on Chinese History, Japanese History, and courses in Philosophy and Religion. But I didn't take my studies too seriously that year in China. I was traveling and soaking up China.

My folks had moved from Berkeley to Denver in 1935. Although I had a scholarship, my year in China had been very expensive with the travel involved, and it was during the years of the Great Depression. So the folks didn't have to persuade me very hard to live at home in Denver during my last two years of college before I graduated in 1938. There I majored in Economics and Sociology, and I took Philosophy, Religion, and Speech courses. I graduated in August of 1938 rather than in June. I had to go to summer school because I hadn't taken a full course in China. I had to make up for the fact that I traveled more than I studied.

People that I admired along the way included Al Hamilton, one of the students at UCLA who refused ROTC. I got to know him later in New York. He was a Socialist Party member and I became a Socialist Party member during my period at Union Theological Seminary in New York.

My first year at the College of the Pacific I met Glenn Young, who was President of the campus YMCA. Glenn had been an exchange student to Hawaii the year before. He influenced me to apply to become an exchange student to China. I respected his ability to speak clearly as he did. We did a lot of talking together about our positions on social and political concerns. We took one trip across the country together. Glenn was a mentor.

Later on my mentors were people like Norman Thomas, Roger Baldwin, and, especially, A. J. Muste[43] who was an influential figure in my life. I met A. J. when I was in Union Theological Seminary when he was the minister of the Labor Temple at 14th Street and Second Avenue, before he was appointed as Executive Secretary of FOR.[25] Muste had been a Socialist, a leader of a wing of the Trotskyist Movement, but he left that and was converted in a religious experience to pacifism. He was one who was living out his own convictions and he became a strong pacifist. I admired his strength and the kind of leadership he gave to FOR.

My father had gone to Boston University School of Theology, which is a Methodist seminary, but I decided to go to Union Theological Seminary in New York. Professors such as Reinhold Niebuhr[48] and Harry Ward were very socially and politically active. Union Seminary was non-denominational, so we had a scattering of denominations and even of religious representatives. I went along with one of my close friends, Francis Hall. We had been very active on the Denver campus in the Student Christian Movement. We traveled together to New York and roomed together our first year.

Our courses included New Testament, Old Testament, Church and Society, Church History, Theology, Sacred Music, and Ethics, which dealt with world issues, Speech, and Preaching. I was stimulated by many of my professors, among them Reinhold Niebuhr[48] was probably the most widely known.

Studying the Bible included the sociology and history of the times when the church was trying to make a place for itself, so this was a very important period for developing my own philosophy and theology.

I refused to register for the draft in my senior year, which was broken up by spending almost a year in prison in Danbury, Connecticut. When I got out and went to Chicago Theological Seminary, I got so involved in FOR work that I did everything except write my thesis. I took the final comprehensive exams and did well on all of them, but I didn't write my thesis, so I could not get the degree. After I had retired from my work with the American Committee on Africa,[1] I wrote to the president of Chicago Theological Seminary and said I fulfilled all requirements except the thesis. I had done a lot of writing in the last few years. Could I send you a sample of this and maybe the committee can decide whether this would qualify for my thesis, or could I come to Chicago and spend a semester? I would like to get the degree. A reply came back, "We understand you're writing a book. Send us sample chapters." So I have a Master's degree from Chicago Theological Seminary. My work was not basically academic but was in the action field. I also got an honorary degree of LLD (Doctor of Laws) from Antioch University in Ohio. They gave me that in 1994, me and Jim Farmer together. I have a picture on the wall here with Jim and me with our doctorate stoles around us and the plaque from Antioch.

I was in western Colorado, a little place called Norwood, when the Selective Service Act was passed in September of 1940. When I returned to seminary a group of us who had worked together in various social action concerns, peace activities, and social justice sorts of things, seriously discussed whether we should register. We decided to refuse to register and wrote a statement.

Here is a brief excerpt:

"To us the war system is an evil part of our social order and we declare we cannot cooperate with it in any way. War is an evil because it is in violation of the way of love seen in God through Christ. We do not accept war and conscription as necessary evils. For these reasons we refuse to comply with the Selective Training and Service Act. We do not expect to stem the war forces today but we're helping to build a movement that will conquer in the future."

We had a two-page statement that twenty students signed originally. Then the pressure began—pressure from parents, newspaper publicity, the government, letters, phone calls, and the seminary. The faculty passed a resolution against our taking the position. After days of struggle, there were eight of us who finally decided we would go through with it.

I decided partly on my own and partly because there were a group of us together. It was unprecedented action. There had never been anything quite like this—the fact that we were seminary students, our having worked together as a group.

Our major supporters included A. J. Muste who said, "Bravo, you're doing the right thing, this is the thing to do." Evan Thomas was the brother of Norman Thomas.

He had been a CO during the First World War and had gone to prison. He was very strong in supporting us.

People like Roger Baldwin supported us on civil liberties grounds, not that they would necessarily take the action. John Haynes Holmes, the Minister at that time of the Unitarian Community Church in New York wrote a letter saying, "I don't agree with your position, but I agree with your strong commitment."

My folks supported my action, not that they would have taken it, not that they weren't sorry to see me take it. My sisters, both older than I, wrote to me in some anguish about the action, but then gave me support. I had telegrams, letters, phone calls from people going back to my grammar school days. They saw my name in the newspaper, in some cases, my picture.

I said to myself, "All right, this is the point at which I have to be prepared to take the consequences. I shouldn't back out." I remember this as a kind of dominating feeling, although I was pretty nervous about it.

The publicity that we got was from all over the world! My Aunt Emma, saw my picture with this group of non-registrants on the *Movietone News* in the theatre and I'm told she screamed. The publicity was both pro and con, with much of it being con. The day we appeared before the Grand Jury down at Foley Square in New York, the paparazzi were out, a totally new experience for us. They followed us and finally had us cornered where we had to stop and talk with them. We were just hounded as a group. The day of our sentencing the courtroom was absolutely packed. And outside there were picket lines. My feeling was, all right, you've taken a stand, you've got to be prepared to take what goes with it.

Although the faculty had issued a joint statement against our position and the President of the Seminary,

Henry Sloane Coffin,[15] had telegraphed our folks and put pressure on them. The night before we were sentenced we had a service at the James Chapel at Union Seminary. The place was packed and there was nothing but a kind of religious support, not necessarily political, for people who had taken this position following their convictions. The service was not confrontational at all, so that support was very important to us.

Our major detractors were the faculty, Union Seminary President Henry Sloane Coffin,[15] the Selective Service Director Lewis B. Hershey[34] and the press, those who were strongly opposed. The publicity wasn't all negative. Some of it was just news, but we were put in the headlines as ones who were refusing to obey the law of the land. All of that was tremendous pressure.

What finally ended any ambivalence was the key meeting that the group of twenty of us had after all this pressure came. We met most of the day and into the night. We had to finally decide what we were going to do. Eight of us didn't register and twelve decided that they would register for one reason or another. It was an agonizing decision for everyone. In one case, his father threatened to commit suicide. I had none of that. I don't know what my response would have been if I had that kind of response from my family. I still have the letters and telegrams that came. My mother said, "I wish that there was some other way."

On registration day, which was October 16th, the eight of us went before the draft board, who came quietly to the Seminary. I'm sure that was by agreement. The Seminary didn't want us followed by the press on the way to registration. They didn't want the publicity. It had already cost the Seminary a lot. I know a lot of people were saying to Coffin, "Kick 'em out." He urged us to go home which none of us did. We handed the draft board our statement and we were immediately given a notice that we should appear before the Grand Jury.

Then we appeared before the Grand Jury. I was one of the two or three who spoke. The jurors asked us, "Do you realize you are destroying your career? Do you realize that you won't be able to get a job any place as a result of this? Why did you decide to take this? Do you realize you're imposing your will against a worthy cause?" The Grand Jury issued a "true bill," that we should go to trial on the indictment of disobeying the Selective Service Act.[57]

We appeared on November the 14th before Judge Samuel Mandelbaum in the Federal District Court. He had received hundreds of communications, which he mentioned, backing us up. He was impressed by that fact. We all made statements in the court on that day. Joe Bevilacqua said "Judge, we want you to know that we don't want any special treatment just because we're theological students. Whatever you are going to do, let it happen." All of us made a small statement of a minute or two. Then we were found guilty. There was a lot of discussion about what sentence we should get. Here were these theological students, these nice young guys, what should the government do with us? Five years and ten thousand dollars was the maximum penalty. He decided to give us a year and a day, which made it a felony rather than a misdemeanor.

We were immediately taken out and handcuffed. I was handcuffed with Joe Bevilacqua. We were taken out the back way of the court into the paddy wagon and taken down to West Street, which is a kind of federal holding place, while they decided where we were going to prison. We spent a week in West Street getting used to prison life before being taken to federal prison. The warden himself came down from Danbury in a car with one of the other officials of the prison and drove us to Danbury Federal Correctional Institution. There must have been two cars because eight of us couldn't fit in one.

Every prisoner had a work assignment. The chaplain, George Siudy, was a student at Yale Divinity School. I think he felt a little guilty that he wasn't one of us. He asked for me to work as his assistant. We gave the prison a lot of trouble. I think they were very glad to get us out of there because we were unusual prisoners to deal with. We organized inside the prison and it must have been tough for the administrators. So we got nine months, twenty days of the year and a day. I got out as I mentioned on September 3rd, 1941, having gone in on November 14th, 1940.

A. J. Muste got in touch with me at Danbury and offered me the position with Fellowship of Reconciliation (FOR)[25] in Chicago, which I was glad to take. I worked closely with Jim Farmer[23] who was a Field Representative for FOR, also located in Chicago. We eventually organized the Chicago Congress on Racial Equality (CORE).[16]

My work was to organize what we called "cell groups." I organized seventeen cell groups on Chicago's south side, at the University of Chicago, at Northwestern University, in Naperville, and in the surrounding area. We had a conference of the groups at least once a year and had an Executive Committee that met pretty regularly. I was the Executive Secretary.

We studied Gandhi's autobiography and *War Without Violence* by Krishnalal Shridharani. He had been a follower of Mahatma Gandhi in the movement in India. His excellent book outlined what nonviolence meant in working for justice in a conflict situation. We adapted that to deal with the problem of race relations.

It was partly out of that experience that the Chicago CORE[16] was organized. One of the cell groups at the

University of Chicago was an interracial group that ran into discrimination on 63rd Street at a restaurant just south of the campus. The first sit-in that we organized took place in the Jack Spratt Coffee Shop on the south side of Chicago. After a period of negotiation of trying to end discrimination with discussion didn't work, we just went in to sit there until we were served. We tried to get enough people so that the restaurant would not have too many seats left for regular patrons. They would either be forced to close the place, serve us, or have us arrested. So, we had the Jack Sprat experience.

The White City Roller Rink, also on 63rd Street, had the ruse of demanding that anyone allowed in must be a member of the club. A white person would never be asked if they were a member of the club. But a black person would be asked, "Are you a member of the club? No? You can't go in." "Can I become a member?" "You can submit an application." Of course they'd never accept it. We had a standing line at the window, with black persons in front. If they weren't served the line would not move. We got big support from the trade unions, from the NAACP, from the students and so forth. That was an important case for us at the beginning.

Jim Farmer[23] had written a memorandum to A. J. Muste outlining what a movement for racial justice on nonviolent lines should be. This memorandum was important for our discussion of the kind of movement we wanted to create. After going through some of these experiences, we had a very important Sunday afternoon meeting about what we should call ourselves. There were lots of proposals made. We came up finally with the Committee of Racial Equality and then it was shortened to CORE.[16] Word of what we were doing in Chicago got around, so pretty soon groups were springing up in New York, Denver, Pittsburgh, Syracuse, Los Angeles, all over the country. I became the executive secretary of the CORE in 1945. I was still continuing with FOR. Bayard Rustin[54] and I became the Co-secretaries of the Racial Industrial Department of FOR.

We had our first national conference in the summer of 1943. We planned as a part of it to have a sit-in at Stoner's Restaurant, a big restaurant in the Loop, the downtown section of Chicago. That became a rather famous case in our experience. The work I got into through FOR led into the organization of CORE. Then I became head of FOR's Office of Action Projects and worked from Cleveland, still maintaining the work with CORE and also with FOR. We held interracial workshops and other projects around the country.

I moved to New York in 1946. At that time my work was still with FOR and CORE. We organized the first freedom ride in 1947. The story of that is written in various places, with pamphlets as "We Challenged Jim Crow" and a TV documentary "You Don't Have to Ride Jim Crow" released on Public Television.

Word came to me primarily through Bill Sutherland that the African National Congress was going to put on a nonviolent campaign against the Apartheid laws in South Africa. As Executive Secretary of CORE, I got in touch with Walter Sisulu, Secretary General of the African National Congress (ANC) in South Africa and said, "How could we work with you?" He encouraged us, so we organized what we called "Americans for South African Resistance" of which I was the Secretary. I got people like Roger Baldwin, Norman Thomas, A. J. Muste, and somebody from the NAACP. We had quite a good Executive Committee organized and we raised funds to go to South Africa primarily through Professor Z. K. Matthews, a distinguished African scholar who was Visiting Professor of World Christianity at Union Theological Seminary in the year 1952-53, just when all of this was happening. Our funds went through him, which helped families whose breadwinner was in prison and also with legal expenses in South Africa.

When the Defiance Campaign, as they called it in South Africa, ended in early 1953 we decided we should organize a committee dealing with the whole of Africa, not just South Africa, because there were only four independent countries in Africa at that time. The campaigns against colonialism were just getting started. It was an exciting ordeal. I took a leave of absence from FOR in 1954 and spent from April to October barnstorming around Africa, where I got acquainted with the leaders in some of the freedom movements.

When I returned, I went on a speaking tour around the country for FOR and realized that I wanted to concentrate on Africa now. So I left FOR and became the Executive Director of this neophyte organization, the American Committee on Africa[1] that had no budget and no staff. A young lady that was working with Doubleday left her job and worked with me, Lydia Zemba. We had office space which was given to us by the Community Church on 35th Street just off Park Avenue in New York. We didn't have to pay any rent. We got started. I began working with the American Committee on Africa[1] in September of 1955.

I thought I would try this for six months to a year and see if we could handle it. We had two children at that time and Jean was working too. I ended up working for twenty-six years and left in 1981 when I reached sixty-five.

In December of 1958, I attended the first All African Peoples' Conference in Accra, the capital of Ghana under Nkrumah's leadership. My job was to be in touch with the leadership of the liberation movements and to do an educational job in the U.S. We put as much pressure as we could on the U.S. government to support African equality and independence. We worked with Congress and the U.N. At the time I retired, our staff consisted of about fifteen people.

In 1956, three countries became independent-- Sudan, Morocco and Tunisia. In 1957, the Gold Coast became Ghana. In 1958 Guinea, previously a French colony became independent. In 1960, seventeen countries became independent. Kenya became independent in 1963. I was there on Self Government Day June 1. Independence came in December. I had gone to the first meeting of the Organization of African Unity, which was organized in April of 1963, and from there I got into Kenya. I had always been a prohibited immigrant in all of the British territories of east and central Africa and South Africa. So I got into Kenya for the first time on June the 1st, 1963 and I have a lot of pictures taken at the home of Jomo Kenyatta on that day. I was invited to two independence celebrations in 1964, July 6th in Malawi; October the 24th, in Zambia.

Each one of these events has a long story. We had sponsored the visit to this country of Tom Mboya who was the head of the Kenya Federation of Labor. He had come in 1956 and again in 1959. By then he was practically a celebrity. His picture appeared on the front of *Time* magazine. That was the one time we had a full house in Carnegie Hall on Africa Freedom Day in April 1959, when Tom Mboya was here. We had celebrities like Harry Belafonte and Miriam Makeba on the program, lots of high level support.

In a few years the American Committee on Africa[1] really grew. It didn't become a mass movement but, as far as Africa is concerned, it was one of the few organizations that one had to pay attention to if one was interested in the field at all. The time was right to get something going. These are the only jobs I ever had, but I maintained my ministerial relationship with the Methodist Church.

Through all this, my CO decision created no road-blocks that I know of. It didn't become the threat that was made by the grand juror who said that I would suffer the consequences. I never suffered the consequences because, in a sense, I was working among sympathizers. Not that there wasn't antagonism out there, not that there wasn't opposition, but it never affected me as far as my work was concerned.

I met Jean just a few days before refusing to register. She had a China background and I had a year in China. Our first date was at the Chinese opera in Chinatown. I remember we walked across the George Washington Bridge together once and went to Fort Tryon Park once. Then I was gone, sentenced to prison.

But she came up to Danbury to visit me for half an hour twice a month because you only got an hour a month. We got acquainted sitting across the visiting table from one another and through some exchange of letters. When I got out of prison, I went to New York. I had forty-eight hours before I was to report to a parole officer in Denver. That was my home, I had to report back there and my folks were there. I had the parole officer out there. So I just had long enough, forty-eight hours in New York to pick my stuff up at the seminary and arrange to go to Denver.

During that time I saw Jean and we met each other, Thanksgiving in New York, Christmas in Chicago, Easter in New York, and we got married in June of 1942. Then I was in Chicago working with FOR. I got strong support from Jean. Pacifism was a part of our life so we didn't have many discussions. We had a life and it was part of our daily experience.

Our children were taught about pacifism through example. Through being in a home that was related to the cause, the people that came into the home, our friends, the meetings we went to, and the activities of their parents. Basically that was it. That would be an interesting question to ask our children, who are no longer children. All of our children grew up here in Skyview Acres. Dave registered as a CO and did alternative service under the act when he was younger. He's now 61. Our oldest granddaughter Emily is involved with work that takes her to Vietnam and to South Africa. They call it "Room to Read" and she is one of their key executives and a program director for this organization. I think there's been a certain influence on our children because of environment.

I have been involved in a lot of pacifist escapades, vigils, marches, in Washington and elsewhere, and CORE activities. My activities have supported liberation struggles in Africa, but liberation struggles have not always been pacifist. How should I as a pacifist relate to a struggle that may take the form of some violence? That's a whole big question by itself. All of my actions have been based upon my particular philosophy of nonviolent struggle.

I don't have any major regrets but I've often thought what my life would have been had I, instead of working with FOR, CORE and the American Committee on Africa,[1] taken a church. I was an ordained Methodist clergyman, a member of the Rocky Mountain Annual Conference. If I had gone that route, I could have been in a church some place.

I never figured that whatever I did was going to change the world. There has been change and I think that we have played a small role in it—the civil rights struggle, the work of CORE, the Freedom Rides. CORE played a major roll in that. Our "Journey of Reconciliation" was in 1947. One thinks of the Freedom Riders in 1961, nevertheless it was our plan in 1947, "You Don't Have to Ride

Jim Crow." We were before our time in a sense, but it led to the up thrust of the movement. It helped in that respect.

The work with the American Committee on Africa[1] recognized the possibility of one of the great developments of the twentieth century, the freedom campaigns from colonial domination. There are disappointments as one thinks about what has happened over the years since 1960, but seventeen countries became independent that year. The American Committee on Africa was the beginning of the movement against Apartheid in South Africa. We initiated the campaign of disinvestment from South Africa with our bank campaign. This was picked up and became a major issue until sanctions were passed by US Congress over President Reagan's veto in the 1980s.

So I have been part of something that has helped to change race relations, and has led to a strong anti-apartheid, anti-colonial freedom movement. I'm proud that in

one area where I did a lot of work, in race relations, there have been significant changes even if racism still exists.

The struggle still goes on. The Portuguese expression, *a luta continua* (the struggle continues) comes out of the African experience. And it always does. It never ends because there's always justice and injustice, peace and conflict. One is confronted by these issues and has to take a position of some sort or another. One must find one's peace in the midst of the struggle.

I believe in taking one step at a time. Each step leads to a new set of choices. Take that first step, one step at a time. "One step enough for me" is a Gandhi motto. These are basic philosophies that I would pass on.

Chapter Seven
Philosopher and Mystic

Chapter Seven
Philosopher and Mystic

Richard (Brad) Angell

Stephen L. Angell

In this last chapter we have another pair of siblings. One knew he was a pacifist when he was in his crib. The other struggled mightily until he made his decision. One is reasoned as he orders his life rationally while the other is a mystic. One became a professor of Philosophy and the other a national leader in social work. After he retired, he traveled the globe converting those incarcerated for violent behavior into insightful citizens. One trusts logos, the other trusts logos and the spirit.

Richard (Brad) Angell (1918)

"I think I have more or less settled on continuing the CO stand. It is the most awful state of confusion, though."

My family were Congregationalists when I began. It was a religious family, not an evangelical religious family, but we went to church regularly every Sunday, and we were expected to go to Sunday school, which we did.

Several summers before I was 15, we began going to a Quaker Meeting[52] in Chappaqua, NY. This was much more satisfying to me than listening to a minister every week, or to my Sunday school teachers, because it was a place where people gave their own individual feelings and expressions and they were not trying to prescribe for others.

At 15 or so I joined the Quakers and subsequently my family joined. How important this is in the question of my being a pacifist, I don't know. My folks were not pacifists. My mother argued against my going into the Army, but I had the feeling this was because she didn't want her children to be in harm's way.

When I was in Bronxville High School, the class of 1936, I started a "peace club." I was quite interested in peace and this is what I seemed to be known for as seen in this excerpt from the Bronxville's yearbook. "Richard Angell loves peace. Therefore he is president of Bronxville's Peace Club. He is a fine actor [and] has won great honors in public speaking."

But also typical of that period is a poem I wrote in the mid-1930s:

The world can go to hell –

And fire all its cannon and shoot up all its shell,

There's just one thing I know – by God I know it well:

Interviewed and transcribed by Terry Engeman

You won't get me to trod that path that's leading you to hell.

You can drop your cans of dynamite,

And spread your yellow gases,

And make your preacher talk like fools,

And make your people asses,

And worry off your diplomats,

And murder off your masses ...

You won't find me a-mingling there

To poison someone else's air.

I've got a life to live, a goal to get;

A sun to reach high noon and then to set.

I'll wander off into the woods and when your war is over

You can come round and talk to me of bees and yellow clover.

At Swarthmore College I was active in the American Student Union, which was the most liberal student organization and part of that I construed as being peace work. I also was active in the International Club and attended Quaker meetings. I was affected by the fact that it was a good Quaker college. This attitude toward pacifism probably stayed with me through that period.

I graduated from college in 1940, and in the summer I went to work for the Department of Agriculture and took surveys of people that were on welfare, that had to do with how they arranged for food stamps. When that assignment was over, in the summer of 1941, before Pearl Harbor was attacked, I came home. I was riding the rails of freight trains at that time. On my birthday I stopped off at a little town in Kentucky or Tennessee because I was required to register for the draft. I registered as a CO.[17]

In 1941, after an interval being employed as a social worker, I went to graduate school at the Fels Institute for Local and State Government at the University of

Pennsylvania. By that time I had decided that I wanted to go into government, because that was where the big problems were being solved. I was very enthusiastic about Philadelphia, and thought I would like to be the mayor some time!

I remember the day Pearl Harbor was attacked. I had two roommates, all of us working at the Fels Institute, and we got up and began marching around, singing, "We're in the Army now!"

I still had to make decisions as to what I was going to do. I went to the draft board in Scarsdale, New York, which was my home town, and there I said that I wanted to be a CO. I cited the fact that I had marched in peace parades, that I had started a peace club, and that I was a Quaker, so I had quite a few things. They counseled me to go cautiously, and they gave me some arguments, but I was registered as one.

On February 28, 1942, while still in the graduate program at Penn, I got a letter from my local draft board Number 742 in the town of Eastchester, New York. With it was an order from the President of the United States "to report for work of national importance" at Petersham in Worcester County, Massachusetts on March 9th. On March 3rd I got a nice letter from the Assistant Director of the CPS¹⁴ Camp at Petersham to welcome me and described what was coming.

"I am glad that you are going to be with us, and trust that despite the disappointment of having to give up your normal way of life, you will find here an opportunity to share in and contribute to an experiment, which if properly done, will carry on the testimony left by those Friends and pacifists who have gone before.

"You will find camp rough physically, with crude plumbing, privies, and relatively crowded living quarters. You will find camp gentle mentally and spiritually. We try to avoid the danger of Christian Anarchism, or license, but at the same time try to have respect for personality which allows problems to be worked out by a mutual sharing between the campers and the staff. Certain things are expected: neatness of person and bunk, promptness, and general kindliness."

I somehow got a deferment that allowed me to finish that semester. In the meantime I began to think very much about what I wanted to do, and to reconsider whether I wanted to be a CO. I worried whether I would be able to go into politics or whether my being a CO would work against it. But that wasn't the only consideration. It was also clear to me that Hitler was not going to be stopped by arguments from pacifists, and that he had to be stopped, probably by force. Other people were out there and they were undergoing danger to their lives, and I thought I ought to be part of it:

Here is an excerpt from was a five-page single spaced letter that I wrote on February 2, 1942.

"I think I have more or less settled on continuing the CO stand. It is the most awful state of confusion, though.

"After war was declared I thought very seriously about it. It seemed for a while that the act of the Japanese was so brutal, or rather deceitful, that they constituted a greater menace to the world than war itself. It seems to me that no society can be run where people don't speak honestly and truthfully, or where they implement their plans with methods of deceit and force. I was so confused that I finally decided to go out to Swarthmore and talk it over with someone out there. When I got there, I went to the room of Don Pelz and his roommate Hewson Swift. Don is the leader of a little pacifist group there. I argued with him for about two hours, the main purpose being to clarify my thought. At the end of the two hours he had convinced me that the Japanese attack didn't change things fundamentally. It was really a part of the bigger strategy of the Axis, and it indicated no new method or purpose. However, I walked out saying that since the war was here there is nothing an individual can do about it, the issue is which side you want to win. And there could be no doubt in my mind that the English and Americans with all their many faults promised a better net result from victory than the Axis. No individual could stop it, I said, and on the other hand what this individual does is not going to affect the outcome. Part of my argument was based on the future effect of being a pacifist on a political career. Since individual action does not affect the outcome in grander terms, why not leave the individual interest to be the deciding factor.

"The next day, after having announced that I thought I would renounce the CO stand, I got a card from the draft board telling me that I was classified as a CO.

"It's funny, I don't know whether I lack resolve, or what, but since then I talked to my roommates, some of the pacifists in Pat's [my cousin's] "Brudercoop," a Friend named Alfred Cope who served in Spain distributing food. I haven't sent the renunciation in. I have varied on an average of twice daily from wanting to join the Air Corps to believing that the Quaker stand is altogether right. Understand I don't want to join the Air Corps because I hate the Japs, ... but if I join the armed forces there is no reason why I shouldn't go the whole way. Once you accept the principle that the war can stop anything, or is going to produce a net good, then all things in the war method are justified. I can't hate the Japs because I always think of Yoko [a Japanese classmate in college] who was about as westernized and well-balanced a girl as I knew in college.

"... My whole approach is from the point of view of a utilitarian ethics. That is, war is justified or not insofar as it contributes to the greatest good of the greatest number. It is conceivable, on the basis of this approach, that war might produce a better alternative, bad as it was, than some other things. That makes the problem become one of weighing all the factors to see whether the net result of the war will be worse than the net result if there were resistance, or, specifically, whether the Axis un-resisted would be worse than the effects of a war to annihilate them."

There follow three single-spaced pages of numbered "points" to consider, both pro and con. In conclusion,

"I want to do the greatest good for the greatest number. I want to do that through a political career. But, a political career will probably be much hampered by the stigma, if it is such, of pacifism. Perhaps I would contribute most to the general good if I took part and then came back and rose to positions of influence, and did the good things in reconstructing. I have wondered about this. The answer seems to be that I believe in a man's being true to himself. Truth, I believe, is essential if a society is to be stable and progressive. Strength of character, [the] ability to deny oneself present pleasures for future [pleasures], is also essential. I may ruin a career, but, men recognize sincerity and perhaps that is more worthwhile keeping than the other."

For weeks I struggled with the various possibilities, and eventually resolved it by deciding to volunteer with the medics in the 20th General Hospital that was being organized by Colonel I. S. Ravdin, a surgeon at the Medical School of the University of Pennsylvania. As a medic, I would not be called upon to kill, but would be in a position to help save lives both of allied and enemy soldiers, and I would be part of the effort to stop Hitler. I went to see Dr. Ravdin, and wrote my parents a letter that reports that interview.

"I saw Dr. Ravdin Friday. He said that I looked like the kind of man that they could use and he sent me down to see a Sergeant Lucas in the Dispensary at the Schuylkill Arsenal. ... He said I would be "an outstanding individual in our organization." ... I think I would rather go into this unit than the New York unit which Col. Salisbury suggested because I wish to be sent from Philadelphia. Also, I think it is definitely fixed that I am attached to a medical unit now, so the worry about getting shunted into something else is dissipated."

So this is what I decided to do. After the semester ended, I reported to Camp Clayburn in Louisiana and underwent training as a buck private. Then they gave various I.Q. Tests and decided to send me off for training in Officers Corps. So I would stay with the medics, but would be sent to Texas, for three months training as a medical administrative officer.

After that I was assigned to the 30th Infantry Division and was Assistant to the division's Surgeon General, the head of its medical operations. I did a lot of record-keeping for the division surgeon's office. A division has about 15,000 people in it, three regiments with about 3,000 soldiers in each, plus a lot of support groups, including a medical battalion. Later on I was sent to the medical battalion where I dealt with supplies and logistics, and kept the records. The real medics, the ones who pulled the soldiers in from the battlefield, were at the company level.

Our battalion was a clearing hospital where we processed not only our own soldiers but enemy soldiers and other people that were injured. Most of our casualties were our own soldiers, but the worst casualties we had in the war, were when our own bombers hit our own people by mistake. I remember one particular day in St. Lo, France. Our division had landed about nine days after VE Day, when we first invaded France. There was heavy bombing to break through the German lines. It succeeded, but in the process they hit the wrong targets, and there were four hundred casualties in that one day alone, almost all our own soldiers, which was the highest number of casualties for any one day.

I was aware that in effect I was part of the Army. I had a uniform, I followed Army orders, and I saluted people. Although we had a little target practice in training, I never carried a gun and of course I never shot anybody.

Immediately after the Nazis surrendered, I went with a fellow officer who was a doctor to a place where the Germans had herded their political prisoners all into a barn, sprayed them with gasoline and set the whole thing on fire. Along the way we noticed prisoner's bodies that lay alongside the road in their striped uniforms. I went with this same doctor to a place where a train was unloaded that had a lot of political prisoners, I suppose most of them were Jews headed for concentration camps, and they were in very poor shape. We helped them along with supplies.

This didn't affect my marriage. I wasn't married until 1949, after I'd been in graduate school at Harvard for three years.

My vocational ideas changed during the war. I became aware of how people had to act if they were going to go into politics. What seemed to me to be political activity, particularly at the division level, was that in order to get things done you have to go around and make friends. You have to make a lot of compromises, although they might be ones you could live with. That just wasn't congenial to my way of thinking.

In high school I tried to start a philosophy club, and in college I loved Philosophy. During the war I got hold of an article from *Fortune* magazine by the best-known American philosopher at that time, John Dewey[19] and I decided I was going to apply to go into Philosophy instead of politics.

Also as a result of the war, I saw how soldiers seemed to lose all of their ethical inhibitions when they got into a situation that it wasn't their hometown where people could watch what they were doing. They stole things and took advantage of people. I decided that maybe Philosophy with its interest in ethics particularly, might have some long-term benefits if we could work out a way to get people to solve problems more rationally.

When I came back, I went to see John Dewey and talked to him about the possibility of going into philosophy. He had written a book called *How We Think* that impressed me a lot. As a result of this conversation I applied to study philosophy in several schools, including Harvard, and was accepted at Harvard.

After leaving Harvard I taught at a variety of colleges and universities, chiefly Ohio Wesleyan and Wayne State University. My interest in peace was not diminished by having served in the Army. I helped found a Quaker meeting in Delaware, Ohio. In 1971 our Friends Meeting in Birmingham, Michigan, hosted an AFSC[4] "Peace Caravan" that came through for two weeks, which resulted in the organization of the Oakland County Center for Peace and National Priorities. I was its President for the first seven years and it is still operating 36 years later. My wife and I also helped start, and served as officers in, a local chapter of the United Nations Association, U.S.A. At Wayne State University I taught courses on Philosophies of Peace and War and served on the Board of its Center for Peace and Conflict Studies.

In recent years, partly as a result of Ken Burns' documentary on the Civil War, which I watched very carefully, I came to the conclusion that I'm not a complete pacifist, because I believe some wars have been beneficial. In particular the Civil War preserved our Union, got rid of slavery, and eventually presented to the world the model of a federation of different states, giving rise to the United Nations. If we hadn't won that war, we would have two countries, with slavery next door to us, and a broken model of federal government.

I think all wars could be avoided if people were sufficiently endowed with rationality and goodwill. Most wars are wrong, and going to war should always be an absolute last resort. I joined vigils against the Iraq War, which I think was utterly wrong, and I even feel that the War in Afghanistan was wrongly instigated. The "War on Terror" is a dangerous misnomer, providing excuses for all sorts of misdeeds. Preventive war based on suspected intent should never be allowed. The United Nations, though imperfect, is the United States' greatest contribution to date to the peace of the rest of the world and it should be strengthened, not weakened.

I believe that Quakerism should continue its traditional peace testimony, including encouragement of complete pacifism for those who can believe in it. I admire people that honestly hold that view and stick to it during wars. We need such people to counterbalance the great majority, but I'm not a good Quaker in that I'm not a complete pacifist.

Stephen L. Angell (1919)

"I know experientially that there is a power well beyond my comprehension that can give direction to my life. ... I have clearly experienced times when the direction for my life seemed to have come from outside myself."

Iknew from a very early age that I am a pacifist. I was born right after the end of World War I and one of my earliest remembrances is hearing the adults talking about the war. I can remember lying in my bed and thinking, this doesn't make any sense—men in trenches just a few yards apart shooting at one another, trying to kill one another. If I were there, I would just get out of the trench and say to everybody, "This doesn't make any sense, why don't we all go home?" I was probably five or six, and so I knew from that time that war didn't make any sense to me. My mother was a pacifist, but my father was not. He wasn't outspoken, he probably wouldn't have signed up as a CO,[17] but he wasn't a warlike person.

My family were Congregationalists. But a few generations back my great-great-grandfather had been read out of a Friends meeting because he married someone who wasn't a Quaker. She actually was a descendent of John Bowne who had opened his home to Quakers in New Amsterdam for worship. My uncle, Stephen Holden, found the Quakers in Chappaqua, New York, which was near our summer home in Pleasantville. The Holdens attended Meeting and introduced us to Meeting when I was twelve or thirteen. Our family joined the Friends Meeting in Chappaqua, however, my parents retained a connection to the Congregational Church in Scarsdale. So I really have been a Friend from an early age.

In those plush days we had two homes. Pleasantville was our summer residence and Scarsdale was our winter residence. Our father was in real estate. Then, during the

---

Interviewed and transcribed by Mary R. Hopkins

Depression, he owned quite a bit of property on which he had to keep paying taxes, but had no buyers. By the time the depression was ending, we had lost both of our homes, and he had lost all of the property he owned. But he never gave up on his business although the business was very poor in many of those years.

My uncle, who was married to my mother's sister, was very much a mentor for me. My parents were also, of course. My father's name was Stephen, my name was Stephen, my uncle's name was Stephen, his son was named Stephen, and we both had sons named Stephen. I had great admiration for my uncle. In the summer we lived in Pleasantville on a small farm and my uncle had horses. We used to go horseback riding together. Of course we had gardens. I had a cousin a year younger and a brother a year older and we did many things together.

I was a kid that generally didn't get into fights. But I remember one boy who used to sort of beat up on me.

So I told my parents I wanted boxing lessons. They were very intelligent parents and I think they recognized I needed to protect myself. They signed me up at the YMCA for boxing lessons. And I got just enough training in boxing that the next time this kid bothered me, I got him in a corner of the playground where the buildings came together and started hitting him. I didn't stop until he went off crying. His parents called my parents and told them what an awful thing I'd done and chastised me for it. My parents didn't say, "Oh, that was fine, Steve," but on the other hand I could tell they thought, "Well, it worked." So, he never bothered me again and I never bothered him again. However, he wasn't one of my good friends. The lesson for me was that I can't just let others push me around. I need to stand up for myself. Punching may have been an age-appropriate response at that time, but there are many other options for a mature individual.

I had two older brothers. Gardner was my protector and Richard was the one who bugged me. But when I was thirteen we just decided this doesn't make any sense and we were the best of friends from then on. In my childhood I loved to ride my bicycle and I was very active in the Boy Scouts, as were my brothers. I tended to concentrate on having one particular friend and we always did things together, like building huts. I wasn't into sports because I wasn't that well coordinated. In grade school I formed a garden club to work on some grounds around the school and make the world more beautiful. I started a school newssheet in elementary school. In high school I was manager of the baseball team and by that means earned a sports letter.

In school, I read what was assigned, but I wasn't a bookworm. I didn't pick up and read stuff at that early age. I wasn't into comics. I guess I just read the available books. Our family always had lots of books around. I still have the bookcases. Math was always a favorite, but also Civics, Social Studies, Geography, and History. Bronxville High School was a regular public high school, but I believe everybody was college prep because Bronxville was like Scarsdale, an affluent New York suburb.

In my early teenage years my father had a really good real estate business. I was the youngest son, but the one who had shown the most interest in selling things.

I was presumed to be the son that would come into my father's business and take it over. I heard this expectation stated now and then. At one point I had to leave a conversation that was taking place with visitors, because I had come to the realization that wasn't what I wanted to do with my life. When my mother or father came to find out what was wrong, I was tearful and told them it just wasn't something that I felt I wanted to do with my life. And I never heard the expectation stated again. They just took me at my word that I wanted to do something different with my life. I did not want to be a real-estate salesman.

I had followed my brother Richard in school, so I was always Richard's younger brother and teachers always expected me to be like my older brother. When it came to college he went to Swarthmore and I decided I was no longer going to be Richard's younger brother. While I was still in high school I liked to sing, so my mother got me a New York City voice teacher at a much reduced rate, and I took voice training for part of a year. We scouted around and found Bard College, which had just been taken over by Columbia University. They offered me a very good scholarship, so I entered Bard College for my freshman year. These were depression times and Bard wasn't doing well enough for Columbia to be satisfied with what the tuition rate was bringing in. Consequently, they doubled the tuition at which point my parents decided, "We can't afford to finance Steve in Bard anymore." Hamilton College was able to give us a good financial assistance plan, so I entered my sophomore year at Hamilton College near Utica, New York.

At Bard I majored in Sociology and Political Science, but Hamilton didn't have any Sociology so there I majored in Political Science and Economics. The Economics course was a fluke. Hamilton wasn't up to it and it was really an economic course for teachers, Education Economics. I didn't get a great deal out of that, but Political Science,

Geology and Mathematics were really my major subjects. My actual degree was a Bachelor of Science (B.S.) because at Hamilton you had to take either Greek or Latin to get a B.A. degree and languages weren't my thing.

By the time I graduated from Hamilton, I was beginning to focus in the social studies area. I was a Camp Counselor in the summer, and had a very good Camp Director, who was also a Guidance Counselor in the White Plains schools. He helped me to focus my attention and gave me some tests. It came out that I had an aptitude for Social Work as a profession.

It was when I was in college that World War II started, but I registered as a CO. My draft board didn't want to have a CO. That was a bad mark on their records, so they gave me a 4-F classification which meant I was physically unfit. I asked them why I was physically unfit and they said I had athlete's foot.

As I finished college, I had help from this same guidance counselor in selecting a graduate school. I applied to the New York School of Social Work and the University of Chicago School of Social Service Administration, which were two of the major schools of Social Work in the country at that point. I got accepted at both places but decided I had been in my home territory long enough and needed to spread my wings, so I chose Chicago.

My first year in the School of Social Work in Chicago was the year the Japanese bombed Hawaii. Then the draft situation changed and draft boards were told to go over all their registrants and re-classify all those who couldn't be substantiated under the new guidelines. They could no long justify a 4-F classification so at that point they classified me as a CO, 4-E. They never questioned my claim. I guess that was because I was a Quaker, and my family was well known. The members of the draft board were all local people. Consequently, they just accepted me and never called me in for further clarification. The

Pastor of the Congregational church was very supportive and gave me a Pocket New Testament, which I carry to this day in my suitcase wherever I go. I did not experience any real situations of rejection on the basis of my having taken the CO stand. If anything, my stand raised people's attitudes toward me. It was never a hindrance in any way that I can recall.

That summer right after Pearl Harbor, I was doing camp counseling work in Huguenot, New York, with boys from the New York City area. I had been re-classified but they stayed my induction because my Camp Director, Spot Noyce, wrote a letter saying that I was in a job of national importance, working with them caring for these young kids. So I didn't enter until September, after the camp season was over.

I went directly to a CPS[14] camp in the mountains of New Hampshire. Since I loved nature and the mountains, they couldn't have found a more delightful place for me. I just loved it there. But my conscience weighed heavily that I wasn't really doing work of national importance. I was just having a damn good time. It was an AFSC[4] unit run by the Quakers, and they were looking around for special projects that individuals could sign up for.

One of the projects was trying to find a powder that would destroy lice that are the carriers of typhus and cholera, potential dangers in the planned invasion of Southern Europe. We had a chance to volunteer to be in this experiment, which I thought was a delightful opportunity. We didn't know what kind of powder we got because they were trying out various substances. We were each given underwear briefs with a patch in it and in the patch were a certain number of lice. We had to wear that same pair of briefs for three solid weeks and never wash them, powder them daily. Once a week we had to turn in our briefs, and the number of lice were counted. I didn't have the assignment to count them, thank goodness.

We were building a road around Mount Moosilauki that could be used in case of forest fires. This was a really important task we were doing. Also we were wearing this underwear. And evidently I didn't have the good stuff because my lice survived. While I was still in the louse camp, AFSC[4] opened up a special service unit in Maryland in a school for black delinquent boys. There was an opening for a Social Worker. I already had a year of graduate school at University of Chicago, so I was switched from the Forestry Camp, which I loved, even with the lice, and went to Cheltenham School for Boys where I was for three years. That was a nifty experience, because that school was sort of neglected. For black delinquent children it didn't have to have the finest facilities. But we were two social workers and two psychologists, and we set up a psychosocial clinic in that institution that far exceeded anything that existed in the institutions for white youth in the state.

The Judge couldn't believe our reports when the boys came up for parole. They got better psychological results from Cheltenham than from any other institution in the state. It was an excellent experience. Then the AFSC[4] decided it could no longer in good conscience run a CPS[14] camp, because it was cooperating too much with conscription. They closed that unit and I was transferred to a mental hospital in Connecticut, a Brethren unit, where they needed a Social Worker. I worked for a year as a Social Worker in that institution which was another excellent experience. I came through my CPS[14] experience really with improved preparation for the profession I had chosen.

I did not have trouble getting a Social Work job. I went immediately back to the University of Chicago after CPS and completed my degree there. The Dean of the School of Social Work, Edith Abbott, was a leading light in Social Work education at that time. I guess she was a pacifist herself. When I graduated I was readily accepted as a caseworker at Family Services in Chicago. There wasn't any prejudicial attitude there. I was a caseworker in Family Services of Chicago for three years and then decided to switch to community organization work. I sent out applications. There was not the slightest indication that my war record was a hindrance. In fact, it was a plus because of the kinds of experiences that I had.

In 1948, just after I had gotten out of graduate school, I got married. When I was in Chicago before the war, Barbara's father, Clyde Allee, an internationally known ecologist, was my counselor who helped me develop my application for CO status. I didn't know her at that time, but I knew of her. When I was in the CPS unit in Cheltenham, I made a trip to Philadelphia and met her there where she was working for the AFSC.[4] Later, she said, "You looked me up and down." When I got out of CPS, I was back in Chicago and she was there, too, in the same Friends Meeting. I started making a list of eligible females and Barbara was on that list. I figured when I finished my professional education, I would need a wife, so I had better start looking. Here I was in Social Work School, surrounded by females. Yes, a couple of them were on the list too!

We thought it was better not to have children too close together because then they would all arrive at college age at the same time and it might be more expensive than we could easily manage. So we spaced them three, four, and four years apart. Barbara was in Early Childhood Education. She had her Master's degree so I will say no more about how we raised them. She schooled me. I can only remember using corporal punishment once, which I immediately regretted. Our children have remained connected to Friends, two more closely than the others. Our oldest son, Stephen Warder, named after his two grandfathers, is the Quakerism professor at Earlham School of Religion. Sam is the one who lives nearby and is quite active in Germantown Friends meeting. Our daughter remains a member of Bulls Head Friends Meeting, but is not active in any meeting. She is quite musical and plays the organ for services in a local church. Our other son, Tom, has a strong Christian commitment, holding worship services in his home and attending meetings where he senses a strong commitment to Jesus Christ.

When I got my first job as a caseworker with Family Services in Chicago in 1949, there were United Fund and Health and Welfare Planning Councils. I decided I wanted to be more in the social planning aspects of the work, so I applied for and was accepted at Hartford, Connecticut, as a staff member in their planning council and was there for three years. After that I held a series of jobs in health and welfare planning. The only way to move up was to move on to other jobs in larger communities. I went from Greater Hartford Community Council to the Health and Welfare Planning Council of Philadelphia, Delaware and Montgomery Counties, where I was Assistant Director in the Delaware County District. From there I went to Allentown where I was the Executive Director of the Planning Council of Lehigh County. From there I went to Nassau County, New York, where I was Executive of a Planning Council serving a population of a million five hundred thousand people. This was an important step up. Nassau County is on Long Island, just outside of New York.

From there I was invited to the national staff of United Community Fund and Councils of America to oversee a project to bring activities of planning councils into better coordination. United Fund's Office of Economic Opportunity program was funded by the Federal Government's "War on Poverty." There was some disarray because the Federal Government came in with this huge program that overlapped with what local health and welfare planning councils and United Funds were doing. They wanted to find ways of integrating those services so they would be working together rather than at cross-purposes with one another.

I was Director of this National Project in Health and Welfare Planning. We planned and executed six conferences, which covered the entire country. In these conferences we drew together not only the top staff of the economic opportunity programs that the government had set up, but the United Fund executives and the Community Council executives. These nationwide institutes served as an informational base for getting people talking together and hopefully working together. As a follow up, I designed a program on coalition planning that looked at specific ways of combining and coordinating these operations.

At that point I decided that I wanted to go into business for myself as a consultant. And since this job had been offered to me at the national level with a known termination period of one year, I said that I'd take the job if they would also approve of my developing my consultation practice in places around the country where they needed help in solving problems in health and welfare planning. When I developed the coalition-planning project, I had them contract with the consulting firm that I established. That way I launched myself into a consulting business that held together for the next twenty-five years. I worked all over the eastern and mid-western parts of the country. Then I retired.

During the Vietnam War, my wife and I were distressed at paying income taxes which were helping to support something which we felt was dreadfully wrong, so how were we to get out of this? Because I had a wage-paying job, our taxes were automatically taken out of my pay. As long as others employed me, I had no recourse.

Going into business for myself gave us the opportunity to regulate our lives so we didn't have to pay income taxes. We moved from Long Island to the family farm in Dutchess County, New York. My cousins sold us five acres and we built our house on that. We were able to regulate my earnings so that we never owed any taxes by setting up a family corporation called Polytypic Enterprises, many types of enterprises, which was the vision. It involved the whole family. The two older children had already gone off to Westtown School and college. The younger boys really loved the rural environment. My cousin was milking one or two cows, so the boys could help with the milking. We also bought beef cattle and had animals that we could sell. Along with their schoolwork, the boys helped my cousin with farm chores, so that was another enterprise besides my consulting business. My wife was hired as a Secretary to the corporation. These were the sources of income, plus we could live more simply and raise a lot of our own food. I kept bees, so we had lots of honey. It was a total immersion in trying to be as self-supporting as we could be, and we were able to avoid paying any federal income tax through the time of the Vietnam War.

It was during this time period that I had the most momentous experience of my life. In June of 1970, President Nixon was in office and it was a time of great national unrest over the Vietnam War. On this particular weekend, I was traveling from Long Island to Washington to attend a meeting of the Friends Committee on National Legislation Executive Committee.[27] It also happened to be the weekend of the largest anti-Vietnam War demonstration which took place following the killing four Kent State University students demonstrating against the war. I had made appointments in Washington in connection with my consulting business that required rather precise planning of my travel time.

Before leaving for Washington, a call had come to me from a Quaker friend, which I was not home to receive. The message was that he had heard I was going to Washington and he urgently wanted to talk to me before I left. I got this message after my scheduled departure time had passed, so I took his number to call him en route. The message was that some Quakers and others would be gathering in Lafayette Park, opposite the White House to hold Richard Nixon in the Light (pray for God's guidance for him) and that he hoped I would be able to attend. I said I could not promise because I was uncertain about all of my other commitments but I would be there if I could.

As I continued on my journey to Washington, the route I found myself taking was not the route I would ordinarily have taken to be where I wanted to be when I arrived in Washington. I was listening to my car radio. Much of the news was about the national unrest, the aftermath of the Kent State killings, the upcoming demonstration in Washington and a report that the President was at Camp David. I was very much focused on my travel progress and getting to Washington for my 1:00 PM appointment and all seemed to be going well.

It was at this time that I got a message that I should go to Camp David and give a message to the President. This took me completely by surprise since I had no previous thought of doing anything like this. First of all, I had no notion of how to get to Camp David and secondly I did not know what the message was that I should give to the President. This had to be a whole lot of nonsense, I thought, and I was right on time to meet my personal commitments. I kept trying to put this out of my mind but it would not let me go.

I kept on driving and found myself in the Catoctin Mountains. I came to a side road that led to the right off the main highway and received the instruction that I should turn there. It was not a road I had ever been on before and I had no notion where it was going. It made no sense to turn there and I refused to do it. I drove on down the highway for about two miles and I literally could not drive any further. I had to pull the car over to the side of the road. This requires another story.

A few months earlier, I heard over the radio that on a given date Norman Vincent Peale, a spiritual advisor to Richard Nixon, was going to have open office hours at his church in New York City and anyone who wanted to come in and talk to him could do so. I got a message then that I should go in to see Dr. Peale and talk to him about his support of President Nixon and the conduct of the war in Vietnam. I tried to put this out my mind as something I did not want to do. However, on the day these office hours were to occur, I was on the subway in New York City. I had no conflicting appointments and could easily have continued on to the proper subway stop and gone in to see Dr. Norman Vincent Peale, but I refused to do so. This left me extremely uncomfortable, so uncomfortable that I finally said "Please let me go this time, I promise if you ever again ask me to do something like this, I will do it." This was the next time!

I turned my car around and went back to the road where I had been instructed to turn. A short way down the road was a billboard advertising an orchard and I thought "good, I will end up in someone's orchard and I can turn around, forget this nonsense and go on my way." The road, however, went right through the orchard and came to a T intersection. I said "OK you're in charge which way do I turn?" The instruction was to turn to the left. I then began to think, well if I am supposed to go to Camp David, maybe I should stop and ask how to get there. But then I thought, "No, if I am supposed to get there, I will get there." I continued to travel down the road I was on and came to a National Park. The instruction was to turn into the park. There was a park office there where I thought I could ask my way but my answer to myself was again, "No, if I am supposed to get there, I will get there." I traveled into the park not a very long distance, rounded a curve and saw a sign, Camp David. This was such an

overpowering experience that I had to pull over to the
side of the road and regain my composure.

Now that I was at Camp David, I had to do it. I
thought they would think I was crazy if I told them I had
a message for the President but I didn't know what it
was. I pulled up to the gatehouse. There were two officers inside. One officer asked me what my business was
and I said I had come with a message for the President.
He said if I gave it to him he would see that the President
received it. I said that I could not give him the message
but I could only tell him how I got there and started to
tell my story. While I was talking to the one officer, the
other one was on the telephone. He finally came over and
spoke to the officer listening to me. The officer then told
me if I would pull my car off to the side, one of the president's staff would come out and speak with me. I did this
and very shortly a man came from inside the compound
and sat down in the passenger seat of my car.

I related my story of how I got to Camp David and
then reached the point of relating a message which until
that moment I had no notion of what it would be. I had
faith that when the time came the words would be there.
My feelings and opinions about Richard Nixon were very
negative. I have no clear recollection of what my exact
words were, but I remember that all of a sudden I had a
great sense of compassion for the man. My words con-
veyed this by acknowledging the great weight and concern he must be under for the state of the country and the
difficult decisions he must make. I went on to say that on
Sunday at 11:00 AM Quakers and others would be holding a Meeting for Worship in Lafayette Park to pray for
him and that he might be well guided in the decisions
that he had to make. I said that we would welcome him
among us, however, we would understand if he could
not be there but hoped that he might worship with us
from inside the White House.

The presidential staff person wanted information about me. It just happened that the most recent issue of the FCNL newsletter was profiling some of the leadership, so my picture was there with an accompanying article. I reached into my attaché case on the back seat of the car and there on top of a pile of papers was this recent publication. I handed this to him and he left.

I was then able to resume my trip to Washington. It was reported that the President had gone from the White House to the Lincoln Memorial to talk with anti-war demonstrators. The President did not attend the Meeting in Lafayette Park. I did, however, write him a letter expressing our regret that he could not be with us. The compassionate feelings that came over me while at Camp David were still with me. A week or so later I received a three or four sentence letter of appreciation for my letter signed by Richard Nixon that appeared to me to be authentic.

The impact of this experience has shaped the remainder of my life because I know experientially that there is a power well beyond my comprehension that can give direction to my life. While I have had no repeat experiences quite as dramatic as this one, I have clearly experienced times when the direction for my life seemed to have come from outside myself.

When the Vietnam War ended I started taking on some jobs, like helping to develop nutrition centers for the elderly and as Executive Director of the local Family Service Agency. This meant some salaried situations where they would take money out of my pay for taxes, but the war was over and we didn't feel as conflicted. I retired from Family Services of Dutchess County in 1984 and began drawing on my Social Security. This part of my life had been geared to try and live out more fully my desire not to participate in funding war while still doing constructive work. I closed out Polytypic Enterprises about 1990.

Retirement didn't actually let up on my work a great deal, because for more than three years I served as a part-time Field Secretary for Friends Committee on National Legislation and I was still doing some of my consulting work, although not with the same intensity as before. In the meantime the Alternatives to Violence Project (AVP)[2] started in New York Yearly Meeting. By the time I was three years into my retirement I was also doing AVP work. That has kept me busy every since.

The Alternatives to Violence Project started in 1975 in New York Yearly Meeting, preceded by the Children's' Creative Response to Conflict. I was Clerk of the New York Yearly Meeting Committee on Peace Concerns, which had oversight of these projects. The Yearly Meeting had worship groups in a number of New York State prisons. Besides having a time for worship, we socialized and talked about what Friends were doing in trying to keep demonstrations against the Vietnam War nonviolent. Since many of them were in prison for violent crimes, the men in prison expressed interest in having workshops that would help them resolve problems nonviolently. Thus AVP[2] came into being.

I was not one of the original designers of the project. Lawrence Apsey was a prime founder and the very first workshop was in 1975 in Greenhaven prison, outside New York City. We brought in people from around the country as facilitators for that workshop. Bernard Lafayette, who was a right-hand person to Martin Luther King, Jr., was one of the facilitators for that first workshop. Barbara and I provided hospitality for him, so this gave us a first-hand exposure to AVP as it was starting. I served on the Board of Directors at the beginning of AVP, but was not one of the designers. Then those who were doing AVP, said to me, "Steve, you ought to know what we're doing." I was still very busy with my job at Family Services and doing consulting. But I took the workshop and I found out some things about myself I didn't know before. Sometimes I could be violent without it looking like violence, like attitudes and responses to children's misbehavior. Even when I took that first workshop, I recognized that this was something I should be doing!

I took the training for being a facilitator and was soon giving workshops in New York prisons with Larry Apsey and others. AVP was very short of workshop facilitators in those early years so we trained individuals inside the prisons to become facilitators and co-facilitate with us. So it wasn't just outsiders coming in, but outsiders and prisoners working together. The co-facilitation was very important because it demonstrated our trust and belief in the capability of the incarcerated men and women to acquire and utilize what the workshops were seeking to teach.

For the first fourteen years, AVP was principally a prison program in the United States. When Friends World Committee had its Triennial in Japan in 1988 I had an opportunity lead an AVP workshop there. In 1989 two women facilitators Janet Lugo and Ellen Flanders were in Britain and they did two sample workshops there.

My wife, Barbara died of breast cancer in 1988 and I was her caretaker for the last year of her life. After her death, friends who we had known internationally were writing me saying, "Why don't you come visit?" I thought, "Oh, that's a good idea." Then I got the message, if I was going abroad I should see if they can arrange for a group to take AVP.[2] This is too good a secret to keep in the United States.

By 1991 I had enough correspondence with folks that I knew around the planet that I started planning my worldwide trip to share AVP. By that time we had developed manuals. Fortunately there were trained facilitators in similar disciplines that could work with me in presenting the workshops. We did some of the workshops in prison settings, others were with interested people in the community. In that first year I was in quite a few areas throughout the United States, as well as Canada, Europe, Central and South America, Australia and New Zealand. By the end of 1995 I had been able to share AVP on six continents.

I was Clerk of FCNL[27] General Committee for nine years, from 1965–1974, and then I was Clerk of New York Yearly Meeting, Representative Meeting from 1974–1977. After that I was Clerk of FGC[28] from 1977–1980. Those were all volunteer responsibilities. I would say I was an active Friend.

My lifetime expectation of myself was to do something that contributed to a more peaceful planet. I chose Social Work to help to build positive lives and better communities. I visited many communities and helped them to resolve problems and develop better human services. This fit my expectations of who I wanted to be during my life. I have spent a third of my lifetime on the AVP program worldwide and in the United States, so I guess, it sort of ranks number one.

I regret that my wife didn't live to come to Kendal. We were both signed up. She would have had a ball here because there are a lot of people from Westtown and Earlham. Through all the major elements of my life, a happy and fulfilling marriage and bringing up three sons and a daughter, I've been blessed. Our four children are all married with 13 grandchildren and two great-grandchildren.

I would like to pass on to future generations this message. Our planet is a precious gift and, if we don't get our act together and learn how to live peacefully and make the badly needed changes in our ways to preserve the environment, preserve the clean air, water, life forms and productive soils, all of which we are totally dependent on, our days on planet earth are severely limited.

Afterword

We have come to know thirty-two men who made the radical decision to declare conscientious objection to war when they were young and vulnerable. Did they act with courage and integrity or were they cowards? At the time most of their fellow citizens thought they were cowards.

It was difficult for lawmakers and draft boards to evaluate the integrity of men claiming conscientious objection to joining the military. The government assessed the reality of these claims largely on previous activity in religious settings.

Returning to the beginning of this book we re-visit our original questions: Why is a pacific human male so rare? What is his character? Was he born a pacifist? How do we parent him? Is the culture in which he grows up paramount? Are religion and education important?

The pacifism of most of these rare pacific men seemed to emerge early in their lives. They honored their family history and culture. Many found inspiration in Protestant youth groups, especially the Epworth League of the Methodist Church. Many who started in mainstream Protestant churches later joined one of the three traditional peace churches.

When we asked the men what lessons they would like to pass on to future generations, they most often told us, "Follow your conscience."

What is conscience? We know when we have been pricked by conscience and have felt better when it is clear rather than guilty. But, are we aware when we are driven by our conscience? Some people live their lives fully in control and confident in what they can weigh and measure in concrete terms. Even though there is no concrete reality to either theology or philosophy, some humans have created creeds, commandments, and other systems to control their behavior and explain their thought processes. A few others, a remnant, are aware of a reality beyond human systems of measurement and thought. They experience and are led by the mysterious and ineffable. They are the mystics. This book begins and ends with mystics.

Is the concrete definition of conscience then the measure of how a man lives out his life as a humanitarian? After reading the life experience of these men in their own words, we come to know that conscience is finally defined not by an act, but by the full life of a humanitarian.

We want to understand what drives each one of us to do good works beyond our personal gain. Self aware or not, we are led by spirit. Can we still the drums of war and stop marching to another's beat? Let us learn to gently blow the windy instrument of our own intuition and joyfully dance lives lived for the benefit of others. I hope that you will be led to speak clearly and courageously as you spread the word about this controversial book.

Mary R. Hopkins

Endnotes *(Websites accessed October 7, 2009)*

1) *Africa Action*

Africa Action was formed by the merger of three organizations that have fought for freedom and justice in Africa: American Committee on Africa, The Africa Fund, and Africa Policy Information Center. Continuing this tradition, Africa Action seeks to re-shape U.S. policy toward African countries. <africaaction.org>

2) *Alternatives to Violence Project (AVP)*

"The purpose of the AVP is to empower people to lead nonviolent lives through affirmation, respect for all, community building, cooperation, and trust. AVP/USA is an association of community-based groups and prison-based groups offering experiential workshops in personal growth and creative conflict management. The national organization provides support for the work of these local groups." <avpusa.org>

3) *American Civil Liberties Union (ACLU)*

"The ACLU is our nation's guardian of liberty, working daily in courts, legislatures and communities to defend and preserve the individual rights and liberties that the Constitution and laws of the United States guarantee everyone in this country. ... These rights include:

- Your First Amendment rights—freedom of speech, association and assembly, freedom of the press, and freedom of religion.
- Your right to equal protection under the law—protection against unlawful discrimination.
- Your right to due process—fair treatment by the government whenever the loss of your liberty or property is at stake.
- Your right to privacy—freedom from unwarranted government intrusion into your personal and private affairs.

"The ACLU also works to extend rights to segments of our population that have traditionally been denied their rights, including people of color; women; lesbians, gay men, bisexuals and transgender people; prisoners; and people with disabilities. ... If the rights of society's most vulnerable members are denied, everybody's rights are imperiled." <aclu.org>

4) *American Friends Service Committee (AFSC)*

"The AFSC is a practical expression of the faith of the Religious Society of Friends (Quakers). Committed to the principles of nonviolence and justice, it seeks in its work and witness to draw on the transforming power of love, human and divine. ...

"The AFSC was founded in 1917 by members of the Religious Society of Friends in the United States in order to provide young Quakers and other conscientious objectors to war with an opportunity to perform a service of love in wartime. In the ensuing years, the Committee has continued to serve as a channel for Quaker concerns growing out of the basic Quaker belief that there is that of God in every man'[26] and the basic Quaker faith that the power of love can "take away the occasion for all wars." <afsc.org>

The AFSC administered many of the Civilian Public Service[14] camps where COs served during World War II. "Early in the war, it was hoped that CPS[14] men would be permitted to serve abroad. British Quakers sponsored a Friends Ambulance Unit in China, and plans were made to send CPS men to serve in it, along with men from Canada, Australia, and New Zealand. A rider attached to an army appropriation bill prohibited conscientious objectors from serving abroad. Seven of eight COs were recalled from South Africa, where they were well on their way to join the team in China. The rider was approved primarily because of resentment toward COs by members of Congress and their constituents. It passed despite efforts of legislators who did not wish to prohibit useful voluntary work abroad for such individuals.

"Such frustrations drove many individuals in the CPS units to acts of defiance. Walkouts, slow-downs, and strikes occurred. Quaker administrators were caught in the middle. In early 1946 after the war's conclusion, the AFSC ended its administration of CPS camps because it was opposed to maintaining the camps in a time of peace. At no time did the U.S. government pay salaries to CPS men or support their families, as it did for families of those who served in the armed forces.

"Even before the end of the CPS camps, vocational counseling was offered to many men. Some Quaker colleges offered scholarships to them, and special loans were made so some men could go into business. Any who were qualified and wished to serve abroad were selected for Quaker service projects. A number of CPS men took the opportunity to do such service and carried out valuable and useful work in war-stricken countries. Many men became valued staff members of the AFSC, which never again cooperated in administering any programs for COs. It did, however, offer a number of alternative service positions for people in later generations who opposed undergoing combat training in the armed forces." (Jack Sutters, AFSC Archivist <afsc.org/ht/d/ContentDetails/i/3847>)

5) *Bacon, Margaret Hope*
Love is the Hardest Lesson by Margaret Hope Bacon,1999. Pendle Hill Publications.

6) *Boulding, Kenneth*
Kenneth Ewart Boulding (1910–1993) was born in Liverpool, England, and graduated from Oxford University, where he published his first paper in 1932, and studied at Harvard University and the University of Chicago. He made contributions in economics, education, philosophy, and social science. He was also known as a poet and a religious mystic. He was a founder of a number of projects in economics and

social science that are still in existence, projects, such as, the Center for Advanced Study in the Behavioral Sciences at Stanford University. Publishing more than three dozen books and over one-hundred dozen articles, he was a scholar of conflict, war and peace, and brought ethical, religious, and ecological concerns to economics. <colorado.edu/econ/ Kenneth.Boulding/>

7) *Brethren, Church of*

The Church of the Brethren was organized in Germany in 1708 as a blend of radical pietism (religion of the heart) and Anabaptist (the same origin as Mennonites). By 1719, growing persecution and economic hardship led Brethren to begin immigrating to North America. They were attracted by the settlement begun by Quaker William Penn, so the first congregation in the New World was organized in 1719 at Germantown, Pennsylvania, a community that had been started by Mennonites in the 1680s.

The Church of the Brethren seeks to find new ways to continue the work of Jesus in the world. They hold the New Testament as their only creed and have a strong pacifist practice. The Church of the Brethren is one of the three "peace churches." <brethren.org> or <cob-net.org/ america.htm>

8) *Bruderhof Communities*

Bruderhof Communities are religious communities, also referred to as "Hutterian Brethren," "Society of Brothers" and "Church Communities International." The first Bruderhof Community was founded in Germany in 1920 by Eberhard Arnold, a philosophy student who had studied the Hutterites, a pacifist, communal branch of the Anabaptist movement started in Austria in the 16th Century. The Hutterites stressed community of goods on the model of the primitive church in Jerusalem. When Arnold discovered that the Hutterite movement still survived, mostly in the western sections of the United States and Canada, he became a Hutterite minister. Bruderhof Communities operate collective farms and remain aloof from outside society, taking no part in politics. Children are educated inside the colony until age 14 or until the minimum age decreed by state or province. <thirdway.com/menno/glossary.asp?ID=16>

9) *California Loyalty Oath*

The text of the California Loyalty Oath in the Constitution of the State of California (Article XX, section 3): "I do solemnly swear (or affirm) that I will support and defend the Constitution of the United States and the Constitution of the State of California against all enemies, foreign and domestic; that I will bear true faith and allegiance to the Constitution of the United States and the Constitution of the State of California; that I take this obligation freely, without any mental reservation or purpose of evasion; and that I will well and faithfully discharge the duties upon which

I am about to enter." <atyourservice.ucop.edu/forms_pubs/forms_work-sheets/upay585.pdf>

10) *Catholic Worker Movement*

The Catholic Worker Movement originated as a newspaper in 1933, in the midst of the Great Depression. It was founded by journalist Dorothy Day and French peasant and esthetic Peter Maurin. "The aim of the Catholic Worker movement is to live in accordance with the justice and charity of Jesus Christ. ... There are over 185 local Catholic Worker communities providing social services. Each house has a different mission, going about the work of social justice in their own ways, suited to their region of the country. The group advocates personalism [a philosophy which moves away from a self-centered individualism toward the good of the other], a decentralized society, and a green revolution. They campaign for nonviolence and protest war and the unequal distribution of wealth in the world." <www.catholicworker.com>

11) *Center on Conscience and War (CCW)*

The CCW is a faith-based organization that advocates for the rights of conscience, opposes military conscription, and serves all conscientious objectors to war. The CCW evolved from several earlier organizations, including the National Service Board for Religious Objectors. "CCW works to defend and extend the rights of conscientious objectors. ... The Center is committed to supporting all those who question participation in war, whether they are U.S. citizens, permanent residents, documented or undocumented immigrants--or citizens in other countries. ... CCW participates in the G.I. Rights Hotline, a national referral and counseling service for military personnel. In the event of a military draft, CCW will assist in the placement of conscientious objectors in alternative service programs. The Center is opposed to all forms of conscription." <centeronconscience.org/about>

12) *Citizens for Global Solutions*

"Citizens for Global Solutions envisions a future in which nations work together to abolish war, protect our rights and freedoms, and solve the problems facing humanity that no nation can solve alone. This vision requires effective democratic global institutions that will apply the rule of law while respecting the diversity and autonomy of national and local communities.

"We are a membership organization working to build political will in the United States to achieve our vision. We do this by educating Americans about our global interdependence, communicating global concerns to public officials, and developing proposals to create, reform, and strengthen international institutions such as the United Nations. ...

"The World Federalist Institute (WFI)[67] serves as Citizens for Global Solutions' think tank by promoting debate, discussion and sharing research on the principle of federalism and its applicability to resolving global problems nations cannot solve alone. One goal of the WFI is to develop pragmatic proposals ultimately leading to the creation of a democratic global political system with a federal structure." <globalsolutions. org/about/vision_and_mission>

13) Civilian Conservation Corps (CCC)

The CCC was a public work relief program for unemployed men during the Great Depression. The men did conservation work like planting trees, building flood barriers, fighting forest fires, and maintaining forest roads and trails. They lived in work camps under a semi-military regime. From 1933–1942, approximately three million men were served by the CCC. <ccclegacy.org>

14) Civilian Public Service (CPS)

"The CPS was established during World War II to provide 'work of national importance under civilian direction' to be carried out by conscientious objectors (COs). In 1940, the U.S. Congress enacted a conscription bill which included a provision that allowed people opposed to being trained for combat to be excused. Three of the so-called 'peace churches'—Church of the Brethren[4], the Mennonite[42] Church, and the Religious Society of Friends[52]—undertook administration of CPS camps for non-governmental work projects.

"The CPS men engaged in numerous activities. Some camps operated for the benefit of the U.S. Forestry Service and other federal agencies. Some men were permitted to work on farms. Approximately 2,000 worked in mental hospitals or training schools for people with disabilities. Another group volunteered to participate in 'guinea pig' experiments. They allowed themselves to be infected in a variety of ways, exposed themselves to starvation experiments, and took newly created medicines. One man died from being involved in an infantile paralysis experiment. The men perceived many of these jobs 'of national importance' to be ridiculous. [Others objected to being used as unpaid labor, calling it 'slavery.' They walked out, notified the FBI and when arrested were sentenced to Federal Prisons.]

"Other work such as that undertaken in mental hospitals resulted in better treatment for patients and raised public consciousness about conditions in such institutions. Reforms were made in the hospitals, and eventually, growing out of this work, was creation of the National Mental Health Foundation, which outlasted the era of Civilian Public Service. Some 12,000 men who did not wish to take the lives of others during World War II served in CPS. The work they accomplished was useful and contributed to the well-being of many thousands of people." (Jack Sutters, AFSC Archivist <afsc.org/ht/d/ContentDetails/i/3847>)

15) Coffin, Henry Sloane

Henry Sloane Coffin (1877–1954) was a Presbyterian minister and President of Union Theological Seminary from 1926–1945. He emphasized the application of Christianity to social problems and led the movement for liberal evangelicalism in Protestant churches. Coffin also sought to improve the quality of theological education. He wrote more than 20 books in the field of religion, but his *Meaning of the Cross* (1931) is the most well known. <en.wikipedia.org/wiki/Henry_Sloane_Coffin

16) Congress on Racial Equality (CORE)

CORE was established by James Farmer and others in Chicago in 1942 to improve race relations and end discriminatory policies through direct-action projects. Farmer had been working as the race-relations secretary for the American branch of the pacifist group Fellowship of Reconciliation (FOR)[25] but resigned over a dispute in policy; he and others founded CORE as a vehicle for the nonviolent approach to combating racial prejudice that was inspired by Indian leader Mahatma Gandhi.

"CORE started as a non-hierarchical, decentralized organization funded entirely by the voluntary contributions of its members. The organization was initially co-led by white University of Chicago student George Houser and black student James Farmer. In 1942, CORE began protests against segregation in public accommodations by organizing sit-ins. It was also in 1942 that CORE expanded nationally. James Farmer traveled the country with Bayard Rustin, a field secretary with FOR, and recruited activists at FOR meetings. CORE's early growth consisted almost entirely of white middle-class college students from the Midwest. CORE pioneered the strategy of nonviolent direct action, especially the tactics of sit-ins, jail-ins, and freedom rides." <core-online.org>

17) Conscientious Objector (CO)

A CO is someone who refuses to participate as a combatant in war on religious, moral or ethical grounds. Because conscription into armed forces is a matter of law, COs have generally been prosecuted for legal violations. However, some conscription laws have made provisions to exempt members of certain pacifist religious groups. During the 19th century, Prussia exempted the Mennonites from military service in return for a military tax, and until 1874 they were exempted in Russia. Such exceptions were unusual, however. The U.S. conscript laws of 1940 allowed some form of service that was unrelated to and not controlled by the military for COs based on membership in a recognized pacifistic religious sect. Objections of a philosophical, political, or personal moral nature were not considered valid reasons for refusing military service. <en.wikipedia.org/wiki/Conscientious_objector>

18) CROP Hunger Walks

The CROP Hunger Walks are a project of the Church World Service (CWS), which is the relief, development, and refugee assistance ministry of 35 Protestant, Orthodox, and Anglican denominations in the United States. CWS was founded in 1946. CWS works in partnership with indigenous organizations in more than 80 countries to meet human needs and foster self-reliance for all whose way is hard. <churchworldservice.org>

19) Dewey, John

John Dewey (1859–1952) was a philosopher and psychologist who greatly influenced thought around the world. He was one of the founders of pragmatism and functional psychology. He was on the faculties of the University of Michigan, University of Minnesota, University of Chicago, and Columbia University. <en.wikipedia.org/wiki/John_Dewey>

20) Epworth League

The Epworth League was a youth organization of the Methodist Episcopal Church, which later became the United Methodist Church. The name "Epworth" came from the English hometown of John Wesley, the founder of the Methodist movement. The Epworth League was formed in Cleveland, Ohio, in 1889 by combining five Methodist youth organizations that existed at that time. The purpose of the League was the promotion of intelligent and vital piety among the young people of the church. The Epworth League was especially strong during the first half of the 20th Century. For example, church membership in the Methodist Episcopal denomination in 1913 was almost 600,000 and there were over 200,000 members of the Epworth League. <en.wikipedia.org/wiki/Epworth_League>

21) Every Church a Peace Church (ECAPC)

"ECAPC is a vision energized by the belief that the church could turn the world toward peace if every church lived and taught as Jesus lived and taught. It is an effort to nurture a global network of creative non-violence among Christians, focused within the churches out of a sense of responsibility to first set one's own house in order." <ecapc.org/history.asp>

22) Ethical Societies

The Ethical Culture movement was started by transcendentalist Felix Alder in 1876. It was felt that disputes over theology or doctrine were distractions from people living ethically and doing good, so the motto of the movement was "Deed before creed." Independent societies exist in many cities in the U.S. and elsewhere. <nysec.org/sitemap/about>

23) Farmer, James

"James Farmer (1920-1999) was an outstanding student with degrees from Wiley College (1938) and Howard University (1941). He and several Christian pacifists founded CORE[16] in 1942. The organization's purpose was to apply direct challenges to American racism by using Gandhian tactics of nonviolence. Farmer's religious beliefs resulted in him refusing to serve in the armed forces during the World War II.

"In 1947 Farmer participated in CORE's campaign of sit-ins which successfully ended two Chicago restaurants' discriminatory service practices against blacks. Articulate and charismatic, Farmer became CORE National Director in 1961. In this position he helped organize student sit-ins and Freedom Rides in the Deep South.

"In 1966 Farmer resigned from CORE in order to direct a national adult literacy project. A supporter of the Republican Party, Farmer failed in his attempt to win a seat in Congress in 1968. Shortly afterwards, the new president, Richard Nixon, appointed him Assistant Secretary of Health, Education and Welfare." <www.spartacus.schoolnet.co.uk/USAfarmerJ. htm>

24) Father Divine

Father Divine was a prominent, but controversial, African-American religious leader of the early 20th Century. He was born George Baker around 1880 and died in 1965. He began preaching in 1907 in Long Island and held free banquets at his home, which attracted an integrated following. He adopted the name Reverend Major Jealous Divine, but was called "Father Divine" by his followers. He formulated doctrines of racial equality and individual economic independence and spoke to large crowds in New York City. His movement spread throughout the country and the world with the help of the publisher of the magazine, New Thought, located in Seattle, Washington. In the 1930s he was a champion of racial equality and an advocate of the economic self-sufficiency for African Americans that found broad acceptance only with the Civil Rights Movement thirty years later. Followers of Father Divine were conscientious objectors in World War II. <en.wikipedia.org/wiki/Father_Divine>

25) Fellowship of Reconciliation (FOR)

"FOR is an interfaith and international movement with branches and groups in over 40 countries and on every continent. ... In 1914 an ecumenical conference was held in Switzerland by Christians seeking to prevent the outbreak of war in Europe. Before the conference ended, however, World War I had started and those present had to return to their respective countries. At a railroad station in Germany, two of the participants, Henry Hodgkin, an English Quaker, and Friedrich Sigmund-Schultze, a German Lutheran, pledged to find a way of working for peace even though their countries were at war. Out of this pledge Christians gathered in Cambridge, England in December 1914 to found the Fellowship of Reconciliation. The US FOR was founded one year later, in 1915. ...

"Today the membership of FOR includes Jews, Christians, Buddhists, Muslims, and people of other faith traditions, as well as those with no formal religious affiliation. FOR "seeks to replace violence, war, racism, and economic injustice with nonviolence, peace, and justice. We are an interfaith organization committed to active nonviolence as a transforming way of life and as a means of radical change. We educate, train, build coalitions, and engage in nonviolent and compassionate actions locally, nationally, and globally." <forusa.org/about/history.html>

26) Fox, George

George Fox (1624–1691) was an English itinerant preacher and founder of the Society of Friends (Quakers). His personal religious experience made him hostile to church conventions and established his reliance on what he saw as the "Inward Light" over scriptural authority or creeds. He recorded his experiences in his journal, published as the *Journal of George Fox*. <britannica.com/EBchecked/topic/215366/George-Fox>

A core understanding among all Quakers comes from a 1636 George Fox quotation: "Walk cheerfully over the world, answering to that of God in everyone." (*Quaker Faith and Practice*. The book of Christian discipline of the Yearly Meeting of the Religious Society of Friends (Quakers) in Britain. 1.02.42)

27) Friends Committee on National Legislation (FCNL)

FCNL is the largest peace lobby in Washington, DC. "Founded in 1943 by members of the Religious Society of Friends (Quakers), FCNL is the oldest registered ecumenical lobby in Washington, DC. <fcnl.org>

28) Friends General Conference (FGC)

"FGC is a Quaker organization in the unprogrammed tradition of the Religious Society of Friends which primarily serves affiliated yearly and monthly meetings. It is our experience that faith is based on direct experience of God. Our lives witness this experience individually and corporately, and by answering that of God in everyone, we build and sustain inclusive community." <fgcquaker.org>

29) G.I. Bill

The Servicemen's Readjustment Act of 1944, better known as the "G.I. Bill," provided for college or vocational education and one year of unemployment compensation for returning World War II veterans. It also provided loans for returning veterans to buy homes and start businesses. <en.wikipedia.org/wiki/G.I._Bill>

30) Geiger, Calhoun D.
Leadings along the Way: Stories from the Life of Calhoun D. Geiger by Calhoun Geiger, 1998.

31) German-American Bund
The German-American Bund, also called "Friends of the New Germany," was an American quasi-military organization in the 1930s supported by anti-Semitic and pro-Nazi elements in the United States. The organization received covert guidance and financial support from the German government. Military drill and related activities were provided for adults and youths at Bund-maintained camps in New York, New Jersey, Pennsylvania, and elsewhere. The Bund included self-designated uniformed storm troopers. Mass rallies were held at such sites as Madison Square Garden in New York City. In 1939 the Bund's total membership was about 20,000. After the United States' entry into World War II, the U.S. government outlawed the Bund. <britannica.com/EBchecked/topic/230640/German-American-Bund>

32) Hays, Samuel P.
Conservation and the Gospel of Efficiency: The Progressive Conservation Movement, 1890-1920 by Samuel P. Hays, Cambridge, Massachusetts, 1959.

33) Heifer International
The Heifer Project, now Heifer International, was begun by Dan West who was a conscientious objector in World War I. In 1938 he returned from serving as a relief worker in Spain following the Spanish Civil War and realized the futility of providing food, which is only temporary relief. The Heifer Project distributes breeding livestock and trees around the world to solve the problem of world hunger. Families that receive these gifts are required to pass the gift on, to give a female animal to another family. <heifer.org/site/c.edJRKQNiFiG/b.201520/>

34) Hershey, Gen. Lewis Blaine
General Lewis Blaine Hershey was named Director of the Selective Service in July, 1941. He held the position until 1970, spanning World War II, the Korean War, and part of the Vietnam War. <en.wikipedia.org/wiki/Lewis_Blaine_Hershey>

35) Isolationism
Isolationism is a national policy of avoiding political or economic entanglements with other countries. It has been a recurrent theme in U.S. history, but is often applied to the political atmosphere in the U.S. in the 1930s. Liberal opposition to war as an instrument of policy and the effects of rigors of the Great Depression led the American people to be less concerned with the threat of Hitler's regime in Europe. The Johnson Act (1934) and the Neutrality Acts (1935) effectively prevented economic or

military aid to any country involved in the European disputes that escalated to World War II. U.S. isolationism encouraged the British policy of appeasement of Hitler's aggression and contributed to French paralysis in the face of the growing threat posed by Nazi Germany. <britannica.com/EBchecked/topic/296317/isolationism>

36) *Jack, Homer*

Homer Jack (1916–1993) was a Unitarian Minister who was active in the Fellowship of Reconciliation (FOR)[25] and helped to organize the first Freedom Ride in 1942. He co-founded and served as Executive Director of the Congress on Racial Equality (CORE)[16] and the National Committee for a Sane Nuclear Policy. He co-founded the American Committee on Africa[2] and served as Associate Director. He served as Secretary General of the World Conference on Religion and Peace, as well as Minister for a number of Unitarian churches. He published a history of the World Conference on Religion and Peace. His papers are in the Swarthmore Peace Collection <swarthmore.edu/Library/peace/DG051-099/DG063HJack.html>.

37) *Jehovah's Witnesses*

The modern history of Jehovah's Witnesses began more than a hundred years ago. In the early 1870s, a rather inconspicuous Bible study group began in Allegheny, Pennsylvania, U.S.A., which is now a part of Pittsburgh. Charles Taze Russell was the prime mover of the group. ... In July 1879, the first issue of the magazine *Zion's Watch Tower and Herald of Christ's Presence* appeared. By 1888 50 people were witnessing from house to house offering Bible literature and now the average number worldwide is about 700,000. <watchtower.org/e/jt/index.htm>

38) *Jones, Rufus*

Rufus Jones (1863–1948) was Quaker theologian, historian, and philosopher. He wrote extensively on mysticism and Quaker history. He was a Professor of Philosophy at Haverford College and part of the group of Friends that established the American Friends Service Committee (AFSC)[4] at the outset of World War I to provide work as am ambulance corps in northern France as alternative service for conscientious objectors. After the war was over, the Committee provided relief to the suffering defeated German population. Rufus Jones and two other Quakers went to speak truth to power to Reinhard Heydrich, the primary organizer of the mass murder of Jews during World War II. Rufus Jones was one of the most influential Quakers of the 20th Century. <en.wikipedia.org/wiki/Rufus_Jones>

39) *Kelly, Thomas*

Thomas Kelly (1893–1941) was born into a Quaker family in Ohio. After graduating from Wilmington College, he went to Haverford Seminary where he trained as a missionary and was influenced by Rufus Jones.

He and his wife worked in the AFSC[4] child feeding program in Germany after World War I, where they helped to found the Quaker community in Germany. He had just learned that the publisher Harper was interested in publishing a devotional book when he suffered a heart attack and died. Douglas Steere submitted his devotional essays, which were published as one of the most well loved devotional books, *A Testament of Devotion.* Other essays were published in a book entitled *The Eternal Promise.* *<en.wikipedia.org/wiki/Thomas_Raymond_Kelly_(Quaker_mystic)>*

40) Ku Klux Klan (KKK)

The KKK was originally organized as a social club by Confederate veterans in 1866 and quickly became a means for Southern whites to restore white supremacy through violent intimidation of the freed men and women. Burning crosses and white-robed klansmen have been the symbol of the KKK. <kkk.bz>

41) Laubach, Dr. Frank C.

Dr. Frank C. Laubach (1884-1970) was an educator, communicator and organizer who focused on empowering people to improve their lives through literacy. He developed a one-to-one instructional program that became known as "Each One Teach One." Dr. Laubach wrote forty books on prayer, literacy, justice and world peace. <laubach-on.ca/laubachchronology.htm>

42) Mennonites

Mennonites were first called "Anabaptists," because they baptized adults, which was considered heresy and persecuted in 16th Century Europe where countries were controlled by the Roman Catholic Church. They believed the church should be a community of believers who choose to turn over their lives to Jesus Christ and be baptized to symbolize that commitment. They sought to return to the simplicity of the faith and practice of the early Christian church. The name "Mennonite" came from a Dutch Catholic priest, Menno Simons, who joined the group in 1536 and became a prominent leader and teacher. <mennoniteusa.org> and <thirdway.com>

Some Mennonites escaped persecution by both the Catholics and the Protestants and moved to Pennsylvania at the invitation of the founder of the colony, William Penn (1644–1718). Others moved to Russia. Their pacifism caused Mennonites to flee to Canada to escape the American Revolution, the American Civil War, and the Russian Revolution.

The Amish separated from the Mennonites in 1693 as followers of Jacob Amman, who felt the church was losing its purity. The main difference was the Amish practice of banning a person who did not live according to the guidelines of the church. The Mennonites believed that a person should be welcomed back into the church if they changed their way of life. <thirdway.com/Menno>

43) Muste, A. J.

"Abraham Johannes Muste (1885–1967) was one of the leading nonviolent social activists of his time. Starting as a minister in the Dutch Reformed Church, he became a socialist and labor union activist, and was one of the founders and the first director of Brookwood Labor College. In 1936, he recommitted himself to pacifism and focused his energy on war resistance, civil rights, civil liberties and disarmament. Over his life he worked with a wide array of organizations, including the Fellowship of Reconciliation,[25] Congress on Racial Equality (CORE)[16] and War Resisters League,[68] and served as editor of Liberation magazine. He continued his work for peace during the U.S. war in Vietnam; shortly before his death, he traveled to North Vietnam with a delegation of clergy and met with Communist leader Ho Chi Minh. A. J. Muste was widely respected and admired in the movement for social justice for his ability to relate to people of all ages and backgrounds, to listen to and reflect on all points of view, and to bridge distances among divergent political sectors." <ajmuste.org/ajmustewhopg.html>

44) National Federation of Integrated Neighborhoods (NN)

NN is the oldest fair housing organization in the U.S. NN is "a nonprofit, civil rights organization that promotes racial and cultural equality by increasing multicultural dialogue and access, influencing public policy, and developing national models that support community development through the Fair Housing, Fair Lending, and Civil Rights Laws." <fairhousing.com>

45) National Service Board for Religious Objectors (NSBRO)

The NSBRO was formed in 1940 as a voluntary association of the religious organizations, Mennonite[42] Central Committee, the American Friends Service Committee,[4] and the Brethren[7] Service Committee to support the administration of the draft of conscientious objectors. The NSBRO Board of Directors also included representatives of the Fellowship of Reconciliation, the Commission on World Peace of the Methodist Church, the Disciples of Christ, and the Federal Council of Churches of Christ in America. The NSBRO was organized into the Camp Section that worked in connection with the selection of sites for CPS camps; the Complaint Section that helped men who were not properly classified or were denied their claim to conscientious objector status; and the Assignment Section that was the channel for transmitting the assignment to the proper CPS camp for the COs who were being drafted.

In 1964 the name of NSBRO was changed to National Interreligious Service Board for Conscientious Objectors and in 2000 it became the Center on Conscience and War.

46) New Foundation Fellowship

"The New Foundation Fellowship and George Fox Fund, Inc., support those who are interested in the message and experience of early Friends. 'Gathered by Christ Jesus Sent to Proclaim His Everlasting Gospel to the Inhabitants of the World,' the foundation of the New Foundation Fellowship is the same as the prophets, apostles, early Quakers and all the holy men of God throughout the ages. ... This foundation is good and right for all mankind, in every age, from all walks of life and from every location. We invite you to examine the foundation you are building your life upon. If it is not the foundation of hearing and obeying the voice of God, then wait, I say, in the Light of Christ Jesus who will show you the way forward." <nffellowship.org>

47) Niebuhr, Helmut Richard

Helmut Richard Niebuhr (1894–1962) was an "American Protestant theologian and educator who was considered a leading authority on ethics and U.S. church history. He was a foremost advocate of theological existentialism. Most of his career he taught theology and Christian ethics at Yale Divinity School. He was the younger brother of the theologian Reinhold Niebuhr. <britannica.com/EBchecked/topic/414555/Helmut-Richard-Niebuhr>

48) Niebuhr, Reinhold

Reinhold Niebuhr (1892–1971) studied at Eden Theological Seminary and Yale Divinity School. He was ordained in the Evangelical Synod of North America in 1915 and served as pastor of Bethel Evangelical Church in Detroit, Michigan, until 1928. His years in that industrial city made him a critic of capitalism and an advocate of socialism. From 1928 to 1960 he taught at New York's Union Theological Seminary. His influential writings forcefully criticized liberal Protestant thought and emphasized the persistence of evil in human nature and social institutions. The outbreak of World War II challenged his earlier pacifism and he developed the concept of "just war." His books include *Moral Man and Immoral Society* (1932), *The Nature and Destiny of Man*, 2 vol. (1941–43), and *The Self and the Dramas of History* (1955). He was the older brother of Helmut Richard Niebuhr. <en.wikipedia.org/wiki/Reinhold_Niebuhr>

49) Paulinist

A Paulinist follows a Christian Theology based on the letters of Paul in the *New Testament*.

50) Pendle Hill

Pendle Hill is a Quaker Study Center in Wallingford, Pennsylvania. <pendlehill.org>

51) *Pickett, Clarence*

Clarence Pickett (1884-1965) was the youngest of nine children, raised in a Quaker community in Iowa. As a Quaker minister, he filled pulpits in Friends Churches in Toronto, Canada and Oskaloosa, Iowa. He was the Executive Secretary of the AFSC[4] from 1929 to 1950, while the AFSC[4] was administering the CPS[14] camps. Four presidents of the United States and Eleanor Roosevelt called upon him for advice when faced with developing programs for relief from poverty and injustice. He later became valuable to government leaders around the world, and helped the United Nations embrace ecumenical religious opportunities for worship and mutual understanding.

52) *Quaker Religious Practices*

By the twentieth century, the Religious Society of Friends had split into three branches. Unprogrammed Friends worship in silence, which is broken only when someone is led by the Divine to speak. These meetings did not have pastors or ministers. Programmed Friends have programs planned and carried out by pastors with music and a sermon. Evangelical Friends have programmed worship and affirm the "inerrancy" of the *Bible*.

"Sense of the meeting" is not synonymous with consensus. Consensus is a widely used and valuable secular process characterized by a search for general agreement largely through rational discussion and compromise. Sense of the meeting is a religious process characterized by listening for and trusting in God. (*Faith and Practice*, Philadelphia Yearly Meeting of the Religious Society of Friends, 1997 p. 23)

A Clearness Committee is a Quaker practice to call together a group to help one think something through or resolve conflicts—to come to "clearness."

53) *Reserve Officer Training Corps (ROTC)*

ROTC is a college-based officer commissioning program designed as a college elective. <en.wikipedia.org/wiki/ROTC>

54) *Rustin, Bayard*

Bayard Rustin (1910–1987) grew up under the influence of his pacifist grandmother who had been raised as a Friend and was very active in the National Association for the Advancement of Colored People (NAACP). NAACP leaders, such as William DuBois and James Weldon Johnson, occasionally stayed with his family. As a student at City College of New York, he became a member of Fifteenth Street Friends Meeting and was active in the Young Communist League until he became disillusioned with that organization. He was Secretary for Student and General Affairs of the Fellowship of Reconciliation (FOR)[25] and a co-founder of the Congress on Racial Equality (CORE).[17] As a pacifist, Rustin refused to serve in the armed forces. He was arrested and charged with violating the Selective Service Act, found guilty and sentenced to three years in Lewisburg Prison. While in prison, he organized protests against segregated seating in the dining hall. <quakerinfo.com/quak_br.shtml>

55) School of the Americas (SOA)

SOA, now called the Western Hemisphere Institute for Security Cooperation, is a United States Army facility at Fort Benning in Columbus, Georgia. Over its 59 years, the SOA has trained over 60,000 Latin American soldiers in counterinsurgency techniques, sniper training, commando and psychological warfare, military intelligence and interrogation tactics. The impact of this program has engendered annual protests with many arrests. <soaw.org>

56) Schuller, Robert H.

Rev. Robert Harold Schuller is an American televangelist and pastor known around the world through his weekly broadcast, "The Hour of Power." He was ordained as a minister in the Reformed Church in America and established the Garden Grove Community Church was in 1955, renamed the Crystal Cathedral in 1980. The Crystal Cathedral is the denomination's largest congregation in terms of membership, and arguably the most renowned. Schuller's teachings are influenced by Norman Vincent Peale and focus on positive aspects of the Christian faith, avoiding condemning people for sin. <en.wikipedia.org/wiki/ Robert_H._Schuller>

57) Selective Training and Service Act of 1940

The Selective Training and Service Act of 1940, also known as the *Burke-Wadsworth Act*, was the first peacetime draft in the U.S. Men between the ages 21 and 30 were required to register with local draft boards. Later the age range was increased to 18 to 65. Between 1940 and 1947 more than ten million men were drafted under this law. Section 5(g) of the Act contained a provision for conscientious objection:

"Nothing contained in this Act shall be constructed to require any person to be subject to combatant training and service in the land and naval forces of the United States who, by reason of religious training and belief, is conscientiously opposed to participation in war in any form.

"Any such person claiming such exemption from combatant training and service because of such conscientious objections whose claim is sustained by the local draft board shall, if he is inducted into the land or naval forces under this Act, be assigned to noncombatant service as defined by the President, or shall if he is found to be conscientiously opposed to participation in such noncombatant service, in lieu of such induction, be assigned to work of national importance under civilian direction." <en. wikipedia.org/wiki/Selective_Training_and_Service_Act_of_1940>

58) Settlement Houses

Settlement houses were started by British social activists who believed that students and people of wealth should settle in poverty-stricken neighborhoods to evaluate that life, provide services, and work for social reform. The first settlement house in the U.S. was founded in 1886 by Stanton Coit in New York City's Lower East Side. Jane Addams founded Hull House in Chicago. They taught adult education classes, provided schooling for immigrants' children, organized job clubs, offered after school recreation, initiated public health services, and advocated for improved housing for the poor and working classes. Because of a shared sense of community, those living in the settlement house viewed the people as neighbors, not clients. <unhny.org/about/settlement.cfm>

59) Stark, Susan

Susan Stark is one of Friends' most gifted and inspirational singer-songwriters and song leaders. Her singing has blessed numerous Quaker gatherings, including FGC. She's recorded four albums, including "Phoenix Sings at Sundown~Lullabies for all Ages." <cdbaby.com/cd/susanstark>

60) Steere, Douglas

Douglas Van Steere (1901–1995) participated in the founding of Pendle Hill in 1929-30 and continued his involvement with Pendle Hill until the 1980s. At different times he served as director and full-time teacher. Following the Second World War, Douglas Steere raised a relief unit that labored in Finland, for which he received the decoration of Knight first class in the Order of the White Rose of Finland. <en.wikipedia.org/wiki/Douglas_V._Steere>

61) Stephenson, Edwin

Journey of the Wild Geese: A Quaker Romance in War-Torn Europe by Madeleine Yaude Stephenson and Edwin "Red" Stephenson, 1999. Pasadena CA: International Productions (P. O. Box 94814, 91109).

62) Swomley, John

John M. Swomley, was born in 1915, graduated from Dickinson College and earned a Ph.D. in Political Science from University of Colorado. He was a minister of the Methodist Church and served as the National Secretary of the Fellowship of Reconciliation. He was active with the American Friends Service Committee[4] and the American Civil Liberties Union.[2] He campaigned against universal military training, serving as Director of the National Council Against Conscription, and as editor of Conscription News. He was the author of books on militarism and the Cold War. Much of his peace and anti-military work was done as an individual rather than as a representative of the Methodist Church. (Swarthmore College Peace Collection <swarthmore.edu/Library/peace>)

63) *Thomism*
Philosophical and theological system developed by Thomas Aquinas, by his later commentators, and by modern revivalists of the system, known as neo-Thomists. <plato.stanford.edu/entries/aquinas>

64) *Tucker, Todd*
The Great Starvation Experiment: The Heroic Men Who Starved so That Millions Could Live by Todd Tucker, 2004. New York NY: Free Press (Simon and Schuster).

65) *United Nations Relief and Rehabilitation Administration (UNRRA)*
UNRRA was created in 1943 by a 44-nation meeting at the U.S. White House in 1944 to assist nations ravaged by World War II. Until 1947 relief supplies and services were provided to millions of displaced persons through coordination of the work of 23 different voluntary agencies. Food, clothing, fuel, shelter, medicines, camps and personnel were provided for repatriation of refugees. They also assisted with agricultural and economic rehabilitation. After 1947 the UNRRA ran out of money and was replaced by the International Refugee Organization. <en.wikipedia.org/wiki/United_Nations_Relief_and_Rehabilitation_Administration>

66) *Victim-Offender Reconciliation Program (VORP)*
VORP is a restorative justice approach that brings offenders face-to-face with the victims of their crimes with the assistance of a trained mediator, usually a community volunteer. <vorp.com>

67) *War Resisters' International (WRI)*
"WRI exists to promote nonviolent action against the causes of war, and to support and connect people around the world who refuse to take part in war or the preparation of war." <wri-irg.org/network/about_wri >

68) *War Resisters League (WRL)*
The United States' oldest secular pacifist organization, WRL was organized in 1923 by men and women who had opposed WWI, many of whom had been jailed for refusing military service. ... During WWII hundreds of members were imprisoned in the US for refusing to fight. The League was radicalized when these resisters left prison after the war. Not only had the prison experience deepened their thinking, but League members were impressed by the drama of Gandhi's nonviolent struggle for India's liberation. ... Through its whole history the League has remained independent of any political party; opposed to conscription and authoritarianism, censorship and racism in any country; and holds to a nonaligned position in international work." <warresisters.org/historyphilosophypolitics>

69) *West, Dan*

Dan West was a farmer and Church of the Brethren[4] relief worker who started the Heifer Project.[33] He was ladling out rations of milk to hungry children during the Spanish Civil War. West returned home to form the Heifers for Relief Committee, dedicated to ending hunger permanently by providing families with livestock and training so that they "could be spared the indignity of depending on others to feed their children."

70) *Wilson, E. Raymond*

Raymond E. Wilson (1896-1987), a Quaker peace lobbyist, helped found the Friends Committee on National Legislation in 1943 and served as its Executive Secretary until 1962. He also helped organize the Committee on Militarism in Education in 1925. From 1931 to 1943, he served as Field and Education Secretary of the Peace Section of the American Friends Service Committee.[4] He was the author of two books, *Uphill for Peace: Quaker Impact on Congress* (1975) and an autobiography, *Thus Far On My Journey* (1976). (Swarthmore College Peace Collection <swarthmore.edu/Library/peace>)

71) *Women's International League for Peace and Freedom (WILPF)*

WILPF is the oldest women's peace organization in the world. WILPF was founded in April 1915, in The Hague, the Netherlands, by some 1300 women from Europe and North America, from countries at war against each other and neutral ones, who came together in a Congress of Women to protest the killing and destruction of the war then raging in Europe. It is an international non-governmental organization with Sections in 37 countries, covering all continents. The International Secretariat is based in Geneva with a New York UN office. <wilpf.int.ch>

72) *Works Progress Administration (WPA)*

WPA, originally named the Works Progress Administration and renamed "Work Projects Administration," was a work program for the unemployed was created in 1935 under U.S. President Franklin D. Roosevelt's New Deal. The purpose of the program was to provide useful work for millions of victims of the Great Depression and thus to preserve their skills and self-respect. During its eight-year existence the WPA put some 8.5 million people to work (over 11 million were unemployed in 1934) at a cost to the federal government of approximately $11 billion. <britannica.com/EBchecked/topic/648178/Works-Progress-Administration>

73) *World Federalist Movement (WFM)*

WFM is a global movement dedicated to the realization of global justice, peace and sustainable prosperity through the development of democratic international institutions and the global application of international law. WFM believes that federalism applied on an international level, inspired by the experiences of the federal political systems worldwide that represent 40% of the world's citizens, is the best way to accomplish these goals. Our vision is of a world where people have a sense of citizenship beyond national borders, to include their region and the global community. <wfm-igp.org>

74) Young Men's Christian Association (YMCA)

In 1844 the YMCA was founded in London, England, in response to unhealthy social conditions arising when the growth of the railroads and centralization of commerce and industry brought many rural young men who needed jobs into cities like London. The first YMCA was started to substitute Bible study and prayer for life on the streets. By 1851 the first YMCAs in North America were established in Montreal and Boston, and in 1853 the first YMCA for African Americans was founded in Washington, D.C., by Anthony Bowen, a freed slave. The YMCA took on war relief for both refugees and prisoners of war on both sides, and worked to ease the path of African American soldiers returning to the segregated South. John Mott, a leader of the YMCA movement in America, received the Nobel Peace Prize in 1946 in recognition of the YMCA's role in increasing global understanding and for its humanitarian efforts. <ymca.net>

Appendix
Announcement and Guidelines

ANNOUNCING THE

Conscientious Objectors Autobiographies Project

Statement of Purpose

We will publish, in one volume, the stories of diverse men who were conscientious objectors at the time of World War II. This book will present the histories of how these men made their decisions. Also, it will show how their consequent experiences played important roles in social progress. Our goal is to help readers to understand and respect the man of peace whom conscience compels to take a position opposed by majority social norms.

We see this publication as a step toward placing on library shelves autobiographies of an indispensable significance now denied by the overwhelming number of books about those who make war.

Signed: Steve Angell, Allan Brick, Terry Engeman, Patricia Hunt, Mary Hopkins.

And so ...

WWII Conscientious Objectors Are Being Sought with other volunteers to interview and transcribe their life stories for inclusion. Guidelines and support provided. Book planned. All material submitted will go into the Swarthmore College Peace Collection.

Our object is to interview these men to discover who they are through their decision making process. They defied all that was sanctioned at the time. What decisions have they made the rest of their lives that echo this early answering of personal principles and leadings? The working title of the book is: *Men of Peace.*

GOALS AND GUIDELINES

GENERAL GOALS

We would like a full text of whatever the subject thinks is important about his decision making process in regard to his Conscientious Objection during World War II and thereafter. This manuscript will go in the Swarthmore College Peace Collection.

If the work is used for the book, we will shorten, not change, the manuscript into a piece which is relevant to the theme of the book: i.e.: we will remove material about what he did while he was serving as a CO We want a character study in the first person.

GUIDELINES

1. For The Conscientious Objector

You are in charge of the content of this manuscript. Please study the questions for a few days before you meet with your interviewer. Try to speak in full sentences and spell out whatever words may not be in common use such as proper names. We are interested in your decision making process and what actions this led you to take during your life. It is our experience that you will forget something on the day you are interviewed! Plan to ask the interviewer back until it is all on the tape.

When you receive the first draft of the manuscript, do not hesitate to make it reflect what you want to say. The computer makes it relatively easy to add and subtract your changes. When you decide it is the way you want it, we ask you to sign and date the last page of the final draft.

If you have letters, papers and other ephemera that apply to those days during WW II, let us know what you have. The Swarthmore Peace Collection would like to hear about them and may be interested in adding them to their collection.

2. For the Interviewer

Give the CO a copy of the question sheet at least a week ahead of time. This also give you time to understand what we are asking of our subject.

Keep your interview low key with your subject in control. Every question does not have to be answered.

Avoid getting interested in something that leads you to spontaneously ask a leading question. If you do this, the answer will have to be typed from the tape and then removed from the manuscript as inappropriate material.

Be prepared to go back for further material that was forgotten during the first interview. You may find yourself returning two, three or four manuscripts for his corrections and additions.

The last page should contain your names, interviewer and subject, street addresses, phone numbers e-mail and, date. If your transcriber is a volunteer, give us their name and etc. so, should we be able to use this manuscript in the book, we can include all the names of the people who have contributed to it.

We suggest that before you begin, you decide to transcribe the tape yourself or find a transcriber. You want to be sure you have the size tape your transcriber can use in their machine. Please mail us a signed, ready to print manuscript on both paper and a computer file.

3. For the Transcriber

We assume you are transcribing onto a computer!

Do not be concerned about page set-up; our production team will reformat the manuscripts that go into the book. However, putting the interviewer's questions in italics is helpful to the reader.

In the first draft, we want all the words you hear in the rhythm in which they are spoken. Unfinished sentences and such are fine. The person being interviewed can finish them later if they choose. In other words:

Plan to clean up the manuscript several times until the subject gets it the way he wants it. If you, in Microsoft Word, go Format>Paragraph>Line Spacing>1 ½ it will give you both sufficient room to mark readable corrections.

On the last page of the last draft, place lines with appropriate names underneath for signature of interviewed, interviewer and yourself if you are a volunteer. Put "Date" at the end of each line.

Place appropriate names with addresses, phone and e-mail information on a separate sheet and include with hard copy.

To you all, we thank you, signed: Steve Angell, Allan Brick, Terry Engeman, Mary Hopkins, Pat Hunt.

Interview Guide

1) How and when did you become aware that you are a pacifist?

2) Family of Origin: Was it a religious family? Were they Pacifists?

3) Childhood: Hobbies, Competitive Sports, Early Mentors

4) Education: Favorite Subjects and Reading Preferences; Philosophy of schools you attended; Reasons for choices of schools, majors, degrees; Graduate: diplomas earned, majors and/or graduate degrees

5) Age at time of Pearl Harbor: How did you come to your decision? Major Influences (Inner and Outer); Major Supporters; Major Detractors; What finally ended any ambivalence?

6) Government Assignments: How many years did you serve?

7) Job and/or Vocation: How did you choose it? What opportunities were presented? What roadblocks did CO decision put up? How did you overcome them?

8) Marriage: Decisions around marriage, family and raising children.

9) Have you undertaken other pacifist activities?

10) Achievements: What are you proudest of? What regrets do you have?

11) Did you hope that by this time things would have changed because of your decision? Have they?

12) What lessons have you learned that you would like to pass on to future generations?

Index

About the Editor

Mary R. Hopkins, using her Master's degree in Social Work, has focused her adult studies on religion, psychology, and art from a woman's point of view. This work culminated in the video tapes entitled, *Women and her Symbols* and *Mother Earth: Revisioning the Sacred*. She was very active in Quaker organizations, resulting in her papers being included in the Friends Historical Library at Swarthmore College. Charmed and inspired by Calhoun Geiger's memoire, she was led to compile stories from other World War II conscientious objectors. When she moved into a Quaker retirement community, she found the wisdom and resources necessary to complete this book.

LaVergne, TN USA
09 May 2010
182049LV00001B/30/P